# Designing Organizations

The very structure of an organization is increasingly rcognized as being central to its performance. In this major new text, Richard Butler explores current concepts of organizational design and relates them to the latest theories about strategic decision making. He integrates many strands of organizational and management theory into a single new model, which can be applied internationally and to any kind of organization.

Practical as well as theoretical in his approach, Butler emphasizes that organizational design needs to strike a balance between too tight and too loose a structure in order to achieve both adaptability and efficiency. Within this model, he covers topics such as the organization of technology, strategy, effectiveness, departmentalization, power and coalition management, reward systems, and learning. He also discusses aspects of co-operatives, voluntary organizations, and Japanese management methods.

*Designing Organizations* will be a useful tool for students of management at many different levels, and will be particularly valuable to those specializing in strategic management theory and organization behaviour.

Richard Butler is Reader in Organization Analysis at the University of Bradford Management Centre. He has published widely on organizational decision-making theory. His recent publications include *Top Decisions* (1986) and *Managing Voluntary and Non-profit Organizations* (Routledge 1988).

# Designing Organizations

A Decision-Making Perspective

Richard Butler

London and New York

First published 1991
by Routledge
11 New Fetter Lane, London EC4P 4EE

Simultaneously published in the USA and Canada
by Routledge
a division of Routledge, Chapman and Hall, Inc.
29 West 35th Street, New York, NY 10001

© 1991 Richard Butler

Phototypeset in 10pt Times by
Mews Photosetting, Beckenham, Kent
Printed and bound in Great Britain by
Mackays of Chatham PLC, Chatham, Kent

*British Library Cataloguing in Publication Data*

Butler, Richard
 Designing Organizations: A Decision-Making Perspective.
 1. Organizations. Design
 I. Title
 302.35

 ISBN 0-415-05331-5
 ISBN 0-415-05332-3 pbk

*Library of Congress Cataloging in Publication Data*

Butler, Richard, 1938–
 Designing Organizations: A Decision-Making Perspective/Richard
 Butler
  p. cm.
 Includes bibliographical references and index.
 ISBN 0-415-05331-5 (HB) – ISBN 0-415-05332-3 (PB)
 1. Decision-making. 2. Organization. I. Title.
 HD30.23.B875  1991
 658.4'02–dc20
                                                    90-8905
                                                      CIP

# Contents

# Figures

# Tables

# Preface

This book presents an integrative approach to organizational design. By this is meant an approach that integrates into a single model the many strands of organizational and management theory that have accumulated over many years. This model is called the institutional model.

As the thinking and the writing have proceeded over the years I have become increasingly aware that the book has roots in my early experiences of working as an engineer in Rolls–Royce. There, I quickly found that my main problems were not technical and that my main need for understanding was for a way of thinking about how organizations work.

Organizations are not only technical systems, they are also social systems. Training as an engineer had given me an appreciation of technology, but a theoretical framework from which to develop an understanding of the interaction between the social and the technical was lacking so I became involved in the social sciences. The Ph.D. programme at Northwestern University, with its strong tradition in psychology, sociology, and research methods, provided the ideal setting for developing expertise in social science research; this was followed by my move to the Organizational Analysis Research Unit at Bradford.

It was at Bradford, in collaboration with my colleagues, that the interest in decision making developed and our study of 150 strategic decisions in 30 organizations was conducted. This tradition of the comparative analysis of organizational decision-making processes has been continued at Bradford through other studies – for example, studies in investment decision making and into the implementation of new technology.

Decision making is an ideal concept for putting at the centre of a model of organizational design. If we accept that decision making is about making choices and taking action then this activity is at the centre of all managerial work. Decision making has analytical, judgemental, political, and inspirational aspects to it; an important part of the skill of managing is to combine these four processes. However, decision making takes place within an organizational setting. The task in designing organizations is to create this organizational setting in such a way as to permit the necessary decision processes to take place effectively. The overall message of the model is fairly simple. If uncertainty is high a fuzzy structure is required to enable the necessary decision-making activity to take place to achieve adaptability to changing cirumstances. If, on the other hand, uncertainty is low, specification and routinization of decisions becomes possible and crisp structures can be created in order to improve efficiency. No organization is completely fuzzy or completely crisp. The problem of organizational design comes down to selecting zones of fuzziness and zones of crispness in order to maintain the balance between adaptability and efficiency.

In developing the institutional model I became acutely aware of the fads and fashions that exist in management theory. Sometimes it seems as if every author has to invent a new vocabulary. On closer inspection new vocabularies are often old ideas in a new wrapping. There seemed to be a need for an integrative model that could provide a framework upon which concepts and theories could be hung. I cannot claim total success in providing this integration; my dilemma has been that some new vocabulary has had to be invented to do this but I believe I have kept it to a minimum. I do claim, however, that a step has been made in the right direction. I believe that the major task confronting organizations during this last decade of the twentieth century is for them to move away from structures in which tasks are broken down into functional specialisms to a more integrated way of working whereby people come to realize that they are working for the whole enterprise. If this is the problem facing organizations then the theory of management must reflect this need for integration. In the future it will become less and less acceptable for business schools to teach separate courses on specialism X or specialism Y without reference to an integrative theory of organization.

The author of any book has many creditors: those people who have, often unknowingly, helped in its formation; those who have given generously of their time and opinions and yet demanded no repayment of the debt. For any book that has been so long in its making

– the actual writing can be traced back for nearly a decade quite apart from any prior gestation period – the list of creditors is too long to give in full. Special mention must, however, be made of my co-authors on the earlier *Top Decisions* book: David Hickson, David Cray, Geoff Mallory, and David Wilson. The time spent working with them on that project has been invaluable in forming my ideas for this book. So too must I thank John Sharp, Peter Clark, Rob Turner, Reva Brown, and an unknown reviewer who gave comments on earlier drafts. Thanks are also due to the many managers in industry, the public and voluntary sectors who gave generously of their time in the various research projects in which I have been involved and who, in a wider sense, provide the raw material of the subject of organizational analysis and theory; in one way or another without their co-operation there would be nothing to write about. Students of all levels and over many years – that most critical of all audiences – who are subjected to the sometimes half-cooked ideas of us academics, must also be thanked since they perhaps give the most potent and valuable of all comments. And, as always, there are Ann, Julian, and Rachel, those three special people for whom husband and father appeared to spend long hours incarcerated on his own doing something, they knew not always what. Well, this, for better or for worse, is the result. Thanks to them for their support and understanding since an author preoccupied with a writing project does not always make the best of companions.

Richard Butler
The Management Centre,
University of Bradford, 1990

# Chapter one

# The institutional model of organization

The overall question addressed by this book is to discover how organizations may be designed for effectiveness. The answer to this question has become ever more urgent as organizations have increasingly become a major feature of our lives, affecting every type of activity we pursue, and so too has the interest in studying and theorizing about them grown alongside the manifest problems of improving their design.

What is it that we are trying to achieve in organizational design? Organizations need to demonstrate fitness for future action within their environments (Thompson 1967: 88); in this way the manufacturer gets support from its customers, suppliers of raw materials, labour and capital, and the wider institutional environment; or the hospital likewise is supported by a wide range of interested parties. Big or small, manufacturing or service, public or private, whatever dimension is chosen to describe organizations they need support from their environments and, most crucially, they must be concerned with gaining support in the future. In order to do this they have to demonstrate their worthiness for such support by adopting appropriate structures (Brunsson 1989, Meyer and Scott 1983).

A typical working definition of an organization might say that it is: (1) a social entity that, (2) has a purpose, (3) has a boundary, so that some participants are considered inside while others are considered outside, and (4) patterns the activities of participants into a recognizable structure (Daft 1989). Although organizations are real in their consequences, both for their participants and for their environments, they are essentially abstractions. They cannot be picked up and dropped, felt or fulfil any of the other tests that we apply to physical things. The hospital, the firm, or the school will have physical aspects to them, the buildings, the plant and equipment and the like, but to understand how organizations work we need to go further than this. The factory has something real and physical about it but this is not the organization; people are doing tasks to which there is a pattern, raw materials are taken in, converted, and distributed to markets; capital is provided by banks and other financial institutions; systems provide information for decision making and co-ordination; people are talking about matters which do not necessarily appear to have anything directly to do with the job, some people remote from the physical plant, perhaps a continent away, are making decisions critical to our factory.

## ORGANIZATIONAL DESIGN AND THEORY

Organizational design is the setting of appropriate structures within which decisions are made and executed. Structure refers to the set of decision rules, or 'rules of the game' (Karpik 1972, Crozier and Friedberg 1980, Hickson *et al.* 1986) that guide the behaviour of an organization's participants during decision making and provide both opportunities and constraints for action; structures become observable as patterns in participants' behaviours although it is often the existence of formalized procedures and rules that are the most obvious manifestations of structure.

### Three source disciplines

Organizational theory provides the theoretical base for the analysis of organizational problems. It is essentially interdisciplinary (Pugh 1966) in its origins drawing particularly upon the three social science disciplines of economics, psychology, and sociology.

### *Economics*

Economics is particularly concerned with the efficient use of the resources at the disposal of an organization. Organizational theory developed partly as a reaction to some over-simplistic assumptions of economics and of its failure to comprehend the complexities of internal organization.

One such assumption of economics may be described as the notion of individualism. Classical economics (Smith 1937) was concerned with the question of how individual purposive human activity could, aggregated over a large number of individual decisions, result in effective meaningful collective outcomes without the participating individuals ever intending to achieve those outcomes. The marketplace, through its use of simple price signals and competition, was the institutional framework of the Industrial Revolution which enabled this process. Economics became primarily the study of individual behaviour as aggregated in marketplaces.

Economics complemented the individual human actor with a collective unit, the firm, but the effect was the same since the firm was assumed to be a single decision-making unit. This was still assumed to be profit driven and so the possibility of disputes amongst the management, or between the management and the owners, over what the firm should be doing, although noted in practice, was largely ignored or reduced to an error term in this theorizing.

Another problem arose from the observation that firms do not necessarily attempt to maximize profits (Cyert and March 1963) and neither do they operate in frictionless markets with abundant free information. Goals other than profit pursuit, such as survival, can take precedence or firms do not necessarily always accept the norm of competition since they can often be observed attempting to set up cartels or taking other anti-competitive moves.

One pathfinding work on the border between economics and organizational theory, *The Behavioral Theory of the Firm* (Cyert and March 1963), pointed to these deficiencies and proposed that the firm would be better conceptualized as a coalition of interests in which agreement amongst participants over a decision is only reached through a social process of bargaining and the making of temporary alliances over specific issues. The authors stressed the importance of uncertainty in making it difficult to reach agreement over goals. The significance of these ideas will be developed throughout this book.

*Psychology*

One way in which psychologists initially contributed to our understanding of organizations was by examining the problems of productivity, individual motivation (Maslow 1943, 1965, Herzberg 1966), morale, group conformity (Asch 1956), or leadership (Likert 1961, Fiedler 1967). The pioneering research of Elton Mayo in the Hawthorne Studies (Roethlisberger and Dickson 1939) moved industrial psychology away from essentially individualistic concerns to understanding the wider role of group norms by emphasizing that workers in factories and other kinds of organizations could not be treated only as an amorphous mass but had to be seen as individuals forming a social structure out of their interactions, beliefs, and values. The Hawthorne experiments are often associated with what became known as the Human Relations movement (Pugh and Hickson 1989: 170), a trend in management whereby attempts were made to create a more benign environment by providing workers with welfare facilities and other social benefits.

While these studies have been useful in developing our under-standing of organizational behaviour at a micro-level they suffer from the problem of reductionism whereby it is difficult to develop a theory linking the behaviour of individuals within an organization to its structure. A theory of organizational design must be able to link individual and small group action to action at the organizational level.

## Sociology

Whilst the research of sociologists complements that of psycho-logists in many areas, such as in Roy's (1952, 1954) classic studies of output restriction (see chapter 8) which parallel the Hawthorne Studies' interest in the informal organization, sociologists have naturally concentrated more upon social structural aspects of organizations and have increasingly taken a critical stance towards organizations.

Some studies have emphasized formal structure and its relation-ship to factors such as technology (Woodward 1965). Sociology in particular has been more concerned with wider issues of social structure outside the factory or organization (Gouldner 1954). It is the setting of organizations within a wider societal and insti-tutional framework that has been the particular contribution of sociology to organizational theory. Sociologists have pointed out that a large proportion of organizations are not profit seeking but pursue other goals (Blau and Scott 1963, Hall 1987). They stress, for example, the vast array of government bureaucracies, voluntary organizations (Butler and Wilson 1990), health and social service agencies, and so forth, are not profit seeking and that organ-izational theory needs to take this into account. Sociologists have also emphasized the importance of power and political processes as an aspect of organizations (Lukes 1974, Clegg 1979) and take a deliberately critical approach to the nature and operation of organizations.

**Three source models**

In addition to the source disciplines it is also possible to identify three source models of organization which have had an influence on the development of organizational theory. These are the closed systems, open systems, and coalition models each of which bears a resemblance to a paradigm (Burrell and Morgan 1979) in which there is a consistent system of thinking about organizations, each paradigm tending to develop its own disciples.

*Closed systems model*

Closed systems thinking can be exemplified by the 'one best way' Scientific Management School of thought based upon the belief that it is possible to scientifically determine various aspects of organization and is especially associated with writers such as F.W. Taylor (1911), Gilbreth and Gilbreth (1917), and Fayol (1930).

In the early part of the century, Taylor, through his experiences of working for the Bethlehem Steel Corporation in the United States, described the organization of the ideal factory workshop. This was to include features such as his system of functional foremen whereby basic workshop management was to be carried out by a number of foremen, such as a cost clerk, a time clerk, an inspector, a repair boss, or a disciplinary foreman, each specializing in some aspect of shop management. This philosophy of management became known as Taylorism and included methods of timing jobs in order to overcome disputes over the rate to pay for particular jobs.

Closely related to Taylorism is Fordism, a rather larger scale theory deriving from Henry Ford's ideas on assembly line production (Wood 1989). By breaking jobs down into precise measurable tasks, linked together and paced by a constantly moving assembly line, Ford introduced a radical philosophy of mass production; the logic was to keep the productive machine going at an even pace to achieve maximum efficiency at producing a given product in order to satiate an ever-hungry market for cars.

In terms of an overall picture of what an organization looks like, the closed systems model has a bureaucratic structure, with a strong hierarchy, rules, and procedures as the main co-ordinating method. The organization is viewed as essentially determinate based upon the possibility of laying down a set of rules for its operation so that once determined it could run effectively with the minimum of managerial intervention. Management under this model becomes essentially a rule setting and enforcing activity.

## Open systems model

The open systems model assumes that an organization exists in an environment, that its survival rests upon its ability to make exchanges with environmental elements, and that it has to adapt to environmental changes (Katz and Kahn 1966, Emery 1967, Buckley 1967).

We can conveniently summarize the main aspects of the open systems model in terms of five sub-system activities or functions (Katz and Kahn 1966: 86) which, it is assumed, all open systems will have to carry out. These are:

1 Boundary spanning. Open systems conduct exchanges with their environments acquiring resources and information, and exchanging goods or services in the environment for further resources. The boundary spanning function is needed to ensure that these exchanges take place and that the integrity of the system boundary is maintained.

2 Technological. At the heart of an open system is the transformation process converting inputs into outputs for exchange in the environment.

3 Control. An open system receives information about its performance from its environment and, through negative feedback, has to make the necessary adjustments to keep its performance on track and to maintain homeostasis.

4 Adaptive. An open system has to adapt to changing environmental circumstances and this means collecting information about constraints and opportunities in the task environment. It is this adaptive function that Beer (1972) describes as the 'brain of the firm'.

5 Institutional. Katz and Kahn (1966) note the Second Law of Thermodynamics stating that systems will degenerate towards ever-increasing disorganization unless steps are taken to prevent this. In the long term, the institutional sub-system is the most important one; externally it has the function of negotiating performance norms for the organization; internally it has the function of interpreting these norms into a set of internal norms, or ideology, to guide decision making.

*Political coalition model*

A major criticism of an open systems model is that it discounts the potential for conflict and goal disparities in organizations; each sub-system is assumed to fulfil its function as do the various organs of a biological system. This leads us to consider a political view of organization and the notion that participants may indulge in political acts and use power to further their own interests rather than the interests of the total system. A number of authors have emphasized the political reality of being a manager in an organization (Pettigrew 1973, Pfeffer 1981, Mintzberg 1983a, Hickson *et al.* 1986) but have not tackled the organizational design implications of this politick-ing. To survive there has to be a sufficient agreement over goals amongst an organization's participants, that is, there has to be a coalition of interests (Cyert and March 1963), and the organizational design question is to create appropriate structures to resolve these disparities.

An underlying source of goal disparity is the division of labour an organization develops over time. The exact nature of these divisions and groupings will vary from organization to organization according to factors such as technology, organizational history, or chance; one logic for these groupings has been mentioned, namely, the sub-system functions that have to be carried out. The coalition may also include external interests in the task environment of the organization such as customer groups, suppliers, financial institutions, government, and any other group that has some stake in the operation of the organiza-tion (Hickson *et al.* 1986).

There has, from time to time, been a tendency to assume that organizations are nothing but politics and power play. This, however, is to ignore the systemic needs of an organization to make exchanges with its environment in order to gain resources and to attend to internal concerns over efficient use of those resources; without sufficient attention given to these matters there would be no organization in which politicking may occur.

## THE INSTITUTIONAL MODEL OF ORGANIZATIONAL DESIGN: ICONIC VERSION

From these foundations has emerged an area of study with a developing body of theory, distinguishable from its source disciplines and organizational in its perspective (Donaldson 1985), that deals with the internal processes and structures of organizations and their relationship to the environment. This is organizational theory; it is a social science based theory of how purposive social organizations work. The general ideas developed above provide a background against which we can now construct the elements of a more precise model of organizational design which we call the institutional model.

A model is a simplified representation of a real system (Daft 1989: 21, Evans and Karwowski 1986: 3). In the physical world, aeronautical engineers might build scale models of aircraft for testing in wind tunnels or develop computer simulations; whether features such as materials used, construction, and size are different from the real thing is

*Figure 1.1* The institutional model of organizations

(a) Environmental

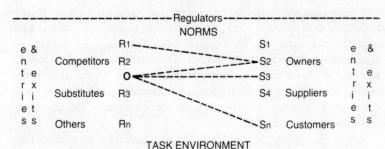

(b) Internal

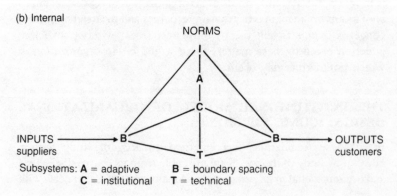

inconsequential providing the model is comparable on the essential variables under investigation such as shape, the proportions of certain dimensions, and so forth.

Social science models have similar aims in that essential variables are chosen for investigation but social science differs from engineering in that there is often less agreement over what perspective and assumptions should be taken. We start our theorizing from the institutional model of organization. This is presented in two versions: first, is what Evans and Karwowski (1986: 5) call an iconic model providing us with a visual picture of an organization within its environment (see Figure 1.1). Much of organizational theory starts from this kind of image of organization; the traditional picture of a hierarchy is another example of an iconic model. Second, will be a contingent model which more specifically develops the appropriate variables and their interrelationship. The institutional model incorporates the main features of the three source models outlined but adds the important extra dimension of the institutional environment.

## Organizations in action

The institutional model starts from a picture of an organization situated within an environment. An organization can be seen as located at the confluence of a number of streams of institutionalized action (Thompson 1967); we identify three such streams in particular: a resource stream, a normative stream, and a technical stream. The underlying organizational design problem is to ensure the co-alignment of these streams. Our iconic model of organizational action helps us to identify the main actors comprising these streams.

We start from the environment of a focal organization (O). This is seen to consist of two primary components, the task environment and the institutional environment.

### The task environment

The open systems model has emphasized the need to gain support via the exchange of resources with task environmental elements, the supporters (S) who may be customers, clients, suppliers of raw materials, finance and labour, and any other element in the task environment with which the organization makes exchanges. The supporters bring with them norms by which they assess an organization's performance and make judgements as to the future ability of that organization to fulfil their needs.

In making this assessment supporters may have available rivals (R) of the focal organization to provide another source from which their needs can be satisfied. Rivals consist of the direct competitors of the focal organization, possible substitutes (Porter 1985), and other less obvious elements who indirectly compete for a pool of resources. From the supporters' viewpoint, competitors are those rivals to which a supporter may exit (Hirschman 1970); the more rivals the supporter is presented with the less that supporter is dependent upon the focal organization.

The more general way to view O's problem is to see O as jostling with a set of rival organizations (Hannan and Freeman 1977), some of which may not be known, in order to attract the attention of a common set of supporters who are potential providers of resources; again, this potential set of supporters is not completely known. Hence, a university receiving government support is quite obviously competing with other universities to attract as much of that support as possible and to attract students, but it also has other less direct rivals, such as health care or social service organizations, which are trying to attract for themselves some of that same pool of government support.

*The institutional environment*

The normative stream of action derives from the institutional environment and appears as beliefs and values, or norms, outlining the range of desired performances for an organization (Thompson 1967) against which an organization's effectiveness is assessed; the need for a firm to make a profit is one example of this but the concept applies equally to non-profit organizations (Butler and Wilson 1990). Hence, the voluntary organization has to respond to norms concerning the types of aid it might provide for various categories of beneficiary and is more likely to be assessed according to a concept of moral worthiness than is the firm.

There are a number of identifiable segments of the institutional environment which can influence the norms to which an organization is exposed; the categories of religious, social, economic, governmental, political, and scientific institutions and groups probably cover the great majority of norm setters found in industrial nations. Increasingly, institutional environments are becoming international and consequently organizations are having to take note of norms concerning health, safety, consumer interests, ecological factors, and the like to a greater degree than ever before.

Norm developing is essentially a political process whereby interests in the institutional environment negotiate over their preferences concerning their preferred outcomes from the relevant task environment; task environment elements can be part of this negotiation. Out of this negotiation process comes a regulatory regime enforced by regulatory bodies; examples of such bodies are tax authorities, health and safety agencies, the Monopolies Commission in the UK, or the European Community.

Action in the institutional environment is potentially of the greatest long-term importance to an organization. For instance, scientific, socio-cultural, and political factors over the last three decades have had a tremendous effect on the tobacco industry (Miles and Cameron 1982). This has acted in a number of ways; scientific evidence became available to users of tobacco products concerning the health risks of smoking; socio-cultural values affected expectations of people as regards health and longevity; and political pressures, arising as a result of the scientific and socio-cultural effects, began to change the performance norms impacting upon the tobacco companies through regulations concerning factors such as advertising or the composition of the tobacco. Changing values of consumers and society can, in the end, be translated into hard regulations constraining the action of organizations in the task environment.

Institutional environments also regulate the extent to which entries and exits to the task environment are permitted, both for rivals and supporters. Regulations restricting the use of the airports in a country to airlines which sign reciprocal agreements with the national government limits the number of actors in the task environment of airlines (Pfeffer and Salancik 1978).

The reality for any but the simplest organization is that there can be different and sometimes contradictory norms arriving from different segments of the environment. An organization is most likely to respond to norms applied by those elements upon which it is most dependent but norms can change due to changes in the institutional environment, as seen above in the example of the tobacco industry. Further, organizations are not passive recipients of norms but can develop negotiated environments in order to change prevailing norms.

*Internal organization*

There are a number of aspects of internal organization which can be outlined as appropriate to our institutional model. The need for order is represented by a hierarchy and specialist positions. Particular sub-system functions need to be carried out as already defined in the open systems perspective, namely, transformation in the technical core of inputs to outputs, boundary spanning to obtain inputs and dispose of outputs, control to ensure that the organization fulfils the performance norms emanating from the environment, adaptation to monitor environmental changes, and an institutional sub-system which has to oversee the total system and negotiate terms with institutional environmental elements.

*The dynamic*

If changes occur in the performance norms applied by powerful environmental elements, the organization is expected to take note and to adapt according to its abilities; these may be introduced by changes in regulatory standards coming from the institutional environment, as the case of the tobacco industry shows, or from the actions of competitors affecting the availability of customers and supplies, and the prevailing industry norm. Internally, adjustments are made to cope with these changes in a search to find more appropriate structures.

If norms change to permit more entrants to a task environment an organization has to adapt its strategy. Such major regulatory changes can occur particularly during privatization (Butler and Carney 1987) and can create major uncertainties for an organization. Finally, an organization is not a passive recipient of performance norms but can act on the institutional environment to change them.

## THE INSTITUTIONAL MODEL: CONTINGENCY VERSION

We now wish to translate our iconic institutional model into an explanatory or contingency model to explain structure and in this way move further towards a theory of organizational design. By a contingency model we mean a model from which it is possible to make statements such as: increases in $X$ lead to an increase (or decrease) in $Y$ or, in more complex versions, increases in $X_1$, $X_2$, $X_3$, etc. lead to increases in $Y_1$, $Y_2$, etc.

Structure is defined as the enduring set of decision rules provided by an organization. So far our model of organization has suggested a central position for uncertainty and we will therefore base our explanatory model upon the processes of decision making which, so to speak, is the driving force of the model, providing the dynamic by which individual actors interact and make choices within an organizational framework.

Decision-making theory has long been a mainstay of organizational theory as seen particularly in the writings of Barnard (1938), Simon (1947), March and Simon (1958), and Cyert and March (1963) within what has become known as the Carnegie tradition (Daft 1989). Decision making is about choosing and acting and involves beliefs about ends/means relationships (Thompson 1967); it has an underlying theory of social action whereby there is an intention to act but a need to take into account the interpretation of a particular decision situation by the participants (March and Simon 1958: 152–3, Silverman 1970, Johnson 1987) in understanding the actions taken. It provides both an interpretive and an interactive theory of organizational processes

## Decision-making capacity and fuzzy versus crisp structures

The organizational design problem can be demonstrated as follows. Imagine ourselves with a 'green field' site and the ability to design an organization to carry out whatever purpose we wish. This might be a manufacturing business, a voluntary organization, or any other type of organization – it matters not. Also let us say that: an organizational structure provides capacity for decision making by setting the degree of elasticity of decison rules; fuzzy structures lead to high decision capacity; crisp structures lead to low decision-making capacity; a fuzzy structure will provide a great deal of elasticity on variables such as who does what job, the extent to which operating procedures can be adapted to varying situations, who can get involved in decisons, who has influence, who reports to whom, how participants get rewarded, the amount of analysis done during decision making, or on any other variable that is relevant to describing what organizational participants do when involved in decision making; crisp structures will provide a low degree of elasticity on the preceding variables.

The list of variables could be modified and no doubt extended; this we will find out as we proceed. At this stage it is sufficient to illustrate the kinds of design questions to be addressed. The terms fuzzy and crisp structures originate from the mathematical theory of fuzzy sets where a fuzzy restriction is defined as 'an elastic constraint as to the values that may be assigned to a variable' (Zadeh *et al.* 1975: 1). Such an idea seems appropriate to what is meant by a fuzzy structure here. The essential point about the fuzzy structure is not that there are no rules but that the rules are not considered as laid down in tablets of stone and are liable to change according to an ill-defined set of circumstances; they are considered flexible by decison makers and it is the intention rather than the letter of the rule that counts.

A number of other terms have been used in organizational theory which capture, in different ways, the meaning of the fuzzy–crisp distinction (see Table 1.1). McGregor (1960) made the distinction between theory Y and theory X management styles, Burns and Stalker (1961) described organic versus mechanistic organizations, Lawrence and Lorsch (1967) the differentiated organization, Cohen *et al.* (1972) the garbage can organization, Butler (1980b, 1983) communes or collectives versus bureaucracies, Ouchi (1980) clans versus bureaucracies, Peters and Waterman (1982) loose versus tight organizations, and Mintzberg (1983b) the adhocracy versus the machine bureaucracy.

The advantage in using the fuzzy–crisp terms is that they are located within a mathematical theory of fuzzy sets which holds some promise for the development of organizational theory (Lerner and Wanat 1983). Further, by showing that the terms capture most of the meanings covered by the above authors and by locating them within an institutionalized decision-making model of organizations, we suggest a needed unifying theme for organizational theory and design.

In general terms, we define structure as providing a relatively

*Table 1.1* Writers on the fuzzy-crisp theme

| Fuzzy | Crisp | Writer(s) |
|---|---|---|
| Theory Y | Theory X | McGregor 1960 |
| Organic | Mechanistic | Burns and Stalker 1961 |
| Differentiated | | Lawrence and Lorsch 1967 |
| Garbage can | | Cohen, Olsen, and March 1972 |
| Collective | Bureaucratic | Butler 1983 |
| Clan | Bureaucratic | Ouchi 1980 |
| Loose | Tight | Peters and Waterman 1982 |
| Adhocracy | Machine Bureaucracy | Mintzberg 1983 |

enduring set of rules for decision making. For the moment, the degree of fuzziness (or conversely the degree of crispness) is a convenient summarizing variable for structure and the nature of these rules; some rules are elastic and fuzzy, others are tight and crisp. We accept that fuzziness is a multidimensional variable the nature of which will be explored as we proceed.

## Uncertainty

We can see fuzzy structures as closely related to the notion of organic organizations and crisp structures related to mechanistic organizations as outlined by Burns and Stalker (1961). As in their theory we posit that the fuzzy structure is suitable for coping with conditions of high uncertainty whereas crisp structures are for coping with conditions of low uncertainty.

## Contextual variables: complexity

Uncertainty emerges from interpretations made by decision makers of particular objective conditions (Brunsson 1985) which we call context. The contextual variables are the set of independent variables seen to influence the dependent structural variables. According to the institutional model of organization so far described there are three main categories or streams of contextual variables: (1) the normative stream, (2) the resource stream, and (3) the technical stream (see Figure 1.2). In terms of the iconic version of the institutional model the contextual variables describe aspects such as the number of rivals and supporters in the task environment, and the norms of performance applied to the organization. Uncertainty will, in part, be an outcome of the extent to which decision makers are unsure about the values of these variables.

As with structure above we seek at this stage a summarizing concept for context; this we call complexity which will also be multi-dimensional and awaits exploration.

## Ideology variables: robustness

The notion of structural and contextual variables, or similar, has been well defined in organizational theory (Pugh *et al*. 1976a, 1976b). Here we introduce another set of less defined independent variables, those of ideology. Ideology is important in that it provides the set of ideas that decision makers take with them to guide decision making and to interpret their context (Brunsson 1985).

We also have a summarizing concept for ideology, that of robustness. A robust ideology is one that contains a rich body of ideas and may be contrasted to a focused ideology which has a highly specific set of ideas. The notion of ideology is developed at different points in this book and again we accept that this is a multidimensional variable awaiting elaboration.

## Linkages in the model

The overall point to appreciate in understanding the linkages in the institutional model outlined in Figure 1.2 is that the model operates at two levels. The first level is an organizational level, as indicated by thicker lines, while the second level is a decision-making level, as indicated by thinner lines.

At the organizational level complexity of context is seen to lead to fuzziness of structure which leads to robustness of ideology, which in turn leads to complexity of context. There is a mutually reinforcing triangle of relationships. Complex contexts are taken to require the flexible non-crisp type of structure to permit the requisite decision-making degrees of freedom, or high decision-making capacity as we will elaborate, in order to resolve uncertainties. But fuzzy structures foster, we will argue, a rich robust ideology with many shared meanings and trustworthy relationships between participants. We will also demonstrate that robust ideologies tend to choose complex contexts, and so the relationships outlined become mutually supporting over time. We could, of course, have argued conversely that simple contexts require only the decision-making capacity of crisp structures and it would be inefficient to provide more than is required, but this would lead to a narrower focused ideology on the part of decision makers which, in turn, leads to reinforcement of simple contexts.

At the decision-making level the model provides for decisions to arise within the context–structure–ideology triangle. Decision making is seen to be about coping with uncertainty. At this stage we will just note that the uncertainty of these decisions is in some way a function of fuzziness, complexity, and ideology, and that an organization will set in motion various decision-making processes to attempt to cope with decision uncertainty. The nature of these processes and their relationship to structure, context, and ideology also awaits exploration.

Nevertheless, two general observations can be made. First, as there is a cycle around the context–structure–ideology triangle so too will there be decision-making cycles but that these cycles are likely to be more frequent and of lesser duration than organizational level cycles. Second, there will be an interaction between decision cycles and organizational cycles. The model is summarized in Figure 1.2.

## THE DESIGN OF THIS BOOK

The contingency version of the institutional model provides a framework for the structure of this book. At present it is a skeleton awaiting a body and each chapter elaborates various aspects of the model. The notion of decision making provides the underlying theory of organizational processes in the model and we need an understanding of these processes; the theory of organizational decision making is presented in chapter 2 along with the Principle of Requisite Decision-Making Capacity; this principle allows us to make a step towards a view of organizational effectiveness. Effectiveness is also treated in chapter 3, but here we concentrate upon decision-making processes. Following some broad notions concerning types of organization presented in chapter 2, chapter 4 presents some more specific notions concerning bureaucratic and collective organizations. In chapter 5 we meet the technical stream of action and investigate some implications for structure. Chapter 6 concentrates upon the resource stream of action in a discussion of strategic choice and environment, and the relationship between the dimensions of environment and structure. Chapter 7 outlines some generalized notions of organizational profiles while chapter 8 returns to the normative stream of action in positing some relations between structure and ideology. Chapter 9 elaborates upon the all-important dynamic to the model through a discussion of organizational change and learning. This theme is continued in chapter 10 in a discussion of coalition management while chapter 11 provides a conclusion and summary.

We present a fairly broad selection of established organizational theories within the framework of the institutional model of organizations but do not claim to have been at all exhaustive in this. The major claim is that the institutional model of organization provides a much needed contribution to organizational theory and design by providing a coherent and unifying theory of organization transferable across time and space.

*Figure 1.2* The contingent institutional model of organization: the framework

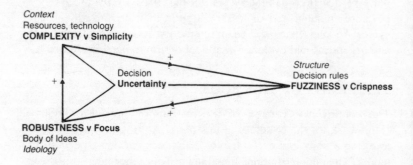

## DESIGN IMPLICATIONS AND SUMMARY

Organizational design needs to take into account the full complexity of the task and institutional environment, and of the technology. The contingent institutional model suggests that structure needs to be fitted to the context – complex contexts needing fuzzy structures, non-complex contexts requiring crisp structures.

Organizational design needs to be approached from the viewpoint of a triangular relationship between context, structure, and ideology at an organizational level of analysis, within which is located the processes of decision making. The organizational design problem becomes that of finding the structure to enable the required decision-making capacity. This notion will become encapsulated in the Principle of Requisite Decision-Making Capacity.

# Chapter two

# Effectiveness and institutional environments

According to the institutional model of organizations the starting point for considering the notion of effectiveness is the performance norms that emanate from action in the institutional environment. Externally, an organization is assessed against performance norms set by powerful elements within the institutional environment defining the essential values the organization is expected to pursue and the beliefs of how it is supposed to achieve those values. Norms provide standards of desirability by which an organization is scored and scores itself (Thompson 1967: 84). External norms get translated into internal norms for purposes of internal score keeping, forming the basis of the organization's ideology. Norms are not necessarily set unilaterally by the external elements but are set through a process of negotiation between an organization and its environment. The extent to which an organization can have a say in this negotiation will depend upon its power relative to other environmental elements (Thompson 1967). The overall design problem is that of achieving isomorphism (DiMaggio and Powell 1983) between the external norms and the norms used to assess the performance of internal decision making.

## KEEPING SCORE: PERFORMANCE NORMS

To help us understand the types of norms that might be applied to an organization two important dimensions of score keeping can be defined which are derived from the idea that there are two major problems in trying to assess performance.

First, is the extent to which the standard of desirability is clear or ambiguous. The correctness, or otherwise, of some performances can be easily assessed agianst a clear standard; the performance of a small manufacturing company can readily be measured by shareholders in terms of dividend yield whereas the benefactors of a charity will find the performance of their charity considerably more ambiguous and difficult to assess. This is the clarity–ambiguity dimension and we can say that, in general, the process of assessment gets more difficult as ambiguity increases.

Second, is the extent to which there are available other similar units against which comparisons may be made. The manufacturing company may be easily compared to other investment opportunities by shareholders whereas benefactors might see their charity as providing a unique service not comparable to any other. This is the comparability–uniqueness dimension. We can say that the process of assessment gets more difficult as uniqueness increases.

From these two dimensions we can identify four types of norms (see Figure 2.1). As norms define the expectations of powerful environmental elements they define the criteria of effectiveness.

**Efficiency/competitive norms**   When the situation is clear and comparable we can see efficiency norms as appropriate. This is the easiest case to assess since there is little room for doubt over the performance being exhibited; these norms are typically those which can be applied in competitive marketplaces and to economic organizations based upon the calculation of an output/input ratio, such as a profit and loss account, which may then be used for comparisons with others in the same industry.

**Moral**   The most difficult situation to assess is one of ambiguity and uniqueness since there is no clear benchmark and the values applied are absolute. Moral norms are typically applied in collective or solidary organizations (Etzioni 1964, Butler 1980b, 1983) where the goals encompass the achievement of some absolute good, and under these conditions assessment takes place in a less overt way than with efficiency norms; 'soft' data, relying upon reputation and trust built up over a long time period tends to predominate in the absence of empirically testable data.

**Instrumental norms**   This is the first of the two in-between situations where standards are clear, in the sense that we know whether a particular objective is being reached, but there is no easily available comparison. This situation can apply to bureaucracies, such as government agencies, where there is only one organization of the type. The Inland Revenue is an example of this; instrumental tests are often the only possible norms that may be applied to such organizations. Hence tax authorities may be assessed by the amount of tax evasion they can avoid or the number of investigations conducted. In other words, assessment means finding targets towards which the behaviour of the unit in question is directed. The problem for the assessors in this situation is that, although they can measure tax collected, they cannot truly assess whether all evasion has been eliminated; in the absence of a comparator it is difficult to judge the extent to which performance could be improved.

**Referent norms**   The other in-between situation occurs where standards are ambiguous but there are available other apparently similar units against which performance may be measured. This is typically the situation for a professional organization since professional work is difficult to assess but where there are other comparable individuals available with the professional peer group providing the referent. Finding other appropriate referent groups becomes the main task of assessment under these conditions. The problem for assessors in this situation is that they have no ready measure as to whether the organization has completed a task correctly.

*Figure 2.1*  Four norms, four types of effectiveness

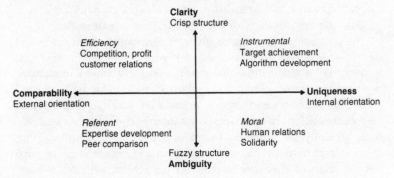

*Sources*: Adapted from Thompson, J.D. (1967) *Organizations in Action*, McGraw-Hill; and Quinn, R.E. and Cameron, K. (1983) 'Organizational life cycles and shifting criteria of effectiveness: some preliminary evidence', *Management Science*, 29: 23-61.

## Effectiveness and the search for isomorphism

The above discussion indicates that the effectiveness of an organization can only be measured relative to norms deriving from the institutional environment. An organization may have to respond to a number of different performance norms emanating from various parts of the environment in order to demonstrate its fitness for future action and future support. These norms can sometimes be contradictory. The fundamental design question is how an organization can achieve isomorphism with its environment by translating these external norms into an internal ideology. We may recall that organizational ideology is the system of internal norms, values, and beliefs that underlie decision making in an organization. The proposition is that an organization needs to achieve isomorphism with the norms used to assess an organization's performance in the environment by reflecting those norms, as far as possible, in its ideology. In this way decision making can be linked as closely as possible to the values expected by the environment.

This problem can be approached from what Daft (1989: 108) calls the competing values approach to organizational effectiveness. Daft suggests that there are two important dimensions to the question of achieving effectiveness, that of structure and that of the externality or internality of orientation of decision making. In our terms structure can be fuzzy or crisp; orientation refers to whether goals are focused onto the environment of the organization or externally.

The competing values approach to organizational effectiveness and the types of norms are combined in Figure 2.1 using the modified terminology of the institutional model of organization. Competitive norms (comparable, clear), it is suggested, will tend to be associated with crisp structures and external orientation: profit, efficiency, and customer relations become important internal goals of the organization, typically the situation found in market organizations. With instrumental norms (unique, clear) structures also tend to be crisp but the orientation is now internal: target achievement and the use of algorithms to make decisions become important internal goals, typically the situation found in agencies such as government bureaucracies. With referent norms (comparable, ambiguous) the orientation is external but structures are fuzzy: expertise development and peer group evaluation become the important internal goals. With moral norms (unique, clear) the orientation is internal and structures also fuzzy, typically the situation found in collective organizations.

The norms that an organization is exposed to are varied and come from many sources in the institutional environment. In practice, organizations often have to respond to different norms from different parts of the environment (Thompson 1967: 88) and have to make choices about which norms to give priority. For example, government may measure a police force quite instrumentally using crime figures, detection rates, and the like. The public living in a particular area may prefer to stress moral norms such as courteousness of the officers, lack of harassment, and the extent to which the police respond to local needs. Since it is not normally possible to score high on all relevant measures organizations may 'satisfice' by holding constant some measures and showing an improvement on a small number of measures used by task-elements upon which the organization is particularly dependent. If there are multiple dependent relationships the result will tend to be satisficing by reaching a compromise between any conflicting demands.

The discussion above sets up a typology of norms but an important dynamic is indicated in Figure 2.1. It is suggested that assessors and regulators will tend to prefer the easier to measure efficiency/competitive norms by seeking non-ambiguous standards and appropriate other units against which comparisons can be made (Thompson 1967). For regulators there is a preference for clarity and comparability. Conversely, the regulated may try to avoid efficiency/competitive norms by pointing to their uniqueness and the inherent ambiguity of their activities. The most difficult type of test to apply is the moral test since there is little in the way of a clear standard of performance and relevant organizations for comparison purposes.

## TYPES OF ORGANIZATIONAL INCORPORATION

There are many ways of classifying organizations (see Blau and Scott 1963, Hall 1987) but from the institutional model perspective the most appropriate dimension on which to do so would be by the type of performance norm applied to an organization deriving from the institutional environment. As we shall see this provides the basis for a typology of incorporation of organizations within the legal structure of the nation-state. Any such typology will vary across nations but it provides a broad framework for thinking about the issue.

Incorporation of an organization refers to the means by which it is made part of the nation-state and whereby it is given certain rights to act and have certain obligations imposed upon it. It is a two-way process whereby the state has an interest in how various organizations operate and sets up regulatory regimes to monitor operations; conversely organizations have discretion to act and can try to negotiate more favourable terms for themselves (Butler and Carney 1985).

## Market organizations

Efficiency/competitive norms predominate for the firm operating in a market where there is competition to enable comparative assessment and a free flow of information to enable the ambiguity of assessment to be minimized. The role of the institutional environment, acting through regulators, is to ensure that the market remains efficient in these terms. Governments attempt to do this by means of monopoly, restrictive practice, anti-collusion legislation, and the like to ensure that the number of rivals in the task environment remains high. At the simplest level firms have to conform to particular standardized accounting and auditing practices in order to make assessment easier. Although in modern industrial societies there are a great many regulations that firms have to conform to covering health, safety, pollution control, employment, and so forth, in exchange for these obligations the firm has a great deal of autonomy to buy, make, and sell what it wishes within a very wide range of markets. Within these constraints regulators leave the process of competition to do the regulating.

## Agencies

These are generally set up by parent organizations to fulfil a specific purpose and are therefore assessed predominantly by instrumental norms. Government agencies such as the Inland Revenue, but also subsidiary branches of large business corporations, can also be predominantly assessed instrumentally when their main purpose is to provide a single product or service only for the use of the parent.

It is worth noting that the organizations which regulate the business firms, as mentioned above, are agencies and therefore act according to instrumental norms since government generally tries to avoid competition amongst its own agencies. For government, agencies fit into some overall plan; hence, the size and powers given to the Inland Revenue fit the government's plan for revenue generation. Generally, the discretion to act is much less for agencies than for market organizations but in exchange for this restriction the agency is usually assured greater security of existence. Competition between agencies is not unknown, however, as we see when, for instance, the Inland Revenue and Customs and Excise (the latter being responsible in the UK for the collection of value added tax) can come into conflict, or rival police agencies trespass upon each other's territory.

Hence regulators will lay down performance targets and measurements and define the number of rivals that are allowed to enter the task environment.

## Professional organizations

Professional organizations consist of a set of professionally-qualified people who serve clients with their expertise. A fairly pure example of a professional organization is a medical or an architectural practice. Larger organizations, such as universities or research institutes, have many of the features of a professional organization although these cases are overlayed by a high degree of bureaucracy.

Referent norms predominate in the professional organization. The basic mode of operation is for the participant professionals to relate to their own clients. With this type of work clients find it difficult to evaluate the performance of their professional because of the inherent ambiguity of the service; they have gone to the professional to seek expertise, and evaluation of the advice given may not be possible until a considerable time later, if ever. Nevertheless comparisons are possible with other similar professionals.

An important part of professional work is the relationship of the professional with other professionals in the same 'trade', a relationship that is controlled through a professional association. The association will serve as a regulatory agency and as an arena for developing expertise by organizing professional meetings and overseeing the training of new entrants to the profession (Hickson and Thomas 1969); for instance, architectural schools will ensure that their courses are acceptable to the professional association.

The professional association regulates by controlling competition, setting numbers for those entering training, forbidding or restricting advertising or controlling the location of practices, and by licensing only those who have experienced an approved training. The professional association often has the backing of the state which, by law, may forbid the practising of that profession by non-licensed practitioners. Through the granting of a virtual monopoly there is an obligation upon the profession concerned to keep their own house in order. Because of the inherent ambiguity of evaluating professional work, the institutional environment is usually aimed at setting up rules to allow self-regulation (Butler and Carney 1985) to take place and the professional association is the main body for carrying out the setting of performance norms. The development of a code of ethics is an inherent part of self-regulation, so too is the definition of appropriate conduct between the practitioner and the client and, ultimately, the use of expulsion for excessive misconduct. Although self-regulation is sometimes criticized as being self-serving, the regulators' dilemma is that if the profession truly has exclusivity of expertise there is no other group of people with the necessary understanding to evaluate the activities in question.

## Mutual benefit associations

Mutual benefit associations are organizations which exist for the benefit of their members. At their inception British building societies were formed by working people who would save small sums of money each week eventually to afford the deposit and obtain a mortgage for the purchase of a house. For working people this was a way of finding credit when bank loans would not have been a possibility. By being privy to data concerning the reputation of a member for thrift and sobriety, gained through savings records, local rumour, and other more qualitative information, the building society could economize on transactions costs in making a decision about a loan (see p. 27ff. concerning notion of transaction costs) compared to the more directly commercial transaction with a bank.

Although British building societies are currently moving away from this tradition and changing their status nearer to that of market organizations, whereby we could anticipate a greater use of efficiency norms, the principle remains the same for those that remain mutual benefit associations. Savings and loans associations found in many countries follow the mutual benefit pattern as do, in a different sphere of activity, communes, clubs, consumer co-operatives, and self-help groups.

The performance norms tend to have a strong moral component and the institutional environment sets up regulations to ensure that the rules of association are kept to, an important purpose being to avoid misappropriation of funds. For example, the rules governing trusteeships try to ensure this by preventing trustees from benefiting from the activities of the organization.

Worker or producer co-operatives have some aspects of a mutual benefit association; if the production was entirely consumed by the membership they would be mutual benefit associations but more usually they have to sell their products in the open market in which case they take on many characteristics of a market organization; this point will be elaborated later.

## Charities

A charity is an organization set up to link givers of money or other benefits to the receivers of those benefits. The charity (alternatively known as a voluntary organization) acts as a broker between givers and receivers (Butler and Wilson 1990). An example is Oxfam, a charity specializing in providing aid to Third World countries; givers in the UK, or in any of the countries covered by Oxfam's subsidiaries, provide benefits (mainly money) which are then used to run schemes such as irrigation, drainage, crop improvement, and the like in Third World countries. The reason why givers give is a complex issue. Titmuss (1970) in his study of the volunteer British blood-doning system summarized this gift relationship between givers and receivers in terms of a bond due to a feeling of common humanity.

Regardless of the motivations of individual donors the problem from the viewpoint of the institutional environment is to ensure that gifts intended for a purpose are in fact used for that purpose. The performance norms of the charity are essentially moral in the sense that the environment expects to be able to trust a charitable organization to run its affairs honestly. Legally, the specific constraints put upon the charity in English law (the law in many American states follows, in broad terms, English practice) requires that a charity operate for the good of the general public and not for the good of its members or for the givers, which distinguishes it from the mutual benefit association. Following this there is a requirement that the trustees do not benefit from the charity.

## THE INSTITUTIONAL ECONOMISTS AND TRANSACTIONS COSTS

Above we have presented a typology of institutional norms and indicated the relationship between these norms and the kinds of internal goals that organizations develop. A useful complementary approach to these kinds of questions illustrating the connection between organizational theory and economics has come from a group who have become known as the Institutional Economists.

Institutional Economics has its roots in the work of Coase (1937), Commons (1970), and Arrow (1974); the underlying question is to investigate the forces that encourage the transference of economic activities from the marketplace to governance from within the authority system of a firm.

Consideration of institutional economics can be approached from the ideas contained within classical economics. Adam Smith (1937) was concerned with the problem of how the intentions and actions of individuals can be co-ordinated to form a joint result without those individuals ever necessarily having the intention to produce that result. He was writing during the early stages of the Industrial Revolution when small firms and traders would independently carry out steps in a whole chain of processes before a final product was produced. The textile industry provides a good example of this; one firm might buy the raw wool and carry out a preliminary cleaning and combing before selling it to another firm for a further stage, perhaps spinning, and so on down the line until a final garment was sold to a consumer. The intention of, say, the woolcomber was not to produce cloth or a garment; it was just to sell combed wool. And yet through market transactions the net result was for garments to be produced.

A complex division of labour occurred, each producing firms specializing in a small part of a total process based upon a specialized expertise, in competition with other firms. At each stage of the process the goods changed ownership with the marketplace acting as the principal institution for co-ordinating these transactions. The goods might only move a short distance down the street to another firm, and the streets of the expanding cities of northern England became part of a great enterprise mainly co-ordinated by market transactions with the extent of this division of labour as determined by the extent of the market; as competition increased so there was an incentive for participants in the market to find further niches by further sub-dividing the overall labour process.

## Market failures

The market system of the Industrial Revolution came to display certain market failures; inefficiencies became apparent, encouraging a move towards encompassing many of these transactions within the managerial framework of single firms. The transactions were still conducted but increasingly under the direct control of a managerial hierarchy and authority system. What Adam Smith called the 'invisible hand' of the marketplace was being replaced by what Chandler (1977) later called the 'visible hand' of organization; unintentional co-ordination became intentional co-ordination.

Williamson (1975, 1985) analysed the nature of these market failures and the conditions under which they occur thereby reviving interest in the notion of different kinds of institutional arrangements for the governance of transactions. He identified two basic problems in co-ordinating transactions: (1) the problem of incomplete information, that is, the problem of bounded rationality, and (2) the problem of opportunism.

In general terms, bounded rationality refers to a condition whereby decision makers' ability to comprehend a problem is limited, a condition created by uncertainty (March and Simon 1958); this term is explained in more detail in chapter 3. For present purposes we may say that bounded rationality can be *ex ante* or *ex post*. *Ex ante* bounded rationality refers to the problem of defining all the conditions and possible outcomes of a transaction at the outset. For example, in purchasing a component for inclusion in a manufactured product, the management of a firm will need to lay down precise specifications defining aspects such as basic design, dimensions, materials, quality standards, quantity, delivery date, and so forth. Many contracts can be extremely complex and require teams of legal specialists to draw them up. Williamson's basic argument is that as these contracts get more complicated there is an incentive to internalize that transaction, that is, to employ people to make that component in order to reduce managerial costs. The direct price paid for a bought item compared to a made item will undoubtedly enter the equation as to whether this is done or not but the managerial costs of controlling transactions also need to be considered. That is, an institutional framework to permit greater decision-making capacity is needed.

*Ex post* bounded rationality refers to the problem of judging whether the management of the buying firm have got that which they requested. In the case of manufactured components this means either having an internal inspection system for goods received or, as is becoming increasingly common and has long been standard practice for large sub-contracting firms such as Marks and Spencer, the buying firm will inspect the production processes and management procedures of the supplying company to ensure that the components are made to standards. Either way, a management cost is incurred. Williamson argues that as the transaction gets more complex, perhaps due to an inherently uncertain technical process, the incentive to internalize and create a hierarchical organization increases.

Opportunism is the tendency of individuals to pursue self-interested behaviour 'with guile' (Williamson 1985: 47). Again, *ex ante* and *ex post* can be identified. The problem of insurance illustrates the distinction between these two types of opportunism. *Ex ante* opportunism refers to the tendency of people seeking insurance not to disclose information as regards the true risk. A company seeking insurance for a plant might not disclose the true danger of the production process; the insurance company tries to guard against this by using inspectors and clauses in the contract making the insurance cover void if certain information is not disclosed or is falsified. This can be done but it increases the cost of the transaction; inspectors have to be paid, contracts written. *Ex post* opportunism refers to the tendency of the insured not to honestly disclose the full conditions surrounding a claim should such occasion arise. Indeed, in the insurance case it might include deliberately making a false claim, perhaps by starting a false fire and claiming an inflated value of stock, a problem sometimes known as a 'moral hazard' (Williamson 1975). Again, insurance companies will attempt to cover this eventuality by the use of inspectors, but at a cost.

Opportunism does not mean that everybody is cheating all the time but that there is a propensity to cheat and that safeguards against this have to be built into the conditions surrounding a transaction. There is an interaction between bounded rationality and opportunism; opportunism breeds off bounded rationality in the sense that if the insurer, in the example above, had perfect knowledge opportunism would not be possible. If all possible outcomes could be foreseen at the commencement of a transaction, there is perfect knowledge and no bounded rationality. It would then be possible to write into a contract all contingencies and to set up appropriate surveillance to guard against opportunism. This, however, is not the situation met in any but the simplest of transactions

One further condition is important in this framework. This is the condition of small numbers. Markets operate upon the notion that a dissatisfied buyer, or seller, can exit to an alternative supplier (Hirschman 1970). Under the condition of small numbers such a choice becomes difficult because of monopoly power. Small numbers is a condition that increases the likelihood of opportunism.

The framework is summarized in Figure 2.2. Bounded rationality and opportunism are two underlying behavioural variables; the first represents the problem-solving ability of people while the second represents the self-interested seeking behaviour. The two are interconnected with the likelihood of opportunism increasing the less it is possible to define the conditions surrounding a transaction (that is, bounded rationality increases) and will increase transaction costs in the sense that the buyer of a supply will try to guard against them through surveillance and defining contracts closely. There will come a point when the marketplace is no longer a suitable institutional arrangement to govern the transaction and the market will be superseded by hierarchical organization and an authority system.

*Figure 2.2* The market failures framework

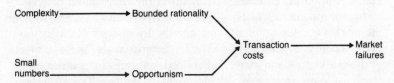

*Source*: Williamson, O.E. (1975) *Markets and Hierarchies: Analysis and Antitrust Implication*, New York: the Free Press.

The market failures framework provides a theory of how transactions shift from market to hierarchical governance (or vice versa) based upon the underlying logic of the minimization of managerial costs. Williamson made a distinct contribution by pointing to the over reliance of classical economic theory upon the notion of markets moving towards an equilibrium point of an optimal marginal price. The classical model assumes near perfect knowledge on the part of decision makers (lack of bounded rationality) and large numbers – that is, good competition. It also tends to ignore the propensity for participants to disguise relevant information from competitors.

One criticism of the markets and hierarchies framework is that it neglects the problem of power (Francis 1983). By this it is meant that neither a marketplace nor a hierarchy (or, more generally, an organization) are situations where participants start on an equal footing. In the market, large firms can exert pressure on the small firms due to greater buying power and ability to move on an international stage. Further, the labour market is not usually a market where employees compete on an equal footing with employers. The transactions costs framework is essentially a theory driven by the logic of efficiency and, over a large number of transactions and over time, the argument is that the quest for efficiency will be the main driving force in determining whether market or hierarchical modes are used.

## The collective as a third method of governing transactions

Williamson is, in effect, proposing the existence of two broad categories of organization: the market and the hierarchy (or bureaucracy) and the conditions under which each will come into existence. A third form of organization has been suggested: the collective form (Butler 1980b, 1983) or clan (Ouchi 1980), which operates upon the principles of moral norms and shared beliefs.

In outlining the variables of the collective form it is useful to put the market and hierarchies theme into the framework of the institutional model of organization. Table 2.1 summarizes the main features of the market, bureaucracy, and collective forms of organization in terms of their structures, ideology, and context. The structural variables of the market can be briefly summarized as consisting of price and exit since this is the primary way in which information flows, and the buyer–seller contract. Ideology stresses the competitive norms while high tangibility of the transactions, low interdependence, and large numbers make up the context most conducive to the market's operation. In an effective market, context, structure and ideology act together to co-ordinate the actors; low interdependence, high tangibility, and large numbers provide the context whereby price and exit is an effective means of communicating preferences but only if the competitive ideology is also present. Likewise, in an effective bureaucracy medium values of tangibility, interdependence and numbers provide the context whereby routines and voice communicate preferences providing the ideological conditions of authority and obedience are present.

The underlying structural features of the collective are those of interaction, consensual decision making and member–membership contracts. The collective is an organization in which trust, shared beliefs, and moral norms form the ideological basis. Structures permitting high interaction can foster the development of moral norms in addition to transmitting technical information. Typical of the collective is the clan (Ouchi 1980) or team where a relatively small number of participants are working closely together, sharing information, and trusting in one another's competence and honesty. It is suggested that the context for which the collective is most suited

*Table 2.1* Markets, bureaucracies, and collectives

|  | Structure | Ideology | Context |
|---|---|---|---|
| MARKET e.g., industry | Price, Exit Buyer–seller | Efficiency – competition | High tangibility Low interdependence Large numbers |
| e.g., divisional structure internal markets | *internal organization begins about here* | | |
| BUREAUCRACY e.g., firm, agency | Routines, Voice Employer– employee | Instrumental – authority – obedience | Medium tangibility Medium interdependence Medium numbers |
| COLLECTIVE e.g., co-operative | Interaction Consensual Member-member- ship | Moral – shared beliefs – trust | Low tangibility High interdependence Small numbers |

*Source*: Butler, R.J. (1983) 'A transactional approach to organizing efficiency: perspectives from markets, hierarchies and collectives', *Administration and Society* 15 (3): 323–62.

is that of small numbers, low tangibility, and high interdependence – a propositon resting upon the notion that large numbers make the development of high interaction and consensual decision making time-consuming and organizationally costly. The collective provides for a further increase in available decision-making capacity over that provided for by the market or bureaucracy.

Overall, the collective is an example of a fuzzy structure whereas a move to the bureaucracy and market implies an increasing shift towards crispness. Table 2.1 also provides for the existence of in-between forms. The divisional structure (which we meet in more detail in chapter 7) is an example and can be seen as an illustration of an internal market form of organization drawing especially upon the characteristics of the market and of the bureaucracy.

### The make–buy decision

One area of application of the transactions costs theory can be to analyse the question of whether a company should make or buy a commodity. This question can apply to a number of factors of production: should a company make a component for assembly in-house or purchase it, or should a service such as maintenance or security be carried out by an internally created department or bought-in?

The obvious answer to this question would be to compare the costs of the two methods. To do this involves calculating internal direct costs of making plus some apportionment of overheads and comparing this to the cost of buying the component. What would not generally be accounted for would be the managerial cost of managing the transaction (Butler and Carney 1983).

Application of transactions costs theory to assess the managerial cost of a transaction would first require us to identify the context. Hence, if a good is tangible, not too highly interdependent, and if there is a ready availability of suppliers, the most cost-effective in terms of transaction costs would be the market; that is, buy rather than make. If, on the other hand, there is some intangibility, some interdependence, and a not particularly ready supply available outside, the internal hierarchical arrangement would be preferred. Further, if interdependence and intangibility are high, but numbers small, a more collective arrangement is to be preferred; these are the operations so central to the organization and where that special knowledge which can only be developed within an organization and not within a market is needed. The firm cannot subcontract its strategic decision-making activity but it can potentially subcontract the purchase of routine used components such as nuts and bolts. In between there is a whole range of hierarchically-managed transactions some of which, if they become less central (reduction in interdependence), or more tangible (due to improvement in technical knowledge), or where numbers have become larger (due to development of the market for the good), might be moved to market transactions. This has increasingly become the situation for many public service organizations which have for decades carried out in-house operations; for example, hospitals previously running their own laundries now usually contract that function out to private sector laundries.

## CHANGING INSTITUTIONAL ENVIRONMENTS: COMPARISON OF JAPANESE AND WESTERN MANAGEMENT PRACTICES

It is when we change nations that aspects of different institutional environments become particularly prominent. This is especially so if we compare the characteristics of 'typical' European or North American companies to 'typical' Japanese companies; both Japan and Europe are highly developed industrially and generally we are comparing organizations in which there is a similar technology so that it becomes easier to attribute differences to institutional arrangements rather than to technical or market conditions. In order to compare the 'typical' Japanese and western company we create characterisms of large corporations in each of the contexts; we will also examine the extent to which these characterisms are justified in terms of their representativeness of industrial organization found in the two contexts.

Holding aside for the moment the risk of over-simplification we can give a summary of the features of a 'typical' Japanese company drawing upon the accumulating evidence on Japanese organization (Dore 1973, Clark 1979, Sako 1988). This literature highlights a number of features of the Japanese company which can be summarized as follows:

**Sense of community**   Japanese company practices emphasize the sense of community whereas western companies are based more upon individual rewards (Hofstede 1980). The collective norm and the need for the employee to work in a team is emphasized in the Japanese company more than in the western. Collectivization in the Japanese company is reinforced by a number of rituals and symbolic gestures which are alien to western eyes; the company song or creed, group exercises in the factory, workers bowing to each other at the beginning of each day and meeting with the supervisor. Workers in a British factory would simply start up their machines and start work (Dore 1973). Work is more individualistic in the western company. Yet, in spite of greater collectivization in the Japanese company there is also a greater respect for authority although this tends to be implicit rather than explicit.

**Lifelong employment**   The great commitment expected from individuals by the organization is reflected by the Japanese approach to tenure. Cohort entry to large corporations is designed to reinforce the mutual expectation that employment in that company is for life. It is, in practice, quite difficult for Japanese workers and executives to move company since there is a stigma associated with leaving the employment of one's company. Employment alternatives, therefore, are generally much less than in the west. Large companies demand a high educational level and set a civil service type of career progression with fine grading and salary levels. In general, salaries and pay are not directly related to performance, the company relying upon a sense of commitment from the individual. Western culture, especially in North America, sees job mobility, at least up to a certain age, as an advantage.

As a consequence of the expectation of life tenure, age, length of service, and evidence of commitment become the main criteria for promotion; the company looks after the employee in return for total commitment. Western culture emphasizes performance and skill, and attempts to marginalize the effects of age and length of service. The Japanese promotion and pay system removes the unpredictability inherent in a western system which more generally puts greater emphasis upon individual performance. Again, the Japanese method can work in a culture that accepts lifelong tenure; it would not work in a mobile, performance-linked system since high-performing workers would quit.

**Collective decision making**   Japanese decision making emphasizes collective responsibility, ensuring commitment to a course of action before taking action. This can often make decision making appear slow to western minds but, on the other hand, implementation can be very speedy as a consequence. Western companies tend to emphasize individual responsibility more.

**Fine status grading**   The Japanese approach to hierarchy reflects the greater acceptance of authority and the greater power distance (Hofstede 1981), and a paternalism reflecting a strong familial culture (Littler 1982: 154–5) in which women are expected to mind the home and the men to earn the living. Hierarchical gradations tend to be finer with workers accepting their position and prepared to move gradually up the promotion scale. Western companies tend to have a greater difference between management and workers. A great deal of symbolism surrounds the equal status Japanese system, such as the wearing of uniforms, fewer job descriptions, and a common cafeteria for all employees.

**Group operation**   The Japanese structure puts greater emphasis on team working and lack of demarcation between jobs in the horizontal direction whereas western companies tend to emphasize individual responsibility.

With its greater emphasis upon social and group pressures to achieve conformity, discipline in the Japanese factory tends to be less overt and based more upon unquestioning acceptance of authority. The western company is more overt in its use of authority and discipline. In the west, particularly in Europe with its tradition of worker–management conflict, work has traditionally been seen as more exploitive than in Japan. Western companies are more likely to rely upon formal sanctions and rules in discipline matters.

**Company based unions**  Japanese unions tend to operate more on the lines of staff associations whereas western unions tend to be more industry based.

## The wider institutional framework

The above summary of the Japanese corporation is a simplification. There is, of course, variation within Japan, although perhaps rather less than there is within western Europe and North America. There are a number of aspects of the wider Japanese institutional environment that, emphasized, will help us to understand the reasons for the nature of large Japanese business corporations and the limitations to this model.

The Japanese have a different attitude to authority. In setting the historical scene of the development of Japanese culture, Morishima (1982) describes how the Japanese took on a modified form of Confucianism from the Chinese. Traditional Chinese Confucianism placed a high value on faith, benevolence, obedience, and symbolism but the Japanese version played down the benevolence aspect and stressed obedience. Consequently, the rise of capitalism in Japan during the nineteenth century took on a less individualistic aspect in comparison to the West and carried forward the strong respect for traditional authority.

Post-Second World War the Americans forced a number of changes on Japanese society (Morishima 1982), in particular the introduction of female suffrage, the right of labour to organize, the abolition of autocratic government, the absolutist monarchy, privy council and peerage, and the break up of large trading companies. In spite of these changes, individualism did not take root and unions remained enterprise unions. The traditional respect for authority, the separate roles for men and women, and many other aspects of a traditional society remained intact (Hofstede 1980).

Dualism (Sako 1988), the large gap between the status and rewards of working for large and small companies, is a marked feature of the Japanese economy. Although the security and tenure aspects of Japanese organizations are commonly pointed to, they only apply in the large prestigious companies for which there is great competition to enter. Only about 30 per cent of the working population work under these conditions (Twaalhoven and Hattori 1982) and even here tenure is a matter of custom and practice rather than of legal contract. The majority of Japanese work in small companies doing subcontract work for the large ones at relatively low wages. Prestige derives from working for a large corporation and recognition is given to an individual according to the status of his employer.

Subcontractors tend to be highly dependent upon their large customer corporations. As far as possible the large corporations try to link the subcontractor into their network through techniques such as Just-in-Time (JIT) management, thereby reducing the small firms' freedom to move to other customers; in this way corporations maintain a high degree of power over their suppliers. We can now see how the large companies are able to maintain the predictability of the employment contract. Any fluctuations in demand can be passed onto the subcontractors.

In many ways the relationships within Japanese organizations mirror those in the wider society (Sako 1988) as seen in two ways. First, are the interconnections between large corporations and other organizations, such as banks, trading companies, and government departments. Japanese managers spend a great deal of effort in developing close industry associations for sharing information and in developing links with the Ministry of International Trade and Industry (MITI) (Ouchi 1984). Second, is the close way in which subcontractors are managed, reflecting the ideology and structures that we see within Japanese companies. The large company sets up close working relationships with subcontractors with frequent meetings and visits.

Table 2.2 shows a summary of the features of the Japanese company already noted compared to the features of the subcontracting system. Here we also see an emphasis upon long-term relationships, high trust, with frequent contacts between customer and contractor, to a much greater degree than would be the norm in Britain (Sako 1988). There is also a fine grading of subcontractors with a hierarchy of status and size. The customer-company may allow good performing sub-contractors to join an association of contractors. The company pays great attention to maintaining frequent contacts with the supplier. These characteristics of the subcontractor–company relationship are reflected in the internal organization of the company and also in the other environmental relationships (see Table 2.2).

*Table 2.2* Japanese company/context relationships: the case of subcontractors

| Subcontractors/company relationship | Company |
| --- | --- |
| High trust | Community |
| Long term | Lifetime employment |
| Association of companies | Collective decisions |
| Fine grading of status | Fine grading |
| Frequent contacts | Group operation |

Adapted from Sako, Mari (1988), lecture delivered at University of Bradford Management Centre, 23 May.

A number of advantages of the subcontracting system accrue to the large corporations in Japan concerning the operation of the labour market. First, the subcontractors provide a pool of low cost labour. The small companies are of low capital intensity compared to the large and so flexibility is achieved in the labour market by using subcontractors to absorb fluctuations in demand. Toyota has approximately half the number of employees of the German motor manufacturer, Daimler–Benz, for a similar turnover. The subcontractors work long hours for low wages and reduce the capital required by large corporations.

One major implication of this analysis of the institutional environment of the Japanese company is that caution needs to be applied in transferring management practices from one environment to another. These practices come together in a cluster or package making it difficult to utilize one aspect without having the other. For example, introduction of Japanese-style teamwork into a British factory would need to be accompanied by a number of other features such as single status operation (Wickens 1987) whereby the symbols of hierarchical differences are removed as far as possible. This must go beyond the merely symbolic gestures of a uniform or a single cafeteria but must extend to pay, working conditions, vacations, pensions, and the like.

The significant theoretical issue is not that Japaneseness is to be preferred to any other type of ideology. The Japanese corporate characterism presents a case study of the general proposition that organizations try to achieve isomorphism with their task and institutional environment. If indeed Japanese society is showing a change in values away from the traditional respect for authority and paternalism we would expect to see organizational ideologies change accordingly.

## DESIGN IMPLICATIONS AND SUMMARY

Organizations are scored and keep score of themselves by performance norms which can be categorized as the efficiency/competitive, instrumental, referent, and moral/solidary types. The norms are derived from actions within the institutional environment. Organizations are incorporated into the nation-state and are thereby expected to conform to certain norms in exchange for permission to conduct transactions within the task environment. Major categories of organizational types can thereby be identified.

Organizations need to achieve isomorphism with the environment by translating external performance norms as closely as possible into internal ideology. Organizational effectiveness is assessed relative to the dominant performance norms to which an organization is exposed. When these are inconsistent an organization needs to satisfice by choosing those norms used by those supporters upon which it is most dependent.

Transactions can be managed by the institutional framework of the market, bureaucracy, or collective. Which is most effective will depend upon the contextual variables of tangibility, interdependence, and small numbers. This has implications for the make–buy decision.

Moving to a different nation highlights the importance of the institutional framework in setting the basic norms for the organization. Japan has been used as an example and the interest in Japanese management methods noted. Aping of managerial practices from other countries is not recommended. Adjustment has to be made for the variation in institutional environments.

Some of the major variable relationships discussed in this chapter are given in Figure 2.3. In general we can say that contextual complexity is increased by ambiguity, uniqueness, disparity, and interdependence; these factors are likely to lead to more fuzzy structures as characterized particularly by collectivism and supportiveness. Markets, as described in relation to the make–buy decision, can be seen as providing relatively simple contexts emphasizing clarity of goals, comparability of assessment, and autonomy. Structurally, markets are individualistic and punitive in the sense that poor performance results in exit rather than in supportive attempts from other participants to put matters right. We have also seen some suggestion of the use of symbolism in the Japanese company as a way of fostering the moral ideology; the converse of this is the use of literalism for the interpretation of rules and procedures as will be developed particularly in chapter 4. We have pointed to the need for moral ideology in collective structures and an efficiency ideology in a market. However, we must not restrict our notion of the robust ideology purely to the presence of moral norms.

*Figure 2.3* The contingent institutional model of organization: variable relationships discussed in this chapter

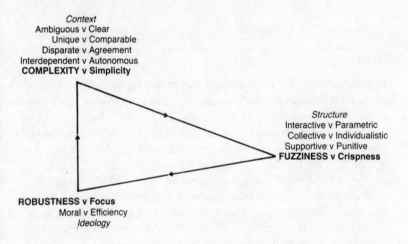

*Context*
Ambiguous v Clear
Unique v Comparable
Disparate v Agreement
Interdependent v Autonomous
**COMPLEXITY v Simplicity**

*Structure*
Interactive v Parametric
Collective v Individualistic
Supportive v Punitive
**FUZZINESS v Crispness**

**ROBUSTNESS v Focus**
Moral v Efficiency
*Ideology*

# Chapter three

# Requisite decision-making capacity

Decision making has been identified as providing the central dynamic of the institutional model of organization and is often seen as a central activity of managerial work (Mintzberg 1973); this chapter develops a model of decision-making processes and indicates how this model relates to the broader institutional model of organization. We also outline how the Principle of Requisite Decision-Making Capacity can give us a theoretical basis for designing appropriate structures.

A decision may be defined as the selection of a proposed course of action. This definition implies a number of features of organizational decision making. First, is the notion that there is some choice as to the actions to be taken; that is, there is uncertainty. Second, there is the intention to act although that intention may not be realized during the decision's implementation. Third, decision making in an organization involves a number of actors; it is seldom that important decisions are taken by one individual.

Uncertainty is a pre-condition of decision making. If there was no uncertainty as to the course of action to take there would be no decision to make. It is possible to consider two dimensions of uncertainty (Thompson and Tuden 1956, Thompson 1967). First, is uncertainty as to the preferred outcomes; this is ends uncertainty or the problem of disparity. In an organization disparity ultimately becomes a political problem involving the interests of different organizational participants and units. Second, is uncertainty about the solutions used to achieve the desired ends; this we call means uncertainty. In an organization means uncertainty is essentially a technical problem of how to achieve the ends which in themselves can be uncertain.

The processes of decision making are what decision makers do in order to cope with these uncertainties. Organizational structures set rules of the game that enable, or hinder, the required processes; for example, an important set of organizational rules defines who should, or should not, participate in decision making – crisp rules defining this very closely, fuzzy rules allowing a great deal of latitude over who participates.

As decision making is fundamental to the perspective on organizational design presented here we examine the various approaches that have developed for the study of decision making. Four such approaches are specified, the rational, the bounded rational, the coalitional, and the garbage can.

## THE RATIONAL APPROACH

By far the predominant view of how decisions ought to be made is the rational approach; there are a number of unifying ideas common to the different versions of this approach which have been well summarized by Mintzberg *et al.* (1976) in terms of a number of distinct steps or stages:

— Recognition. The environment is constantly surveyed for new opportunities using many different kinds of information, financial, industry reports and the like, or informal information. The essential idea is of decision makers who are constantly alert to opportunities.
— Diagnosis. The problem is defined in terms of the decision maker's objectives.
— Search. Information is sought concerning possible solutions.
— Design. Possible solutions are created to solve the problem.
— Evaluation. Each solution is thoroughly assessed.
— Choice. The optimal solution is selected according to objectives.
— Authorization. In an organization the choice usually needs to be authorized at a higher level to ensure co-ordination with the overall organizational objectives.
— Implementation. Since the optimal choice has been selected implementation will follow.

The overall picture presented by the rational model is of active, highly alert decision makers, clear about their objectives, who search until they are in command of a great deal of information and who are knowledgeable about possible solutions, who are then in a position to choose the best course of action which then proceeds to be authorized and implemented. Decision making is a sequence of steps which, if followed, should lead to the best solution; that is, to action which optimizes the decision maker's utilities.

Some decisions do nearly follow this rational model of decision making. Examples would be the routine reordering of bought-in components in a manufacturing firm, or acceptance of undergraduate students on university courses where large numbers are involved. In both cases an organization will lay down a crisp set of decision rules for gathering information about available suppliers or about the qualities and past performance of students. This information will be assimilated and categorized (Lerner and Wanat 1983) in the organization, perhaps using computers, and the decision choice will become fairly obvious; it falls out of the figures, so to speak. In the case of stock reordering the answer may depend upon information about prices, quality, and delivery dates of different suppliers. For the university, school reports and exam results and grades will play a dominant part in categorization. In both cases the decisions can be delegated to a fairly low level in the organization providing the boundaries set by the decision parameters are adhered to. These are programmed (March and Simon 1958) for routine decisions which recur frequently. They can also be described as computational decisions in the sense that it is assumed that formulae, or algorithms, exist for the solution of problems.

## Insight: a fairly routine decision at Automotive Components

For a motor components manufacturer, such as Automotive Components (AC), the introduction of a new product happens quite regularly. It is a competitive market with a number of home- and foreign-based firms chasing custom from an automobile market increasingly dominated by the large multinational manufacturers. There has to be constant awareness of trends in types of components needed and anticipation of future demands. In this sense the decision to introduce a new product, called a gas spring, may be a matter of adapting an existing component or launching a product which had already been worked out and is, so to speak, waiting on the shelf for use.

The launching of the gas spring is an example of this general approach to new product decisions. Making telescopic shock absorbers is one of the main product lines. These could easily be adapted to different car models by altering the basic dimensions but the principles of operation and manufacturing remain the same. The gas spring uses the same engineering principles.

Within the company, the marketing director (Stan Hughes) and chief engineer (Rod Smith) had three years previously noted the introduction of gas springs on a number of cars and saw this as a possible market opportunity. During this phase a number of enquiries were made about competitors' products and information collected about their design and the implications for manufacturing, and some preliminary designs were drawn up. At the end of this phase it was noted that the market was hotting-up with increased demand and a widening range of cars needing gas springs. Stan Hughes had kept his board in touch with what Rod Smith and himself had been doing to gather information but now Stan informed the board about the changing market. He also informed them that one German supplier now had a dominant position in the British market.

The chief executive, Bob McGregor, now authorized a full-scale development of the product to a point where it could be launched quickly. Stan Hughes was requested to progress this through and he immediately started detailed discussions with Rod Smith who undertook the engineering work. Prototypes had to be built and tested and more information found about the likely performance parameters. This included specifying the strength of the spring and its ability to withstand repeated cycles.

Generally, the board were in full agreement about the need to develop this product. McGregor put his full weight behind it. Opposition, however, was met from the Product Group manager who favoured extending the existing range of shock absorbers rather than developing a completely new product which might show new problems. Both Stan and Rod felt that this manager was dragging his heels and trying to block the new project. This was reported to McGregor and the manager was fired.

After three months, design and development was completed and production facilities available for a full-scale market launch were ready. Stan reported this to the board but he also reported that their price could not be much lower than that of their German competitor. He therefore advised waiting for the German supplier's price to rise which he thought would happen since they had already announced two rises. The board agreed to launch in principle but delegated the final launch decision to Stan when the price should appear right. It was all a matter of timing. The organization had geared itself up to go given the appropriate conditions and the launch took place thirteen months after the agreement by the board.

In this gas spring decision we see a number of features of the rational decision approach in spite of the fact that it was quite a major and complex decision problem. We see the emphasis upon efficiency norms through the use of extensive search procedures, an alertness for opportunities, a specifying of objectives, and the evaluation of alternatives in so far as this was one (admittedly important) product to be compared alongside other new products in the offing. In the end the decision to implement the gas spring product was partly a matter of calculating the possible future returns.

In seeing this decision as a purely rational matter, however, we would be overlooking a number of aspects of the process which cannot be adequately seen in that light. One aspect is that it is the beliefs of the decision makers that determine the mode of decision making. If decision makers believe that there are algorithms that can be applied to make the decision then this is what they will do; they interpret the situation. Whether those algorithms are correct in terms of some higher purpose may come to light later, but until there is a feedback from the outcomes of the decision, decision makers will proceed upon this assumption.

If decision makers approach a decision in this way the danger they can face is to assume the decision to be amenable to solution through rational processes when a more elastic process might do better. From the organizational design viewpoint the structure likely to induce a rational type of decision process would be a crisp structure defining an inelastic set of rules. We can see that likely decision-making errors of the crisp organization would be those of insufficient decision-making capacity to cope with uncertainties; these would be errors of decision under-capacity.

## THE BOUNDED RATIONAL APPROACH

A number of writers on organizations and decision making (Simon 1947, 1957, 1960; March and Simon 1958; Cyert and March 1963) have pointed to the limitations of the rational approach when compared to the way in which actual decisions are made and this has led them to propose an alternative bounded rational model. The essential point about the proposed alternative model is that it emphasizes the need for managers to make decisions with incomplete information, under time pressures, when there may be disagreements over goals, and to accept that an optimal solution cannot always be achieved within these constraints. Rationality, therefore, is bounded.

The bounded rational approach to decision making accepts a number of features which are opposite to those of the rational model. These are:

1 Problemistic search rather than complete alertness. This means that managers respond to problems rather than going out of their way to find them. A firm may revamp its products because it finds sales and profits falling rather than as a result of a systematic-continuous searching for opportunities. The spur to decision making may be outer- rather than inner-directed. Decisions often lie around a long time before becoming active within the decision arena. This gestation time can run to years while decision makers ponder whether to make the issue more public and perhaps give the game away to others (Hickson *et al.* 1986).

2 Cognitive limits exist in this search process meaning that the human mind is limited in its comprehension of problems thereby making it impossible to achieve the synoptic ideal of mapping out the complete decision tree showing the paths to possible solutions. Part of the synoptic ideal (Lindblom 1959) is setting objectives and finding paths to achieve them. A complex decision's objectives may not be known beforehand. It is simply felt that there is a problem and something must be done, but what is to be done evolves out of the process of decision making. Thus, in the Cuban missile crisis of the early 1960s when the Soviet Union started building missile bases on Cuba, the US government knew they had to do something but objectives were not clear after or during the decision process (Allison 1971).

3 Time pressures frequently apply which may cut short complete search. A decision has to be made even with incomplete information.

4 Disjointed and incremental decision making often occurs (Lindblom 1959) rather than the smooth continuous process of the rational model. Disjointedness might come about because complex problems cannot always be solved, so to speak, in one sitting. Managers may let the issue rest before taking it any further and so the decision process appears as discontinuous with stops and starts. An incremental approach may be used in some cases by breaking the problem down into small steps and taking these one at a time. Marks and Spencer experimented with the North American market through opening a few stores in Canada fourteen years before opening in New York. Even then they moved

cautiously and in steps by selling a limited number of lines before trading under their own name.

5 Intuition and judgement may have to be the basis for making a decision rather than computations. Computations may be made to inform a decision but managers realize that the answer cannot fall out of the figures. In the gas spring decision (see pp. 44–6), the marketing director had to make a final judgement as to the state of the market and the pricing changes made by the main competitor. Experience becomes a key aspect of intuitive decision making. It is not in any way irrational but by drawing upon a reservoir of previous successful and unsuccessful practice a manager can judge the correct action to take although it may not be possible to fully explicate reasons. Bits and pieces of information gleaned from a variety of sources, especially informal sources, can be used to let a pattern of a solution evolve (Issack 1978, Eisenberg 1984, Simon 1987).

6 Satisficing rather than optimal solutions are arrived at. The word 'satisficing' was invented to describe the idea that managers will suffice with satisfactory solutions rather than continuously searching for the ideal (Simon 1957). Thus minimum performance standards are set and once achieved the problem is considered solved. In the gas spring decision notional profitability and rates of return were set and when it looked as if there was a reasonable chance of reaching these the product was launched. There was little in the way of systematic checking back or post-decision audit to see whether these had been achieved.

Another example of satisficing would be seen if a student, searching for a job on nearing completion of a degree course, stops search after receipt of the second offer because the job fulfils a number of minimum performance criteria. The number of all possible potential offers will be unknown and can never be known but must run higher than two for most graduates. In this case satisficing involves setting some key targets and proceeding upon the assumption that complete search is impossible and pointless; the rule of thumb becomes to accept that which first comes to hand which fulfils the minimum performance level (March and Simon 1958: 142).

## Conditions for rational and bounded rational decision processes

As descriptions of two possible types of decision processes, the rational and bounded rational approaches provide useful insights but do not, as yet, explain the conditions under which one of them might be more appropriate for managers to use or give any indication of the possible organizational consequences of each.

Generally we can say that the rational model is more appropriate for routine decisions and the bounded rational for non-routine. Routine decisions are likely to be recurring, such as a stock control decision or aspects of the gas spring decision, or at least reducible to recurring and familiar elements. An important aspect of this routineness is that the decisions tend to be programmed into an organization's systems so that particular events stimulate particular actions; that is, there are crisp structures defining what should be done. This is comparatively clear in a stock control decision which is often stimulated by stock falling below the reorder level. Conversely, the bounded rational approach is appropriate for non-programmed and more disparate issues. Here problems are unfamiliar and non-routine but also more likely to be contentious. The bounded rational approach is likely to fit best within a fuzzy structure.

## MINTZBERG'S INVESTIGATIONS OF THE STAGES AND CIRCULARITY OF DECISION MAKING

Mintzberg *et al*. (1976) examined the processes of decision making used in a range of decisions by comparing twenty-five decision cases in a variety of organizations. They used a model which attempted to describe the decision-making processes in terms of three phases which in turn consist of six routines.

First, there is the identification phase which contains the problem recognition diagnosis routines; then the development phase contains the information search and solution design routines; finally, the selection phase contains the choice evaluation and authorization routines, authorization being required when the individual making the decision does not have the authority to commit the organization to a course of action.

To this point the model appears as another version of the rational approach where decision making is supposed to proceed in logical sequential steps. As Figure 3.1 shows, the model allows for the possibility of feedback loops between the beginning and end of the routines. Problem recognition may occur first but thereafter routines can be brought in at any time, or completely missed out, or revisited during the decision making.

*Figure 3.1* Mintzberg *et al.*'s stages and circularities of decision making

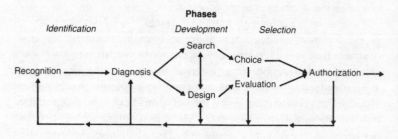

*Source*: Adapted from Mintzberg, H., Raisinghani, D., and Therot, A. (1976) 'The structure of "unstructured" decision processes', *Administrative Science Quarterly*, 21, 2 (June): 246–75.

From this basic model Mintzberg *et al.* (1976) were able to collect data concerning the extent to which the various routines were used, and concerning other factors such as the duration of each decision, the extent to which interruptions (interrupts) occurred in the process, and the number of branches and recycles that occurred in the sequence suggested by the model.

The organizations investigated covered manufacturing, service, and government organizations. The duration reported varied from less than one to more than four years. From their analysis of the data collected they attempted to generalize as to possible patterns of decision making. In order to do this they classified decisions according to: the stimulus giving rise to the decisions as to whether it was an opportunity, a crisis, or a problem to be solved; whether solutions were given at the beginning of the decision, conformed to a ready-made organizational solution, was a modification of an existing solution, or was a custom-made solution for that decision; finally, a description of the overall process.

Types of decision which provide generalized descriptions of the overall decision-making process emerged as follows:

— Simple interrupt. Stimulus by problem, solution given, recognition, and diagnosis stages used with a lot of interruptions. These were the non-complex decisions with given solutions which got blocked.
— Political design process. Given solutions or modifications to

ready-made solutions were used in these decisions but interruptions were more extensive due to intensive political activity.
— Basic search. This type of decision would appear to come nearest to the rational type in that there were few interruptions and the emphasis was upon rational search processes and finding solutions in accordance with organizational precedence.
— Modified search. Represents a rather more complex basic search type in which ready-made solutions are modified to a particular decision.
— Basic and dynamic designs. These decision types appear to move towards the bounded rational type in that custom-made solutions are found following considerable design and evaluation effort.

Mintzberg's study represents an attempt to derive patterns of decision-making processes by comparing twenty-five cases. Obviously this is a great improvement upon studies which attempt generalizations from one case but their research does indicate how difficult it is to make sense of such complex processes. Above all, they emphasize the essential circularity of decision making even over fairly simple issues.

## THE POLITICAL APPROACH

The political model of organizational decision making is based upon the idea that an organization is made up of a number of interests not necessarily sharing the same goals and often pursuing their own views of organizational effectiveness (Butler *et al*. 1974, 1977/8). As explained in chapter 1 this approach, therefore, challenges the assumptions traditionally made by economic and systems theories of organization which have tended to see the firm as a unitary whole, as if there were a single corporate mind which could speak for everyone.

The political approach sees the processes of organizational decision making as involving shifting coalitions of interests and temporary alliances of decision makers who can, for the purpose of a decision, come together and sufficiently submerge their differences to make a decision (Cyert and March 1963). A coalition may be formed just for one decision but it is also likely to involve trade offs in which, say, A supports B against C for this issue providing B supports A in the future over another issue.

An explicit notion of political behaviour in organizational decision making was emphasized as the reality of organizational life by Allison's (1971) analysis of the US government's handling of the

Cuban missile crises in the early 1960s, by Pettigrew's (1973) analysis of the purchase of a computer in a firm, and by Mintzberg *et al.*'s (1976) analysis of decision making. The Insight of the gas spring above has also indicated that dissent can arise during decision making although in that case the dissent was firmly quashed. A more complex case of political decision making is given by the Insight, Reorganization of Pathology Services.

## Insight: reorganization of pathology services

The story of reorganization in the British National Health Service (NHS) has been that of creating ever-larger units. Following various recommendations from the Department of Health and Social Security (DHSS), a move was started to centralize pathological services into the City Royal Infirmary (CRI) as the Health District had evolved out of the amalgamation of a number of separate hospitals which already had their own pathology services. Pathology provides a service to clinicians in all the hospitals throughout the area and the advantage of centralization would be that more economical use could be made of developments in medical technology. Against this argument was the concern of clinicians associated with the outlying hospitals that samples would have to be sent to CRI for analysis and hence there would be a delay in getting results.

Dr Richards, the chief clinical member on the district management team, proposed centralization with the aim of achieving economies of scale and better specialist facilities. A fast turn round time was to be guaranteed for the outlying hospitals. The proposal was generally supported by the rest of the management team and by many other clinicians at the CRI who saw this as a chance to get improved facilities. However, opposition built up from clinicians who were strongly associated with outlying hospitals; unions and nursing staff were also opposed to the proposal since there were possibilities of job losses. Other peripheral interests involved were the haematology and blood transfusion services which were generally supportive of centralization. As the CRI was a teaching hospital the adjacent university medical school also had an interest in seeing improved pathological services and favoured centralization.

Dr Richards and other members of the management team held discussions with the opposing clinicians over a four-year period but this simply seemed to entrench the two camps. The opposition presented figures to deny the increase in efficiency claimed by Dr Richards and his side.

All of a sudden events acted as a catalyst to resolve the dispute. First, there was a shortage of the skilled technical staff needed to run the various dispersed pathological services. This strengthened the case of the centralizers. The second and final impetus for centralization came about because one of the main leaders of the opposition, a senior consultant, died, and then the other main opposer announced his retirement. Within six months the decision to centralize was authorized and implementation ensued.

## Analysis

This shows how a decision that starts as an apparently simple fairly computational type, begins to take on a political complexion as different interests are drawn in. To reorganize pathology from a technical viewpoint was a relatively straightforward matter of weighing up the pros and cons of a particular course of action. However, interests entrenched in the more dispersed and decentralized older structure were affected and resisted the change. The problem was only resolved upon the unexpected removal of the main opponents. On getting agreement over the pathology services decision Dr Richards had to develop a coalition to support his views. Here, the support of the district administrator was vital but the management team did not initially have enough authority and power to override the opposition.

## THE GARBAGE CAN APPROACH

A colourful and apt description of the way in which some decisions are made in organizations has been introduced by the Garbage Can Model (Cohen *et al*. 1972, March and Olsen 1976). In this approach events and decisions in organizations are not necessarily even as systematic as the bounded rationality model suggests but approach those of an 'organized anarchy' and exhibit three distinct features:

1 Problematic preferences. Problems, alternatives, solutions, and goals are ill-defined. Ambiguity characterizes each aspect of a decision process.
2 Ambiguous technology. Cause and effect relationships are difficult to identify.
3 Fluid participation. There is a turnover of participants and they have only limited time to allocate to any one problem or decision. Participation in any given decision will be fluid and limited.

The garbage can characterizes organizations as experiencing rapid change and a collegial, nonbureaucratic, and fuzzy context. No organization fits these organized anarchy circumstances all the time but most organizations will occasionally find themselves in positions of making decisions under problematic and ambiguous circumstances particularly at the strategic level. An important characteristic of the garbage can model is that the decision process is not a sequence of steps beginning with a problem and ending with a solution, as problem-identification and problem-solution stages may not be connected to each other. Ideas may be proposed as a solution when no problem exists. Problems may exist and never generate a solution.

The reason problems and solutions are not connected is that decisions are the outcome of independent streams of events within the organization. Four streams of garbage can decision making can be seen:

1 Problems. Derive from a gap between current and desired performance. They represent points of dissatisfaction but are distinct from choices and solutions since a problem may or may not lead to a solution, and adopted solutions may not solve the problem.

2 Solutions. Participants have ready-made solutions which represent a flow of ideas and alternatives through the organization, with people bringing in new ideas. Participants may be attracted to certain ideas and push them as logical choices, and attraction to an idea may cause an employee to look for a problem to which it can be attached. Solutions can exist independently of problems although, over time, there may be a merging of the two.

3 Participants. Participants vary widely in their ideas, perception of problems, experience, values, and training. They can come and go and solutions recognized by one participant may not be those recognized by others. Time pressures lead participants to allocate different amounts of participation to a given problem or solution.

4 Choice opportunities. These are occasions when an organization makes a decision and an alternative is authorized and implemented. Choice opportunities occur when any specific stimulus occurs such as the signing of a new contract or a new product is authorized. These opportunities may be precipitated by specific events such as a crisis, an idea, or perhaps a supplier who is pressing for an order to be placed.

From these independent streams emerge patterns in organizational decision making. Problems, solutions, participants, and choices flow through the organization and, in one sense, the organization acts as a garbage can in which these streams are stirred and problems, solutions, participants, and choices drop in to connect at one point; in this way problems may get solved, or not solved if connections are not made.

Any problem and solution may be connected when a choice is made but the problem does not always relate to the solution and the solution may not solve the problem. Organizational decisions are not simply the result of the logical step-by-step sequence of events that other descriptions of decision making imply. Participants are intendedly rational but events are so ill-defined and complex that decisions, problems, and solutions are independent. By using computer simulations Cohen *et al.* (1972) and Cohen (1989) have been able to demonstrate some consequences of this approach to decision making:

— Solutions are proposed even when problems do not exist. A participant may support an idea and may try to sell it to the rest of the organization. To some extent we see this in Dr Richards' selling of pathology reorganization given in the Insight on pp. 52–3. Another example would be if a finance director tries to sell a complex financial appraisal scheme because he had been on a course. In some cases these schemes fall into disuse, in others they get taken up by the organization.
— Choices are made without solving problems. A choice made with the intention of solving a problem may not solve that problem. Conversely, choices sometimes happen without there being a problem.
— Problems may persist without being solved. Participants get used to problems and give up trying to solve them. Or participants may not know how to solve a particular problem. For example, a 'rogue' professor in a university persisted in his post in spite of causing considerable problems for his colleagues because nobody knew how to get rid of him (Hickson *et al.* 1986).
— Some problems are solved. Over many decisions, things somehow work in an organization in spite of the chaos; solutions do, on the average, connect with choices and the organization does move in the direction of problem reduction. In the above instance, the 'rogue' professor was eventually encouraged to move when an attractive opportunity opened up to him outside the organization.

It is suggested that to work effectively the garbage can will need to draw upon a moral ideology in order to ensure that the participants are committed to some higher ideal as a means of resolving disparity. The garbage can approach is essentially a fuzzy process whereby decision makers muddle their way through to a conclusion without fully understanding the process. As a structure for resolving uncertainty the garbage can provides tremendous decision-making capacity.

The danger with an organization designed as a garbage can will come from errors of decision overcapacity whereby the rules are too elastic. Participants may spend too much time and effort talking, arguing, interacting, pushing favourite solutions, and so forth. Inefficiency may result from these conditions and decision makers proceed upon the false belief that their world is more uncertain than it really is and miss the opportunity to apply crisper structures.

## THE PRINCIPLE OF REQUISITE DECISION-MAKING CAPACITY

The institutional model of organization reveals a picture of an organization that is part determined through the application of institutionalized norms but is also indeterminate in the sense that those norms can be inconsistent; exits or entries of rivals and/or supporters from the task environment provide a potential for uncertainty, and technical knowledge can also change as a result of action in the institutional environment. Overall we can see the organizational design problem as finding suitable structures to manage the conflux of the normative, resource, and technical streams of action.

If an organization was completely determinate there would be no uncertainty and no decisions to make. Once set on course the organization would run as a perfectly reliable clockwork mechanism or as a computer program without any managerial intervention. It is because an organization is also indeterminate – there is uncertainty and decisions have to be made – that managerial activity is needed.

Fuzzy structures set elastic rules for decision making, thereby enabling the process of coping with uncertainty, but at the same time impose organizing costs (Lerner and Wanat 1983) because of the lack of clear guidelines which lead to greater time demands and decision-making activity in general. One aspect of the organizational design problem is to design the structure to reduce that cost.

However, reducing the cost of decision making is not the only aspect to the design problem. Again recalling the institutional model we should note that uncertainties for an organization can derive from unexpected movements in the norms that are applied to assess an organization and in the actions of elements in the task environment. An organization needs to have sufficient decision-making capacity to ensure future adaptability. There is, therefore, a technical aspect to effectiveness, that of achieving efficiency by means of perfecting internal procedures (what Thompson (1967) calls technical rationality), or an adaptive aspect to effectiveness (what Thompson calls organizational rationality) whereby goals are externally oriented towards understanding and testing the environment of the organization.

## Definition

The Principle of Requisite Decision-Making Capacity has been referred to from point to point above but as yet not fully defined. This we now do.

The Principle of Requisite Decision-Making Capacity states that: an organization needs to design a structure of the requisite capacity; that is, one sufficiently crisp to minimize decision-making costs and sufficiently fuzzy to achieve adaptability. This is the overall organizational design problem.

Our Principle of Requisite Decision-Making Capacity might be more picturesquely stated: fuzziness is needed to cope with indeterminateness. In this respect the argument bears comparison to that put forward by cyberneticians. For example, Ashby's (1956) Law of Requisite Variety states that variety is needed to destroy variety in a control system; if the system being controlled is highly variable in its behaviour, highly variable information is needed to control it. For instance, it is not possible to control a car safely under the variability of normal road conditions with a simple information system that would only permit stop–go speed and left–ahead–right steering commands; the variation in available speed and steering positions would not normally be sufficiently high to cope with the variation in road conditions. In a similar vein Weick (1969, 1979) sees the process of organizing as equivocality removal, meaning that when the conditions met in an organization are highly equivocal (i.e., indeterminate) this equivocality can only be coped with by many cycles of no-less equivocal behaviour.

However, this only gives one side of the equation. An organization is usually limited in the amount of resources that can be devoted to decision-making activity. The constraint comes from the need to operate with limited resources and hence account has to be taken of the need for efficiency. There is a continual tension between the need for crispness and the need for fuzziness, a kind of balancing trick in which to err on the side of too much crispness would be to provide insufficient decision-making capacity; to err on the side of too much fuzziness would be inefficient. We can, therefore, define two types of error:

1 Errors of decision overcapacity. These are the errors of inefficiency, of permitting too much fuzziness when greater crispness could be achieved.
2 Errors of decision undercapacity. These are the errors of the straitjacket, of trying to force too much crispness onto what needs to be an essentially fuzzy process. If the set of organizational rules does not allow sufficient capacity there will be lack of scope for uncertainty coping.

These error types are closely related to Hofstede's (1981) discussion of two types of error in management control and is analogous to Type I and Type II errors in statistical hypothesis testing. A Type I error, equivalent to an error of overcapacity, leads to rejection of a true hypothesis: an example of this would be management neglecting to use basic cost accounting methods to assess the worthiness of a cost reduction proposal where the information and techniques are available with great precision. A Type II error, equivalent to an error of undercapacity, leads to acceptance of a false hypothesis: an example of this would be management making a major investment decision based entirely upon a rate of return calculation but where the data fed into that calculation are highly dubious with regard to what is meant.

Huber and McDaniel (1986) introduce a decision-making paradigm of decision making; the basis of this idea is that organizations should be designed to facilitate the making of decisions, in particular ensuring that structures respond to the frequency and criticality of decision making. One way of doing this, Huber and McDaniel (1986: 582) state, is to create the degree of specialization commensurate with the complexity of the decision situation.

We can now make a prescriptive statement based upon the Principle of Requisite Decision-Making Capacity that can guide us in designing organizations, namely: find the structure that provides the requisite decision-making capacity; this is the framework that avoids errors of decision regarding both overcapacity and undercapacity.

## A CONTINGENCY MODEL OF DECISION MAKING

From the understanding of the processes of organizational decision making acquired from the different approaches discussed above and from our definition of the Principle of Requisite Decision-Making Capacity, we can now more specifically develop a contingency model of decision making which can fit within the institutional model of organization.

The organizational design and managerial question is: is there something we can say about the type of decision-making process that is best suited to particular situations which will enable the above state-ment of the Principle of Requisite Decision-Making Capacity to be made into something more than a high sounding sentiment? A contingency model of decision making put forward by Thompson and Tuden (1956), and further developed here, allows us to draw some conclusions towards this end. The model is summarized in Figure 3.2. Here we see the two dimensions of uncertainty about ends and uncertainty about means.

Generally, factors which would increase ends-uncertainty derive from the politicality (Hickson *et al*. 1986) of the decision topic. The

*Figure 3.2* The contingencies of organizational decision making

|  | Means Uncertainty → | |
| --- | --- | --- |
| | **Computation** rational crisp | **Judgement** bounded rational fuzzier |
| Ends Uncertainty ↓ | **Bargaining** coalition fuzzier | **Inspiration** garbage can fuzziest |

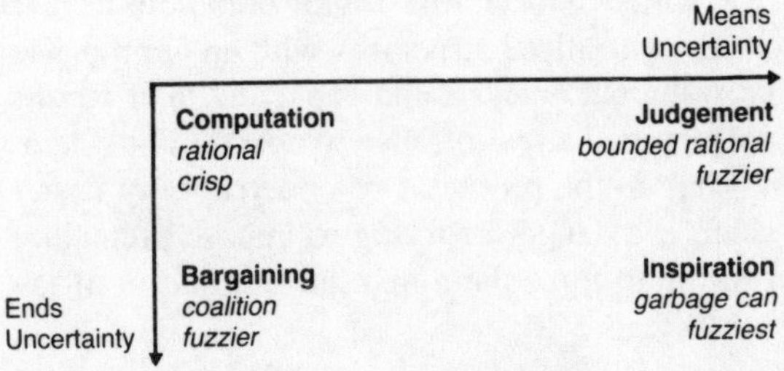

*Source*: Adapted from Thompson, J.D. and Tuden, A. (1956) 'Strategies, structures and processes of organizational decision', in J.D. Thompson, *Comparative Studies in Administration*, University of Pitsburgh Press, pp. 195–216.

greater the number and variability of interests involved or the more outside influences that exist, the greater the propensity for disparity. Some factors which might be seen as leading to ends-uncertainty are:

1 Incompleteness of knowledge as in new technologies.
2 The 'object' worked on is dynamic as in therapeutic programmes to modify personality.
3 Unpredictability of the behaviour of others outside the organization such as rivals, supporters, or norms setters in the institutional environment.

The combination of high and low scores on these dimensions leads to the possibility of four types of decision process in order to manage these underlying problems of decision making (Thompson and Tuden 1956, Thompson 1967).

## Computation: suitable for certain ends and means

Decision makers may not know the optimal solution to a problem, indeed if they did there would be no decision, but they may be confident that such an answer is available through the use of particular computational procedures and proceed upon this belief. The computations may be complex but the expectation is that an answer will come out of the figures. This clarity over ends/means relations will be matched by agreement over ends amongst decision makers. The processes of computation are essentially the processes of the rational/programmed approach to decision making. The overall organizational structure appropriate for computational processes is crisp; specifically we would expect this organization to feature formalized, demarcated, centralized structures with an appropriate number of experts carrying out analysis and expecting their results to be acted upon. Ideology will stress efficiency norms. The dilemmas of computation relate to the problems of undercapacity rather than overcapacity; there is a danger of trying to impose premature closure on issues or trying to force them into the straitjacket of too tight a control.

## Judgement: suitable for certain ends, uncertain means

This is the process whereby decision makers cope with the problem of technical ambiguity. These are essentially the processes of the bounded rational model of decision making, i.e., problemistic initiation, cognitive limits to search with limited choice generation and satisficing solutions.

The organization that is suitable for judgement will tend to be fuzzier with specialization professionally based, with more lateral communication than vertical, high participation, and expert-based influence. Because of the high need to use technical specialists the referent performance norms will be prominent.

## Bargaining: suitable for uncertain ends, certain means

This is the process of decision making whereby participants attempt to resolve conflicting objectives. The underlying factor leading to bargaining is disagreement over the desired ends. Two outcomes of bargaining would seem possible: first, a compromise is reached between involved parties, or second, one party wins and another loses. Both these suggest that underlying the processes of bargaining is the power that different participants can bring to bear upon a decision issue. This dimension therefore captures the politicality of decision making.

## Inspiration: suitable for uncertain ends, uncertain means

This is the most difficult decision situation and the most demanding in terms of communication and informational requirements. We need to be careful in using the word inspiration since this might imply a decision that is made almost haphazardly or without care. Although as outsiders we may observe some decisions being made as if on the spur of the moment we should not disregard the feel and intuition for a situation that experience can bring (Issack 1978, Simon 1987).

Overall, we would expect the organization for inspiration to look like that of the garbage can where solutions, problems, participants, and choices are proceeding in parallel waiting for appropriate opportunities to make connections. Interaction will be high and many of the rules implicit rather than formalized. There is likely to be a shifting leadership and the only way in which this kind of organization is likely to get decisions made is through the development of a robust ideology. The likely errors are those of overcapacity rather than undercapacity of decision making.

## THE DYNAMICS OF DECISION MAKING

Decision topics are issues or problems that arise through a combination of an organization's context and structure (Hickson *et al.* 1986, Pettigrew 1990); context sets the scene for decisions in terms of technology, task environment, and norms, and structure sets the scene in terms of rules for making decisions. Complex contexts and fuzzy structures give rise to uncertain topics in terms of both ends and means. Outputs follow from the processes, one component of which is the substance of the action taken in the organization, whether it be an investment made, a new product introduced, and the like. Further, a decision need not stay within one type of decision process but may shift over time to another (Rowe 1989).

The other component of output is a feedback to the structure. According to the Principle of Requisite Decision-Making Capacity the feedback to structure is the process of the organization learning to improve its decision-making rules for future decisions. The logic is to crispify structure by developing algorithms in order that future decisions can be made in a more computational way. For each round of the decision-making cycle we can imagine, according to the Principle, an increment of algorithm development taking place. This we call inner loop learning which is to do with learning about the task. If decision makers are intendedly rational they will be trying to push the decision towards the computational type in order to reduce uncertainty. This dynamic is depicted in Figure 3.3.

*Figure 3.3* The cycle of decision making

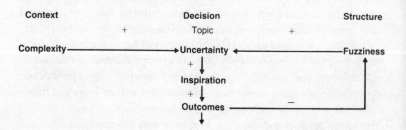

## The importance of time

The model presented would surely suggest that the process ought to be allowed to proceed until sufficient learning has occurred for algorithms to be developed, permitting a decision to be made by computation. That is, for the cycle of inner loop learning to proceed until decision makers approach the ideal rational approach to decision making.

There is, however, a critical limitation – the limitation of time. The above prescription has discounted the value of time, but time enters into the equation in two ways (Sharp 1989): first, through the notion that decision processes take managerial time and therefore impose a cost upon an organization, and second, through the opportunity cost of possible benefits foregone while the search for algorithms goes on.

Managerial time comprises the total of the time spent by the various participants in the decision summed over its duration and, in principle, a time cost could be allocated to this. The effort put into making a decision, therefore, becomes no different to any other investment. The organization is 'spending' managerial time in anticipation of a future return, not necessarily in the form of a single lump, but over time as the decision proceeds. Managerial time can become a surrogate for money and we can see the impact of the time dimension beginning to emerge; increments of time are 'spent' at Times 1, 2, 3, etc., in anticipation of a future delayed return; this is a classic investment problem which, given enough information about costs and discount rates, could be solved by means of a discounted cash flow calculation. Decision makers, according to this argument, would carry out a kind of intuitive cost–benefit analysis balancing time spent on perfecting decision making against expected greater return.

This argument becomes more forceful if we extend the notion of opportunity cost. A discounted cash flow assumes an opportunity cost; managerial time (the surrogate for money) 'spent' at Time 1 has a net present value greater than the same amount of time 'spent' at Time 2, but there is a potentially more important aspect of opportunity cost due to opportunities lost in the environment of the organization while a decision is being made. This can be illustrated in the case of market-oriented decisions where time spent perfecting a decision whether or not to launch a new product may lose valuable opportunities in the market as other firms take up the challenge. In other words, as a decision is being made the environmental conditions are changing. Assumptions made at the beginning of the process may no longer hold as competitors enter, and prices and costs change. This aspect of lost opportunities helps us to explain the satisficing solution adopted by the job-hunting student described above; undoubtedly, more complete search will always yield more job opportunities but jobs are always coming onto the market and leaving the market. It is a search process that can never be finished and the rule of thumb to take the first that satisfies the minimum realistic performance criteria would seem to be an intuitive way of acknowledging the opportunity costs of time spent making decisions.

Conversely, there are occasions when letting a decision lie can improve the quality of the outcomes as new understanding develops or environmental conditions turn favourable. Waiting for the favourable moment was the distinctive feature of the new product decision at Automotive Components, met in the Insight on pp. 44–6. It is here that we need, perhaps, to distinguish between delays due to deliberate blockages (see the Insight on the Reorganization of Pathology Services, pp. 52–3) and delays waiting for conditions to improve (Hickson *et al*. 1986).

Kanter (1984) has put the same problem another way by considering the time taken to make decisions and the rate at which events in the context unfold. The basic prescription is to say that the time taken to make decisions needs to be less than the time between surprises arising in order for an organization to maintain adaptability. When time between surprises is short decisions are likely to be made rapidly, thereby approaching the inspirational mode.

Errors of decision undercapacity would be an outcome of premature closure but might be justified on the grounds of opportunity costs; errors of decision overcapacity would be an outcome of tardy closure but might be justified on the grounds of waiting for favourable conditions to become available. The choice is to err on the side of believing the world more certain than it is by risking acceptance of a false hypothesis, or to err on the side of believing the world less certain than it is by risking rejecting a true hypothesis.

## DESIGN IMPLICATIONS AND SUMMARY

This chapter has concentrated upon the processes of decision making but to summarize the implications we now need to relate the decision-making cycle to the institutional model of organization and the organizational cycle. This is shown in Figure 3.4. The figure also notes some of the main variables discussed in this chapter.

We have noted that uncertainty about ends and means in decision making leads to a shift from computational to inspirational decision processes. The notion of inspirational decision making is a summary concept describing decisions which are quick, intuitive, based upon experience rather than analysis, and where the emphasis is upon taking action. Computational decision making uses algorithms and is taken within a time frame emphasizing the need for the analysis to be done before action is taken.

*Figure 3.4* The contingent institutional model of organization: salient variable relationships discussed in this chapter

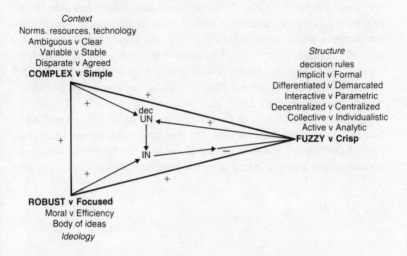

*Notes*: UN = uncertain; IN = inspiration; dec = decision

Decision topics arise as a result of an interaction between context and structure and will carry with them degrees of uncertainty according to the degree of complexity and fuzziness of structure. The processes of decision making describe the activities decision makers use to cope with the uncertainties. These processes, we suggest, are also affected by ideology; decision makers bring with them a set of ideas about how decisions should be made, an inspirational decision process requiring a robust ideology with its underlying moral norms.

The outcomes of decision processes include both the actions taken and the feedback upon structure; hence the decision cycle will, if an organization is following the Principle of Requisite Decision-Making Capacity, lead to learning and the development of crisper structures for future decisions, denoted by a negative feedback loop in Figure 3.4.

Hence the decision cycle makes contact with the organizational cycle via context, structure, and ideology. The design problem is to find the structure that is suitable for a particular context that will provide the requisite decision-making capacity. The model points out that crispifying structure will lead to a reduction in ideological robustness and potential loss of adaptability for an organization.

One major implication of the model is to highlight the organizational tension between the decision cycle, with its attendant inner learning loop representing a shift towards increasing efficiency, and the organizational cycle, with its attendant outer learning loop representing a requirement for organizational adaptation. Over time the dangers with the inner learning loop are those of developing artificially crisp structures – that is, incurring errors of decision undercapacity; the dangers with the outer learning loop are those of developing structures which are too fuzzy – that is, incurring the errors of decision overcapacity.

The main relationships of the institutional model have been outlined. The task in the ensuing chapters is to illustrate and support the operation of this model and to demonstrate how it can be used to analyse and integrate many aspects of organizational design.

# Chapter four

# Bureaucracies and collectives

The institutional model of organization has been posited as a general model of organization outlining the variables of structure, context, and ideology. The Principle of Requisite Decision-Making Capacity gives us the process interrelating these variables. Although some suggestions have been made as to their nature, our task is now to build upon available evidence to add substance to our model. In this chapter we do this by examining two contrasting forms of organization: the bureaucracy and the collective.

## THE SIMPLE HIERARCHY

Consideration of the simple hierarchy is a useful starting point for thinking about bureaucracy since hierarchy is a ubiquitous feature of organizations. It is unfortunate that the term has become confused with the notion of power and authority in the sense that someone at the top of a hierarchy is presumed to have greater power than those lower down. Hierarchy can be seen from a technical point of view as a device to co-ordinate the activities of a number of people working together on a task (Thompson 1967). From this technical viewpoint, as a hierarchy is ascended, each successive level takes a more encompassing view of the organization but possesses less detail of the activities of the lower levels.

A number of prescriptions for the running of hierarchies have been handed down through the Scientific Management tradition (Koontz and O'Donnell 1959) and may be summarized into the principles of:

1 Unity of command. This states that a subordinate should only report to one boss.
2 Accountability. This states that there should be a clear reporting

relationship through which individuals can be required to answer for their actions.

3 Limited span of control. This states that a boss can only manage a limited number of subordinates, a number of approximately six usually being suggested.

The shape of a hierarchy can be measured by three variables: span of control (S), levels (L), and total number of participants (P), which can be linked together by the formula:

$$S = L \sqrt{\quad} P$$

This formula tells us that a given number of organizational participants can be spread 'thick' or 'thin' to give us a short–wide hierarchy (SW) or a tall–narrow (N) hierarchy as shown in Figure 4.1. Each hierarchy has 13 participants but TN has 3 levels and spans of control of 3, while SW has 2 levels and a span of control of 12. The process by which activities are co-ordinated and decisions made will be different in the two cases as can be demonstrated by a simple example. If we call the participants who actually produce the final product of this organization, workers (C), TN has one top boss (A), and three middle managers (B). Hence the managerial ratio for TN is 4:13. SW has a smaller proportion of indirect administrative participants – only one top boss (A), giving a managerial ratio of 1:13. On this basis SW is clearly the more efficient organization.

*Figure 4.1* Two simple hierarchies

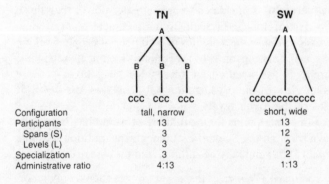

| Configuration | tall, narrow | short, wide |
|---|---|---|
| Participants | 13 | 13 |
| Spans (S) | 3 | 12 |
| Levels (L) | 3 | 2 |
| Specialization | 3 | 2 |
| Administrative ratio | 4:13 | 1:13 |

*Notes*: A = top boss; B = middle managers; C = workers

Another difference between the two organizations is that TN has greater specialization than SW; this is worked out on the assumption that A, Bs, and Cs are different types of jobs, and hence there are at least three types of jobs in TN and two types in SW. If the Bs also do different jobs and likewise for the Cs, specialization will be greater.

On the face of it SW appears to be the more productive organization but perhaps there are some advantages for TN? After all TN comes nearer to the prescription of a limited span of control. If we start from what appears to be the most efficient case, SW, we can consider the conditions under which A's decision-making capacity might get exceeded. A number of contextual variables are suggested as leading to decision overload for A (Child 1977).

First, is task ambiguity which occurs if the Cs' task is ill defined; this will lead to decision overload because the Cs are likely to keep on coming to A with problems needing a decision and it becomes more difficult for A to monitor the Cs' activities. A's decision-making capacity is more likely to be exceeded as the dissimilarity or heterogeneity of tasks done by the Cs increases, as their spatial dispersion and remoteness from A increases communication difficulties, as the amount of any extraneous duties undertaken by A increases, and as the interdependence between the work of the Cs increases.

If we assume that, because of the nature of the hierarchy's task, increases in all of the above variables cannot be avoided there will be a pressure to reduce A's span of control in order to reduce decision overload for A. The dilemma is that for a given number of workers A's span cannot be decreased without inserting a level in the organization – that is, the organizational structure has to shift towards that of the tall and narrow TN. Instead of having to cope with the problems of 13 Cs, A would now have to cope with the problems of only 3 Bs, who in turn cope with the problems of Cs. The cost, however, is that an extra level of management has been inserted.

In addition to the greater managerial cost, possible disadvantages of TN over SW, supported by some experimental evidence (Carzo and Yanouzas 1969), is a likely slowing down of decision making due to the need to refer decisions up through an extra level in the hierarchy. If a C has a problem needing higher level approval it will be referred to a B who will have to refer to A. However, it has been found that although tall structures tend to slow down communication they can achieve faster conflict resolution (Carzo and Yanouzas 1969).

There is, however, another strategy that could be employed to resolve the problem of A's decision overload – that is, to change ideology. For the moment we can take this as to increase both the competence and co-operation of the Cs. Increasing the competence of the Cs is particularly to do with improving their technical ability by training them to carry out their job efficiently (instrumentalism), while increasing co-operation is concerned with increasing the commitment (morality) of the Cs to the goals of the organization in order to reduce the tendency to opportunism and increase the ability of A to trust the Cs to strive towards organizational goals without monitoring (see Figure 4.2).

## A cycle of learning

A classic study by Worthy (1950) describes the policy of Sears, Roebuck and Company deliberately to force a large span of control on their store managers by making a large number of merchandising managers report to them, thereby eliminating a middle level of management. It was found that as store managers had so many subordinates reporting to them they were forced to decentralize and to delegate responsibilities. This improved the morale of the merchandising managers and generally improved their performance. Given the right conditions, delegation encourages learning on the part of subordinates; we can interpret this as an indication that increasing span can provide a positive feedback loop to the variables of competence and co-operation as illustrated in Figure 4.2.

*Figure 4.2* Factors affecting span of control

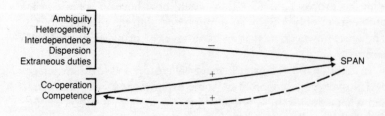

This discussion of span of control can be put into the more general terms of the Principle of Requisite Decision-Making Capacity. Figure 4.2 shows interrelationships between contextual, ideological variables and a structural variable, span of control. In terms of decision-making theory the essential point about increasing span is that it leads to an increase in decentralization. A superordinate's decision-making capacity is limited. If there is evidence that a hierarchy's decision-making capacity is insufficient, the remedy of this problem can be approached by means of increasing the span of control and thereby encouraging a more competent and co-operative ideology; or, ideology can be directly affected by means of appropriate training, socialization, or other processes to be discussed in chapter 8; or, context can be affected to reduce the value of the variables of ambiguity, interdependence, or remoteness; or, and more appropriately, the problem can be simultaneously approached from all three groups of variables.

## BUREAUCRACY

With a long history going back to early Chinese civilization, bureaucracy is probably one of the best known models of organization in use but it is the statements made at the turn of this century by the German sociologist Max Weber (1968) that have had most affect upon modern organizational theory.

In order to fully understand Weber's development of the bureaucratic concept it is necessary to put it in the wider perspective of his approach to authority. He was particularly interested in the historical development of modern bureaucracy as an authority system distinct from two other authority systems which, historically, had greater dominance. Traditional authority rests upon 'an established belief in the sanctity of immemorial traditions and the legitimacy of those exercising authority under them' (Weber 1968: 215); an example is the authority accruing to the hereditary head of a nation. Charismatic authority rests upon 'devotion to the exceptional sanctity, heroism or exemplary character of an individual person' (Weber 1968: 215), and on the particular norms and standards of behaviour set by that person; an example is the authority accruing to the entrepreneur-founder of a firm that has become a great business corporation and who may become surrounded by a sense of mystery reinforced by stories of how great difficulties were overcome in the early years.

The third type of authority, associated with bureaucratic organization, is rational–legal authority, which rests 'on a belief in the legality of enacted rules and the right of those elevated to authority under such rules to issue commands' (Weber 1968: 215). An example is the authority accruing to specialists in an organization who have shown their competence according to some predetermined set of rules; these may include academic qualifications, aptitude tests, or past job performance record if consistently and objectively recorded. Rational–legal authority is centralized in the sense that it assumes superior knowledge at higher levels with commands flowing downwards, and literal in the sense that procedures are interpreted according to the letter and not in a figurative or metaphorical way.

Inherent in the three types of authority defined above is the notion that those subject to the authority believe in its rightness and that they follow the authority more or less without question. If this is the case, the authority can be said to be legitimate and one of Weber's concerns was to show how western civilization had come to accept rational–legal authority as the dominant form of authority. The essential point to note is that legitimate authority involves an almost unquestioning automatic acceptance by its subjects. For example, if students accept that their admission to a university place should be determined upon the basis of exam results rather than upon an inherited position (as they generally do), they accept the basis of rational–legal authority. Any disputes that may occur centre upon how the rules should be made more effective; perhaps a better system of exams should be instituted which more effectively measures the innate ability of the student. Whatever formula is created, such striving is a striving towards rational–legal authority.

Authority and power clearly have an aspect in common in the sense that they both influence the behaviour of those subject to them. The distinction is in the almost automatic and willing acceptance of legitimate authority, whereas power is a more conscious act to influence others and does not imply willing acceptance of that power; the less powerful may simply be complying because there is no alternative. The concept of power is developed further in chapter 9. Authority is also related to the notion of culture (see chapter 8) since both concepts involve a system of beliefs. Charismatic authority, for example, is surrounded by various symbols and myths – an important aspect of the reinforcement of culture.

## The functions and dysfunctions of bureaucracy

According to Weber (1968: 973) 'the decisive reason for the advance of bureaucratic organization has always been its purely *technical* superiority over any other form of organization'. It is due to its speed, unambiguity, ability to store information in an impersonal way, and machine-like precision that has led to the great dominance of bureaucratic structures. It is this claim for the efficiency of bureaucracy that we now examine.

As mentioned, the basis of the bureaucratic organization is rational–legal authority. In practice this means that a great deal of the activity in a bureaucracy is directed towards making laws or rules. The other side of rule making is the need to have people obey the rules, and the norms within a bureaucracy will therefore be heavily weighted towards the instrumental type (see chapter 2). Hence Weber defined the following factors as the main ingredients of bureaucracy (quotes are from Weber 1968: 217–20):

1  Rational–legal authority as explained above.
2  Standard operating procedures for 'a continuous rule-bound conduct of official business' and these procedures get interpreted in a literal way. In this way uncertainty is controlled and predictability imposed.
3  Specialization, where participants have 'a sphere of competence'. The overall task of the organization is broken down through 'systematic division of labour' where the participant has a job definition and is given the necessary authority just for carrying out that job but does not have authority over other spheres of activity.
4  Hierarchy where 'each lower office is under the control and supervision of a higher one'.
5  Standard employment rules and norms 'which regulate the conduct of an office'. A job holder has to demonstrate adequate technical competence and appropriate attitudes which will be determined by rational–legal procedures. Heredity, friendship, or nepotism cannot be the basis for appointment to bureaucratic positions.
6  Separation of management and ownership. Participants 'attached to the administrative staff do not themselves own the non-human means of production and administration' and there is 'complete separation of the organization's property and the personal property of the individual' which extends to the separation of living quarters and working premises.
7  Separation of work and non-work. Participants, while devoting their working lives to the bureaucracy, will tend to lead a second private life away from the workplace.
8  Separation of jobs and people; there is 'a complete absence of

appropriation of his (the official's) position by the incumbent'. The job holder does not own the job, the bureaucracy does and when someone leaves the job is filled by a successor according to rules of appointment. Hence bureaucracies have an existence independent of their participants.

9 Formalization in writing of 'administrative acts, decisions, and rules . . . even in cases where oral discussion is the rule'. This record keeping provides a kind of organizational 'memory' reinforcing the ability of the bureaucracy to exist independent of individual participants. Today, this organizational memory can include information held in computer systems.

The above points outline the essential functions of what Weber called the 'ideal type' of bureaucracy. The term 'ideal type' does not imply that such an organization is without problems but rather how it would function if operating according to these principles. It is possible to indicate a number of dysfunctions of bureaucracy. Dysfunctions are the converse of functions in that they are unintended consequences which can lead to ineffectiveness.

In general we can see that bureaucracy is an efficient way of dealing with the administration of routine matters, while the dysfunction is that rigidity can set in and the organization becomes incapable of adapting to change. Another function of bureaucracy is its independence from its participants so that it is relatively insensitive to turnover. The opposite of this, if turnover is high, can be a loss of a great deal of implicit knowledge and skills that cannot be contained within written procedures. Bureaucracy also has an ability impartially to apply rules which are set by a higher authority. For example, the administration of social security is based upon the principle that a politically accountable legislature makes the rules as to who gets what under particular conditions but that the social security agencies have the task of implementing the rules regardless of the officers' personal views on the merits of various cases. The dysfunction is that officials may lose touch with the clients that they are trying to serve. This has been called the problem of the bureaucratic personality (Merton 1968) with reference to the kinds of attitudes that officials in public bureaucracies can have towards their client-public; because they are trained to interpret the rules as precisely as possible officials can appear as impersonal, incompassionate, and rigid. Closely related to the bureaucratic personality is the notion of the agentic state whereby lower-level officials can come to feel themselves absolved of moral responsibility for their actions because they were following orders (Milgram 1975). Because of the independence of bureaucratic positions from the people who fill them and because of the separation of work and non-work, bureaucracy demands minimal commitment from participants particularly at lower levels. This can often suit certain types of participant who do not necessarily want to take work home with them. The dysfunction of this separation of the individual from the bureaucracy is that there can be a lack of commitment to the bureaucracy's goals.

The characteristics, functions, and dysfunctions of bureaucracy are summarized in Table 4.1. Errors of decision undercapacity are the dysfunctions that tend to predominate in bureaucracy since the reliance upon precise procedures and rules makes it difficult for bureaucracy to adapt to any change in conditions.

*Table 4.1* Bureaucracy: characteristics, functions, and dysfunctions

| *Characteristics* | |
| --- | --- |
| 1. Rational–legal authority | 6. Separation of management and ownership |
| 2. Standard operating procedures | |
| 3. Specialization | 7. Separation of work and non-work |
| 4. Hierarchy | 8. Separation of jobs and people |
| 5. Standard employment rules | 9. Formalization |

| *Functions* | *Dysfunctions* |
| --- | --- |
| 1. Efficient for routine tasks | 1. Lack of adaptability |
| 2. Insensitive to turnover | 2. Loss of skills |
| 3. Impartiality | 3. Bureaucratic personality, agentic state |
| 4. Small commitment needed | 4. Lack of commitment |

## TOWARDS FUZZY STRUCTURES: ORGANIC AND MECHANISTIC ORGANIZATIONS

Weber's concept of bureaucracy provided a starting point for research examining the various aspects and types of bureaucratic organization. Burns and Stalker (1961) introduced the notion of mechanistic and organic organizational types whilst observing attempts to introduce new electronics technology into British firms, noting that those firms which were successful in absorbing the new technology generally had organic rather than mechanistic structures.

The mechanistic structure is typified by a Weberian bureaucracy whereby: tasks are broken down into specialisms somewhat unrelated to the overall goals of the enterprise and are rigidly defined, there is a strict hierarchy of authority, knowledge is assumed to be centralized on top management, vertical communication predominates thereby locating problem solving at the top of the organization, and commitment and loyalty becomes concentrated upon the superior rather than upon the overall task of the organization. The overall aspect of the mechanistic organization that Burns and Stalker emphasized was the demarcation of participants' jobs from one another's, and the overall organizational task. Bureaucracy and mechanistic organization are clearly crisp structures allowing little room for coping with indeterminateness.

As Table 4.2 shows, the organic structure is the opposite on all these dimensions. Although technical advances and knowledge required the use of professional experts in the organic structure, these efforts were always related to the overall goals of the enterprise rather than just to their own professional development. To assist this, tasks were seen as fluid and adjustable; participants would communicate with each other and tasks were in a process of continuous redefinition. Rather than vertical rule-bound control the organization developed a network of working relationships wherein it was accepted that knowledge was diffused and horizontal communication was accepted as normal; there was no assumption that managers at a higher level were omniscient. Commitment and loyalty to the overall enterprise was constantly emphasized rather than just loyalty to a person's immediate manager.

By observing that those traditional mechanistic firms which had been long established were largely unsuccessful in absorbing the new technology, whereas those newer firms adopting an organic

*Table 4.2* Mechanistic and organic systems of management

| Feature | Mechanistic | Organic |
| --- | --- | --- |
| 1. Specialists and organizational goals | separate | related |
| 2. Task definition | rigid | fluid |
| 3. Control | vertical, rules | network |
| 4. Knowledge | centralized | anywhere |
| 5. Communication | vertical | horizontal & vertical |
| 6. Commitment and loyalty | to superior | to organization |
| *Context* | | |
| 1. Environment | stable | variable |
| 2. Technology | clear | ambiguous |

*Source*: Adapted from Burns, T. and Stalker, G.M. (1961) *The Management of Innovation*, London: Tavistock.

management system were more successful, Burns and Stalker give us an example of a contingency theory which may be expressed thus:

When the environment of the organization is unstable and technology is uncertain, develop an organic (or fuzzy) organizational structure.

When the environment of the organization is stable, develop a mechanistic (or crisp) organizational structure.

These propositions can be explained in terms of the Principle of Requisite Decision-Making Capacity. Mechanistic organization is suitable for steady-state conditions because a large number of decisions are contained within its procedures. Because procedures can only be written after a particular set of conditions and problems have been encountered a number of times, by the time the procedures have been written the conditions can no longer be new. If environmental and technological conditions are changing rapidly the procedures will of necessity be lagging behind actual conditions facing the organization and will be inadequate to meet those problems. Mechanistic organizations are likely to suffer from errors of decision undercapacity.

The organic organization, because of its fuzzy structure and emphasis on horizontal communication, can develop the decision-making capacity to cope with changing conditions and indeterminateness. If procedures are developed they are likely to have a short shelf life before modifications are needed. The sacrifice, however, will be in terms of steady-state efficiency. Organic organizations are likely to suffer from errors of decision overcapacity.

## DIMENSIONS OF STRUCTURE: THE ASTON STUDIES

Weber's description of bureaucracy provides what he called an ideal type which gives a useful benchmark against which the characteristics of actual organizations may be compared. As we have seen, Burns and Stalker's work alerts us to the possibility that the extent to which organizations exhibit bureaucratic features might vary according to certain contextual variables. Research conducted by the Aston group in Britain set out to explore further the different dimensions of bureaucratic structures and how this varies with organizational context.

Taking Weber's factors of bureaucracy as a starting point, they identified and created measuring scales for particular variables (Pugh *et al.* 1968, 1976a, 1976b) so that organizations as a whole could be measured and compared, rather in the same way that psychologists measure characteristics of people through psychometric measurement. Six source variables were identified:

1 Specialization. The degree to which an organization's activities are divided into distinct jobs or roles.
2 Standardization–technical. The degree to which an organization lays down rules and procedures for carrying out the basic task.
3 Standardization–employment. The degree to which an organization lays down rules for recruitment and promotion.
4 Formalization. The degree to which rules and procedures are written down.
5 Centralization. The degree to which the authority to make decisions is located at the top of the management hierarchy.
6 Configuration. This measures the shape of the hierarchy, i.e., the chain of command or levels, the size of the spans of control, and the percentage of support staff or personnel.

Table 4.3 gives examples of the kinds of questions that were used to measure the above concepts across a sample of fifty-two organizations covering a wide variety of private/public and manufacturing/service organizations.

By applying the statistical technique of factor analysis to the data three underlying structural dimensions were exposed, each of which can be seen to indicate different modes of organizational control:

**Structuring of activities** This dimension links together specialization, technical standardization and formalization, and non-workflow personnel (i.e., those indirect staff who advise rather than do). If an organization scores high on this dimension this means that its basic method of control is to structure the activities of participants by defining jobs closely in a written form. An organization that is predominantly controlled in this way tends to have a high percentage of non-workflow personnel in specialist departments, such as planning and quality control, generating the routines to control the operations, and may also have a large research and development component. This organization can be relatively decentralized because so many decisions are written into the rules. This represents the highest order of rational–legal authority.

**Centralization of decisions** This dimension is seen when decisions have to be referred up the hierarchy before action can be taken.

*Table 4.3* Sample questions for Aston dimensional variables

*Specialization*
Extent to which individuals exclusively perform the following
activities, e.g.:
1. Public relations
2. Sales and service
3. Buying and stock control
4. Research and development
5. Training
6. Market research

*Standardization*
Extent to which procedures exist to define, e.g.:
1. Operator's task
2. Research and development, market research processes
3. Marketing policy
4. Stock control system

*Standardization of employment practices*
Extent to which procedures exist to define, e.g.:
1. Recruiting and interviewing
2. Selection of supervisors and manager
3. Discipline

*Formalization*
Extent to which procedures are written down, e.g.:
1. Employment contract and handbook
2. Organization chart
3. Job descriptions
4. Agenda of meetings

*Centralization*
Extent to which decisions are referred up the hierarchy for,
e.g.:
1. Pricing of products
2. Promotion of supervisors
3. Launching of new product
4. Creating a new department

*Configuration*
Shape of hierarchy, e.g.:
1. Span of control of chief executive
2. Span of control of supervisors
3. Percentage of indirect personnel
4. Levels in hierarchy

Adapted from Pugh, D. S. (1976) 'The Aston approach to the study of
organizations', in G. Hofstede and M.S. Kassen (eds), *European Contributions to Organization Theory*, ch. 3, Van Gorvan, Netherlands.

Typically, a highly centralized organization is one in which the top management (board level or even corporate headquarters) are closely involved in a whole range of decision issues. There is little structuring of activities in this type of organization except that there is a tendency to standardize recruitment policies, showing a concern to ensure that people are carefully selected. These organizations are typically government departments, subsidiary branches of large companies, or directly-controlled medium-sized companies with a fairly routine operation.

**Implicit control**   This type of control is characterized by narrow spans of control at the operating level. An organization using implicit control will be leaving operational control in the hands of the people actually doing the work of the organization, and their direct supervisors. This type of control tends to be found in small independent non-routine firms which have grown up around a founder-entrepreneur who has managed to develop a loyal workforce which needs little in the way of direct supervision or formal procedures since so much is done through common understandings gained during common experiences. This kind of system does not fit well with large size since people need to be able to communicate directly with one another, and is often found in professional or collective organizations.

The idea that organizations can be classified in this way on the basis of their actual systematically-observed characteristics represented a breakthrough in organizational theory. If we now apply the Principle of Requisite Decision-Making Capacity to explain the existence of the three dimensions of control, an organization is free to choose any control mechanism that it wishes, but the observation that organizations tend to be one thing or another suggests that there are some economies to be had by concentrating upon a particular type of control. For example, an organization that has gone to the trouble of setting up systems for structuring of activities will not need to involve a lot of top management time in direct decision making. To operate both forms of control would be inefficient.

## Context

As well as measuring dimensions of structure the Aston group also measured certain aspects of organizational context (Pugh and Hickson 1976a), notably organizational size (number of employees), aspects of technology, and dependence. Dependence refers to the extent to which the organization relies upon a small number of customers and a small number of suppliers. An example of a highly-dependent organization is one that has to supply virtually all its output to a parent company and which has to take its supplies from one other subsidiary of the parent. An organization that is highly dependent in this sense is highly determined. Technology is discussed in chapter 5.

A major finding was that organizational size tends to lead to structuring of activities; as has already been mentioned, this is accounted for by the need of an organization to develop impersonal forms of communication as it gets bigger. Another finding was that dependence is related to centralization indicating that as the power of a small number of external elements increases top management increase their influence over decisions in order to ensure that the organization is presented in the best light to these external elements. Both structuring and centralization are ways of coping with determinateness; centralization does it by concentrating the locus of decision making, structuring by writing decision expertise into rules. Implicit control allows scope for dealing with indeterminateness through the common understandings contained within participants' experience.

## Simplified profiles

The three underlying dimensions of control give us a simplified way of looking at the issue of organizational structural profiles which is of practical use. The approach is illustrated in Table 4.4 by taking three hypothetical organizations. If each dimension is scored from 'a little' to 'a lot', profiles of the three organizations emerge. They are all business firms thereby controlling to some extent along the profit/non-profit dimension of context. Firm 1 is a high-technology company driven by the founder-manager, still quite small but well past the start-up stage, having had time to develop a culture of loyalty and long service based upon the charisma of the founder-entrepreneur. In this type of organization much is carried out by dint of common understanding between participants and hence the prominent structural feature is implicit control with only a little structuring and centralization.

Firm 2 is also run by a founder-manager but in a relatively routine retail trade with around a dozen stores all within the same metropolitan area. It is a company run by the founder travelling around and personally making decisions and overseeing the store managers. The founder still makes the major buying and pricing decisions and makes decisions concerning the opening and closing of stores. Here the prominent control mechanism is centralization.

Firm 3 is a large manufacturing company mass producing a range of products for a variety of markets. Technology is relatively well understood and so this organization can undertake strategic and production planning. Here the prominent control method is by structuring.

This simple example illustrates that firms (and other organizations) will tend to alter their structures to differing conditions. The smaller firm generally has less overall structuring effort. Although organizations tend to develop a predominant form the three dimensions are not mutually exclusive.

*Table 4.4* Simplified structural profiles

| Firm | Struc | Cent | Impl | Overall | |
|------|-------|------|------|---------|---|
| 1. Founder-manager | 1 | 1 | 2 | 4 | Small size, high-tech, manufacturing |
| 2. Retailer | 1 | 3 | 1 | 5 | Medium size, chain of local stores, price cutting |
| 3. Manufacturer | 3 | 1 | 1 | 5 | Large size, mass production |

*Notes*: Control dimensions - Struc = structuring of activities; Cent = centralization; Impl = implicit control; Overall = sum of the three dimensions as approximate measure of overall management effort.
*Scoring*: 1 = a little, 2 = some, 3 = a lot.

## The dynamic

Organizations vary over time and a firm that is controlled by a particular mode at one stage in its history is not necessarily going to stay that way. The research reported shows that as firms grow in size, structuring becomes the major control mechanism as more bureaucratic procedures are used. In order to get from an implicitly structured organization to a structured one, however, need not be a smooth progression of change. A new chief executive taking over from a founder-manager may initially centralize in order to gain personal control over the organization while a process of planning and structuring is undertaken. The skill that this chief executive will have to master will be to know when to reduce centralization to allow structuring to work and hence, during the actual process of change, we might see an organization both centralized and structured before centralization is finally relaxed.

## CO-OPERATIVES

Co-operatives are a form of collective organization in which owner-ship and control lies in the hands of the membership, a different prin-ciple to the bureaucracy where there is a separation between those who control the organization and the majority of the participants. This form of organization also has a well-established, but lesser-known pedigree. Two main types of co-operative can be distinguished: the consumer and the producer; in the producer co-operative the workers are the member-owners whereas in the consumer co-operative it is the consumers who are the member-owners.

One of the best-known examples of a consumer co-operative was that set up by the Rochdale pioneers in Britain in the mid-nineteenth century by factory workers to overcome their exploitation by local shopkeepers who used their virtual monopoly power to sell poor quality, diluted food at excessive prices to workers. Some workers gathered together and opened a small shop selling goods to member-consumers. Workers and their families would join the co-operative and in return receive a proportion of the profits in the form of a dividend at the end of the year. The principle involved a two-way relationship: the organizers of the co-operative were committed to the concept of non-exploitation of their members and to the notion of a fair price but in return for loyalty to the co-operative on the part of consumers. Consumers would be shareholders and their voice could, in principle, be heard through shareholders meetings.

As the consumer co-operative grew it could not rely so much upon moral commitment as a management principle and had to develop more formalized organizational arrangements. Although the consumers were the owners, decision making would become clum-sy and slow if everyone's views were listened to over all issues. Consequently, paid officials and full-time directors were appointed but voted in by the member-consumers. In principle, unsatisfactory managers could be voted out but as membership became more dispersed this became more difficult in practice.

This kind of consumer co-operative proved very durable and may be seen in a number of countries covering a range of different activities – for example, farmers' co-operatives where a number of farmers may combine together to buy equipment or seed and, in a somewhat different form, building societies where people would save to acquire the deposit for purchasing a house, or workers' savings schemes. In terms of the types of organization outlined in chapter 2 these are mutual benefit associations. It should be noted, however, that in recent times strains set by competition in the marketplace have tended to shift these kinds of organization towards their capitalist counterparts. This trend has been seen in the co-operative retail and building society movements in Britain.

## Producer co-operatives: the case of Mondragon

Producer co-operatives have had more problems in surviving than the consumer co-operatives. Underlying this instability are two fundamental problems: the high degree of a stable capital base needed for manufacturing, and the need to produce a product to sell in a marketplace where the other actors are predominantly capitalist firms. One of the best known, most enduring, and successful producer co-operatives has been the Mondragon Co-operative in the Basque region of Spain. Mondragon presents an interesting case to illustrate some of the general principles of co-operative organization.

In the twenty years leading up to the 1980s, the village of Mondragon has grown into a major industrial area in the Basque region of Spain largely as a result of the Mondragon experiment. By the early 1980s there were more than eighty industrial co-operatives belonging to the overall complex, the largest being ULGOR – its 3,400 workers making it the largest domestic appliance manufacturer in Spain. Generally the Mondragon industrial co-operatives are capital intensive and they therefore give a particularly useful case of how this kind of organization might survive. Other co-operatives also make agricultural plant, plastics, and a whole range of other manufactures. By the mid-1980s ULGOR made over 300,000 refrigerators per year (of which 25 per cent were exported) and 100,000 consumer durables such as washing machines, cookers, and spin dryers. There are also bank, research and development, insurance, welfare, and education co-operatives serving the producer co-operatives (BBC 1980).

### Control and ownership

In principle, ownership and control lie in the hands of the members. At Mondragon the eighty or so primary producer co-operatives are owned by the co-operators, each of whom has to contribute approximately £2,000 upon joining. For those who cannot afford this, the money may be borrowed at a low rate of interest. Members can only withdraw their money when they leave and then their shares have to be sold back to the co-operative. This protects the co-operative from ownership moving outside the organization but leaves the departing member in the hands of the remaining membership to set a fair price. In the absence of a market valuation this may be difficult whereas in the public company ownership can pass to outside shareholders who can buy and sell shares at market valuation.

## Ideology

Co-operatives emphasize goals other than profit and put an emphasis upon developing a moral ideology. In the case of Mondragon an important aspect of the ideology is the feeling of solidarity within the Basque nation.

## Decision making

The emphasis in co-operatives is upon consensual decision making but once a co-operative gets above a small size it becomes more difficult for the whole membership to participate in all decisions. As already mentioned this has led to the development of a system of representative councils at Mondragon. The first step in setting this up was to limit the size of each producer co-operative to about 600 members. Each of these co-operatives has a management board consisting of elected members with the membership replaceable every two years by voting. A general manager is appointed by the board to carry out the decisions of the board and can be sacked from that position. Being a board member requires an extra commitment as shown by the expectation that they should meet outside normal working hours, usually at 7.00 a.m. At the highest level of the organization is the general assembly to which producer co-operatives send representatives.

## Power and status

Co-operative principles emphasize equality of power and status. Election of supervisors and fixed terms of office may be used to ensure this; also jobs are rotated and participants are accountable to an assembly of all members of the co-operative. Job rotation has a potential cost to the organization in that it means that the best person for the job is not necessarily available. However, it does put a great emphasis in the organization upon the need for training which can pay off in the long run. Bureaucratic principles require appointments to jobs to be made mainly on the basis of skills and qualifications.

Following from this ideal in the co-operative is the potential negative tendency of the co-operative to develop an oligarchy whereby power tends to gravitate into the hands of a relatively small number of people. This can be by default of the rest of the membership as much as through deliberate manoeuvring on the part of people to gain power. Participation imposes a cost upon the membership in terms of time and commitment which in the short term may not seem worthwhile to the individual.

*Profit sharing*

The pay range, that is the difference between the lowest and the highest paid worker, is generally less than that found in the equivalent Spanish for-profit firm; in Mondragon, the highest paid worker generally earns no more than three times that of the lowest. Profits are shared out according to a formula which gives 10 per cent to the local community, 20 per cent to reserves, and 70 per cent to the co-operators themselves. It is from this 70 per cent that the pay of the co-operators is drawn but they cannot withdraw the remainder until they leave the co-operative and then this share must be sold back to the co-operative. On average, co-operators take out about £20,000 plus a pension upon retirement (mid-1980s figures). If a co-operative makes a loss, 30 per cent is made up from reserves and the rest from the co-operators themselves.

*Selection and advancement*

Because of the need for the co-operative to develop solidarity and moral norms, the presence of appropriate attitudes becomes an important variable in the selection of people and may take precedence over technical skills. Although there is a potential cost to the organization this could be made up for by a reduction in the need for supervision. The Mondragon co-operative achieves a lower than average supervisory ratio for the industry (Bradley and Gelb 1983, Thomas and Logan 1982) although it would be wrong to assume that they do not also put emphasis upon technical skills. In a bureaucracy, rightness for a job is assessed by formal certification in the first place. At the managerial level attitudes may become important but the bureaucracy does not emphasize this through the organization.

Advancement in the co-operative, therefore, tends to take greater account of the moral commitment and attitudes of the participants, whereas a bureaucracy will tend to emphasize formal procedures of job grading and incentives will be linked to the appraisal of an individual on these procedures. This is more difficult for the co-operative to do since moral commitment is hard to assess.

The co-operative finds it difficult, but not impossible, to fire people because of bad performance; it has happened at Mondragon (BBC 1980) but it is a relatively traumatic event requiring a vote of the general assembly. This is not to suggest that firing is an event that bureaucracies relish but nevertheless it is a decision made by the management and does not generally require anything approaching a consensual decision.

## Sensitivity to turnover

As already noted, the co-operative needs to avoid high turnover of members in order to keep a stable capital base so as not to lose the skills of the members which will tend to be more general-purpose than in the bureaucracy (Abell 1988). When members leave they can take their original capital sum plus any accrued profits and this makes the capital base of the co-operative potentially very sensitive to high turnover compared to a capitalist enterprise. The rule at Mondragon that members cannot sell their shares whilst they are members and that they have to be sold back to the co-operative upon leaving helps to reduce this problem.

## Context

The fundamental dilemma of the producer co-operative is that it usually has to exist in its environment primarily as a market organization, in competition with other non-co-operative firms. However, there are a number of features of Mondragon that enables it to operate efficiently at the same time as, generally, preserving the co-operative principle.

First, is its history. Mondragon cannot be understood without appreciating the solidarity of the surrounding Basque community developed during the Spanish Civil War and its antagonism towards the Madrid government. It was from this background that the founders of the co-operative were able to draw upon the moral commitment of workers to do something positive to help the community. This solidarity was increased through a strong religious feeling and a common language. It would seem, therefore, to be an organizational form less suitable for a pluralistic urban environment in which market forces predominate.

Second, the system of secondary co-operatives is an important aspect of the Mondragon system. Surrounding the primary co-operatives is an extensive system of secondary co-operatives which act as a kind of buffer zone from the environment. The most important of these is the co-operative bank. This was started in the first place as a co-operative bank for small savers; its assets have grown from £4.5 million in 1966 to £275 million in 1979, at which time it had 900 workers. It is financed by profits from the producer co-operatives but can only lend to the Mondragon co-operatives. The board of the bank consists of four bank and eight industrial workers. This board approves and monitors all new projects including the financing of new co-operative ventures. In doing this work it may also draw upon the use of outside experts and consultants. Other secondary co-operatives include a technical college, a co-operative university, a research and development co-operative (IKERLAN) which carries out research and development work for the producer co-operatives, and a social security co-operative since the Mondragon workers count as self-employed and cannot join the state scheme.

Third, co-operatives may draw upon additional support from customers who also expect something other than a profit-making motive. In the case of Mondragon the co-operative had the purpose of creating jobs and building up a community. A similar aspect applies to the financial support and means of gaining capital. In Mondragon the co-operative bank plays a vital role in not applying the same kind of criteria as a conventional commercial bank. The co-operative bank cannot, for instance, lend outside the co-operative system. Generally, the regulatory environment of the co-operative needs also to be relatively benign.

## Evaluation

The efficiency of co-operatives compared to for-profit firms has often been questioned (Thomas and Logan 1982). Bradley and Gelb (1982) report that on economic criteria Mondragon performs favourably compared to other similar local and national firms in Spain at the time of their study. Industrial relations are better, management costs lower, and profitability good.

Bradley and Gelb argue that an important ingredient in this success is the solidarity of the local population in the face of a history of hardship and hostility towards the Madrid government rather than the 'Basqueness' of Mondragon. For a co-operative to work, low turnover of the workforce is necessary and integration of the organization into the community is more important than some particular ethnic quality of the people. One important factor in helping this solidarity is the Basque language which is unique to the area, widely spoken, and taught in the schools.

Lockett (1980: 184) argues that if co-operatives and firms in similar stages of development and of similar sizes are compared, the survival rate of co-operatives is slightly higher. Further, if measurements of some of the non-economic goals of co-operatives are taken – of participation, equality of influence in decision making, and satisfacton, for example – co-operatives generally tend to come out slightly higher than normal firms. If, however, economic difficulties are encountered and survival is threatened, the co-operative tends to degenerate rather easily and score less on these factors.

## Implications

The co-operative form of organization provides an example of how moral norms can work to produce an efficiency that compares well with more bureaucratic types of organization. In this respect, it provides an institutional framework that has some of the features of the Japanese company as described in chapter 2. There we were at pains to point to the need for an organization to achieve isomorphism with the environment. Again this has been demonstrated through the Mondragon example. Co-operatives provide fuzzier structures than bureaucracies particularly through their use of participative and consensual decision making. Their dilemmas arise from the errors of decision overcapacity; the fuzzier structures than would normally be found in capitalist counterparts, to be successful, have to be directed towards developing greater commitment on the part of participants. It is easy for this kind of organization to slip into oligarchy, in the same way as trade unions (Michels 1949), whereby the effective decision-making power becomes concentrated upon a relatively small number of people.

## DESIGN IMPLICATIONS AND SUMMARY

Hierarchy is a ubiquitous feature of organization. The problem is to provide the requisite decision-making capacity. The short–wide hierarchy economizes upon managerial cost but is liable to errors of decision undercapacity when the context is interdependent, heterogeneous, ambiguous, and spatially dispersed. Ideological factors, such as competence and co-operation, can overcome the problems of the short–wide hierarchy. Once a wide span has been achieved, a positive feedback learning loop helps to reinforce the ideological factors.

Bureaucracy is liable to errors of decision undercapacity. These can be attenuated by means of using alternative forms of bureaucracy in particular by shifting towards the organic form.

Studies of different bureaucratic forms reveal three dominant control dimensions. These are: structuring, centralization, and implicit control. Although not mutually exclusive, the Principle of Requisite Decision-Making Capacity would suggest that organizations would tend to specialize in one type of control dimension according to context. For example, large size, as measured by the number of participants, tends to lead to structuring whereas high dependence upon a small number of environmental elements tends to lead to centralization of decision making as a control mechanism.

We can compare the co-operative to the bureaucratic organization within the framework of the institutional model of organization (see Table 4.5). The co-operative can provide an alternative model of organization resting upon the moral ideology permitting some economizing of managerial costs particularly due to a reduction in opportunism. We have noted how this form of organization is particularly suited to a context where clear efficiency goals are not the only important norms of assessment and that more ambiguous norms are also taken into account.

In terms of structure, the co-operative attempts to reconcile the need for efficiency and crispness with the need to maintain the co-operative ideology. Its structure is both bureaucratic and collective. Although a great deal of formalization is needed we suggest that there will also be a high degree of implicitness and shared meanings, reinforced by a greater use of symbolism based upon an understanding of how the organization was founded and the ideals that existed at that time. Although specialists may be extensively used demarcations between jobs can be broken down by means of job rotation and training. The co-operative encourages a more interactive structure through elimination of status barriers and the use of representative councils as a common feature. Collectivism in the co-operative is built in by means of common ownership and profit sharing; rules about the sale of shares attempt to prevent ownership moving outside the organization.

Reward systems in a bureaucracy have a punitive aspect to them in the sense that redundancy or firing for poor performance may occur; the co-operative will try to emphasize positive policies, such as retraining, if there is a downturn in labour requirements. Bureaucracy tends to be literal in its interpretation of rules whereas the co-operative can draw upon symbolism; if, for example, a proposal to move into a new market is disputed in the co-operative, decision makers may draw upon the ideals of the founders to ask what they would have done.

*Table 4.5* The contingent institutional model of organization: salient variable relationships discussed in this chapter

| Bureaucracy | Co-operative |
|---|---|
| *Context* | |
| clear | some ambiguity |
| | some uniqueness |
| | some interdependence |
| | *more complex* |
| *Structure* | |
| formalized | implicit by shared understandings |
| demarcated | differentiated by job rotation |
| hierarchical | interactive by representative councils |
| centralized | decentralized by councils and autonomous units |
| individualistic | collective by ownership and profit sharing |
| punitive | supportive by commitment to tenure and training |
| literal | symbolic by story of foundation |
| | *more fuzzy* |
| *Ideology* | |
| instrumental | morality important |

The co-operative has particular problems in achieving the requisite stability of capital base. Providing a secondary co-operative bank to act as a 'buffer' between the production co-operatives and the uncertainties of the wider financial markets helps to make the task environment more stable. Similarly, other buffer secondary co-operatives also increase stability for the supply of services such as research and development and various community services. In this respect the case of Mondragon suggests that the co-operative needs to design its context to provide this buffering.

The comparison of the capitalist enterprise, with its predominantly bureaucratic structure, to the co-operative, is meant to demonstrate that the co-operative is a form of organization with particular characteristics suitable for a rather special set of conditions. We do not suggest that the co-operative is inherently superior.

# Chapter five

# Technological variables

It is in the technical sub-system of an organization that the processes of transformation take place converting given inputs into outputs to be exchanged in the environment for further resources, where what might be recognized as the 'real' work of the organization occurs, and where most workers are situated. In the factory one is immediately aware of technology; there is noise, vibration, heat, and the obvious expenditure of energy in the machinery. Non-manufacturing organizations also have their technology. In a hospital there is the application of medical treatments such as surgery, nursing, radio-therapy, and orthodontics in various parts of the organization; in insurance, there is the process of assessing risks associated with the various categories of insurers and balancing these against various investment opportunities and risks.

## TECHNICAL AMBIGUITY AND VARIABILITY

Technology is the application of knowledge to effect a change in the inputs of an organization to produce a desired output. That knowledge concerns beliefs about ends/means relationships in the search for the instrumentally best way to reach a given end. To achieve a desired end, physical equipment will usually be required even if it is as simple as paper and pencil; but technology is more than just machinery or equipment although this is what frequently dominates the discussion of technology in manufacturing organizations. It is the interaction between people, machines, and the knowledge of how to use those machines that needs to be considered. A machine on its own is inert without people to operate it but this requires knowledge of how to operate it.

As technology is seen as the interaction between machines and people with knowledge and beliefs interposed between the two, we need specifically to introduce this dimension into our consideration of organizational technology. Here we present the typology developed by Perrow (1970) which looks at the basic operating unit of an organization. Two dimensions are identified as significant in determining the activities and structures of these units: the ambiguity and the variability of the task.

## Ambiguity versus clarity

Technology is concerned with beliefs about end/means relationships; this can be seen especially when these beliefs are ambiguous and it is difficult to analyse how to reach a given end. Teachers may dispute over the 'best' way to teach handicapped children to read or do mathematics, but ultimately the skill of any teacher rests upon the ability to adapt existing beliefs about the best way to effect a change in a child to the circumstances of a particular child.

In general, when the transformation process is analysable, activities can be well understood by the operators. Knowledge as to whether effect B follows act A is precise; for instance, the assembly of standard 'chips' into circuits with different operating characteristics is well understood and analysable. In medical treatment the actions of some drugs (chemo-therapy for the treatment of cancer, for example) or of some surgery are not well understood as their precise outcomes are unpredictable. The degree of ambiguity depends upon the 'state of the art', the extent to which scientific knowledge has developed understanding of the particular process, and upon the knowledge and skill of the operators concerned (Withey et al. 1983).

## Variability versus stability

When the operating unit is presented with many new tasks and exceptions the technology is variable. Variability is seen in therapeutic fields where each psychiatric patient presents a new problem, and in manufacturing where prototype production of an advanced computer or jet aircraft presents new problems. Again we are concerned about knowledge. Whether a task is perceived as a new problem will depend upon the experience of the operators. As an organization learns technology, tasks can be categorized according to previous experience and organizational routines developed accordingly.

By taking the combination of different values of ambiguity and variability four broad categories of technology can be defined (see Figure 5.1):

*Figure 5.1* Technology and unit structure

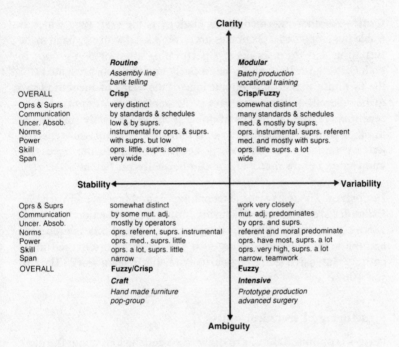

| | Routine | Modular |
|---|---|---|
| | *Assembly line* | *Batch production* |
| | *bank telling* | *vocational training* |
| OVERALL | **Crisp** | **Crisp/Fuzzy** |
| Oprs & Suprs | very distinct | somewhat distinct |
| Communication | by standards & schedules | many standards & schedules |
| Uncer. Absob. | low & by suprs. | med. & mostly by suprs. |
| Norms | instrumental for oprs. & suprs. | oprs. instrumental. suprs. referent |
| Power | with suprs. but low | med. and mostly with suprs. |
| Skill | oprs. little, suprs. some | oprs. little suprs. a lot |
| Span | very wide | wide |

Stability ← → Variability

| | | |
|---|---|---|
| Oprs & Suprs | somewhat distinct | work very closely |
| Communication | by some mut. adj. | mut. adj. predominates |
| Uncer. Absob. | mostly by operators | by oprs. and suprs. |
| Norms | oprs. referent, suprs. instrumental | referent and moral predominate |
| Power | oprs. med., suprs. little | oprs. have most, suprs. a lot |
| Skill | oprs. a lot, suprs. little | oprs. very high, suprs. a lot |
| Span | narrow | narrow, teamwork |
| OVERALL | **Fuzzy/Crisp** | **Fuzzy** |
| | **Craft** | **Intensive** |
| | *Hand made furniture* | *Prototype production* |
| | *pop-group* | *advanced surgery* |

Clarity (top) / Ambiguity (bottom)

*Source*: Adapted from Perrow, C. (1970) *Organizational Analysis: A Sociological View*, London: Tavistock.
*Notes*: *suprs* = supporters; *oprs* = operators; *med.* = medium; *mut. adj.* = mutual adjustment; *Uncer. Absorp.* = uncertainty absorption; *Span* = span of control of first line supervisor.

**Routine**  The most routine technologies are clear and stable. Examples are: from manufacturing, assembly line production; and from services, bank telling. In both cases the worker is presented with a uniform task and precise knowledge of how to do it.

**Modular**  Modular technology is variable and clear. Here the emphasis is upon putting essentially standard components or processes together into different 'mixes' of outputs. In manufacturing, standard units or sub-assemblies are assembled in different mixes to effect a variation in products. In vocational training standard units of knowledge are reassembled to produce different kinds of courses for different types of student.

**Craft** Another intermediate technology is the craft type which is stable but ambiguous. Examples are: from manufacturing, hand made furniture; and from services, a performing artist or pop group. In both cases the craft operator has a fairly uniform task presented (for the furniture maker only dimensions of the items of furniture have to be altered, for the pop group the same 'turn' might be used repetitively), but the means of doing it cannot be easily transmitted to other people, cannot be written into standard procedures, and a lengthy period of experience is needed to acquire the necessary knowledge before the operator can be really proficient.

**Intensive** The least routine technology is ambiguous and variable. Examples are: from manufacturing, prototype production; and from services, advanced research. In both cases a novel task is presented and the knowledge of how to do it has yet to be discovered in its entirety. Intensive technology usually results in team work (Thompson 1967).

## Structuring of technical units

Perrow's outline allows us to draw some conclusions about the most appropriate unit structures for each type of technology. Here we are concerned with the internal structure of the units that are involved in the actual task of producing the organization's output.

We consider two types of people, their interrelationships, and their relationships with the wider organization in looking at the kinds of structures that might emerge in these types of technology. First, are the operators themselves, the people who carry out the actual task itself and, second, are the technical support people whose function it is to directly help the operators. The exact way in which these two types of people work and relate to one another and become involved in decisions will vary with the type of technology.

Figure 5.1 summarizes some important aspects of structure and how this might vary to provide the requisite decision-making capacity in order to cope with ambiguity and variety. With the routine technology only a low decision-making capacity is required and we will generally see a crisp structure; we see supporters and operators as distinct groups of people. What uncertainty there is, is absorbed by the supporters who have power to make decisions and plan operating procedures, although the power of both groups is relatively low within the organization since top management in this structure tends to hold the power. There are wide spans of control and overall training, and skill levels are low especially for operators. Norms will be essentially instrumental.

Both the modular and the craft systems can be seen as needing in-between amounts of decision-making capacity. Both exhibit a lesser degree of crispness in their structures than the routine, but in different ways. The essential difference between them lies in the different roles played by the operators and the supporters. In the modular technology the idea is to keep the operators working routinely and hence crisply organized but to let the supporters absorb the uncertainties raised by increasing variety of output. Intensive planning is now needed since the production schedule has to be continuously updated to keep up with the changes in products. Norms within the operating group will still be essentially instrumental but the support group will contain professionally-qualified people and hence referent norms will predominate here. In the craft technology it is the operators who are fuzzily organized and have the discretion, power, and referent norms, while the supporters' role is a relatively routine one needing instrumental norms and is controlled by the demands of the operators. Typically the supporters are bookkeepers and people fulfilling other administrative tasks.

As we shift to the intensive technology we see a move to a fuzzy/team structure for both operators and supporters, non-formalized communication, more equal power for both groups relative to each other and relative to higher management. High within-unit decision-making capacity is required and both groups will be involved in absorbing uncertainty. High skill levels are required for both groups probably with external professional training. The emphasis here is on team operation with uncertainties being absorbed more by the operators than by the supporters, although supporters are heavily involved in this as well. Norms will be referent and moral since commitment to the team working will play an important part. At the limit the distinction between operators and supporters will disappear. Advanced surgery teams illustrate the vital role of support people; the surgeons will need many highly-skilled support people, anaesthetists and the like.

## The dynamic

What is particularly useful about the above typology is that it can be used to trace out possible organization design changes as the underlying dimensions of the technology change and an organization adjusts itself to provide the requisite decision-making capacity. This can happen in any direction. A strategy emphasizing efficiency, variety reduction, and price cutting would drive technology towards the routine type. Hence we would expect to see a crisper structure, greater formalization, a greater separation of operators and supporters, greater power in the hands of supporters, and less skill requirements for operators.

A strategy emphasizing innovation and adaptability with lesser concern for efficiency would drive technology and associated structures towards the intensive. This could apply equally to manufacturing or service organizations.

The overall logic of technical rationality, however, is towards an ever-increasing routinization of operations. The ideal efficient operating system is one which is non-ambiguous and non-variable, operating almost as a closed system, sealed off from environmental variation, and instrumentally perfecting its routines.

## SOME EVIDENCE: WOODWARD'S STUDY

One of the first studies to investigate systematically the relationship between technological and structural variables was conducted by Woodward (1965, 1980) and her colleagues. They devised a classification for technology consisting of eleven categories which may be summarized as covering the four broad categories of unit and small batch production, large batch, mass production, and process production. The researchers assessed the dominant, or modal type of technology in an organization relative to this scale which was then interpreted as a scale of technical complexity, with unit production as the least complex and process production as the most complex. They investigated the relationship between the technology type and various aspects of structure in 92 manufacturing firms, although the actual results are based upon slightly fewer than that.

Two main kinds of relationship between technology and structural characteristics were found. First are those factors which increase linearly from unit through batch-mass to process production. These are:

— number of management levels in hierarchy,
— ratio of indirect to direct workers,
— ratio of managers to total personnel,
— ratio of total costs to labour costs,
— span of control of chief executive.

This set of results indicates that management effort as a ratio of total personnel generally increased from unit through batch-mass to process production as machines come to do more and more work and proportionately fewer operators are needed. With unit or craft production it is the direct workers (operators) that matter; they are the ones that do the work and control its organization. At the other extreme with process production there are very few direct workers; at the limit jobs can be done by automatic processes and robots, and hence the control of the organization is in the hands of technically-qualified personnel whose job is to ensure that production is efficiently controlled. Mass and batch production occupies an intermediate point on this scale.

The second set of results shows low values at the unit and process ends of the scale and high values at the middle batch-mass production point. These are:

— span of control of first line supervisors,
— unskilled to skilled worker ratio,
— separation of administration from production,
— amount of written communication.

This set of findings indicates a greater routinization and structuring of activities at the batch-mass middle point of the scale than at the extremities. Consequently, supervisors can supervise more people, more unskilled workers are used, and there is an army of supporting bureaucrats to keep production going by carrying out functions such as production control and planning. Generally this kind of organization is crisp.

Another set of variables shows the same curvilinear relationship with technology type – that is, low scores at the two extreme points of the scale (unit production at one end, process production at the other):

— management–worker conflict,
— specificity of job definition as regards pay and conditions,
— use of sanctions and control procedures.

These are essentially the industrial relations type of variables describing the quality of relationships between management and workers. The unit end of the scale may be interpreted as craft technology in Perrow's terms with skilled workers making decisions about how to work. The process end of the scale is marked by the lack of direct operators; here personnel surrounding the technical core are more 'white coated' (rather than blue collared) technically qualified people who need to understand how the equipment operates and whose function is to ensure continuous smooth operation; with this type of technology there are very few direct and unskilled workers with whom conflict can occur. The middle mass-production point of the scale has many unskilled workers doing highly routine, repetitive, and boring work, and is usually highly unionized. In the chronological development of technology these are jobs which in the future could become mechanized in a shift towards the automated continuous type of production. In the meantime human beings continue to do machine-like jobs. Conflict becomes endemic in this situation.

Another part of Woodward's study examined the relationship between performance and the fit between technology and organizational structure. Performance was measured by ranking firms in terms of commercial success. The main conclusion from this analysis was that the more successful firms adopted structures close to the average of their technology category.

## INTERDEPENDENCE

In complex organizations technologies cannot be operated by individuals acting singly. This brings us to our third basic dimension of technology: interdependence. Thompson (1967) pointed to the effect of interdependence upon structure; according to the Principle of Requisite Decision-Making Capacity the summary proposition is that increasing interdependence needs increasing decision-making capacity.

### Interdependence and co-ordination types

Activities in an organization are interdependent in the sense that work flows from one unit, individual, group, or department, to another. Interdependence requires decision-making activity in order to achieve co-ordination. In general we can say that as interdependence increases in complexity so too does the decision-making capacity have to increase. What we need, therefore, is a way of describing and measuring the complexity of organizational interdependence.

Thompson (1967) suggests a scale of three types of interdependence. The lowest degree of interdependence complexity is pooled interdependence, which is seen when organizational units are not directly dependent upon one another but are individually dependent upon a pool of resources. An example of this is the kind of interdependence that the divisions in a multidivisional company have where, assuming that there is no flow of products between the divisions, they each look to the headquarters for capital investment funds and other central resources. Here, according to Thompson, co-ordination can be provided for by means of simple rules laying down certain minimum conditions of performance that must be attained in order to gain access to the pooled resources. This we call parametric co-ordination. In the multidivisional company this might be achieved by laying down a particular rate of return on investment and other financial targets. Providing interdependence remains pooled such simple summary performance parameters provide the requisite decison-making capacity; so long as central management does not need to understand in great depth the internal operations of each division, this highly economic method of co-ordinating is adequate. Because reliance upon parameters can filter out much rich informal information this co-ordination type is particularly susceptible to errors of decision undercapacity.

When technologies are based upon pooled interdependence, Thompson (1967) calls this a mediating technology. The aim in a mediating technology is to connect a number of independent users who wish to make a transaction. A telephone exchange does this by connecting callers, banks do this by connecting a lender to a borrower, estate agents do this by connecting a seller of a house to a buyer. The essential problem is to summarize the needs of the transactors into as few simple parameters as possible. The telephone exchange has simple rules covering subscription levels and the pricing of calls, the bank has simple rules covering requirements for depositers and borrowers in order to reduce chances of defaults on loans, the estate agent uses simple parameters to describe houses categorizing them into price, location, type, and the like. Because the mediating technology needs precise categorization it rests upon the ability to develop crisp rather than fuzzy structures. In this type of technology interaction between participants is lowest.

The mid-point on the interdependence complexity scale is sequential interdependence. This is seen when work flows serially between organizational units – that is, unit A's output is passed to unit B who passes work to unit C, and so on down the line and is perhaps best typified by the assembly line type of production. Sequential interdependence is clearly much more open to disruptions from contingencies than the pooled type since any interruption in the work of an upstream unit due, say, to a breakdown will mean that the downstream units cannot do their work. Under these circumstances co-ordination is clearly more difficult and needs to be achieved by scheduling. Here the essence is to synchronize activities of the different units precisely. There will have to be a production schedule to ensure that the correct outputs are available when wanted and contingencies, such as breakdowns, need to be guarded against through measures such as planned maintenance programmes. Scheduling allows for greater decision-making capacity in that schedules have to be written and updated periodically. The greater the uncertainty the more frequently the rescheduling has to occur but this is more costly than co-ordination by parameters since it is more demanding upon managerial time. Scheduling can be susceptible to errors of decision undercapacity or overcapacity.

Technologies based upon sequential interdependence are of the long-linked type. The aim in the long-linked technology is to join together a number of operators who are performing tasks that have to occur in a certain order. The assembly line is an example of such a technology; long-linked technologies can also be found in hospitals where patients go through stages of diagnosis and treatment in a prescribed order, or in education where students go through stages of teaching in a certain order because it is assumed that A has to be learned before B, which has to be learned before C, and so on. As indicated above the problem is to synchronize the stages.

The most complex interdependence is the reciprocal type. Here work flows back and forth between individuals or units and is typically found in non-routine types of production such as may be found in advanced prototype manufacturing in the aerospace industry, where technology is still relatively indeterminate. People have to work closely together in these situations and, although there will probably be parameters and schedules, these will take second place to the need for mutual adjustment as the main co-ordination method. Mutual adjustment means the ability to have two-way communication and high interaction as the task proceeds. Through this process of feedback individuals can quickly adjust their activities as new information comes to light and conditions change; feedback is not impossible with scheduling but it has to await the advent of the next planning cycle. Mutual adjustment clearly enables the transmission of much richer language than parameters or schedules. In moving to mutual adjustment we have moved to a yet more costly co-ordination type but one which gives the greatest decision-making capacity. To use this when the cheaper parameters or schedules will suffice is inefficient; this type of co-ordination is most susceptible to errors of decision overcapacity.

Technology based upon reciprocal interdependence is the intensive type (Thompson 1967) which has already been described above. It is in this type that the degree of interaction between participants is highest.

What we can see from this outline of interdependence, co-ordination, and technology types, summarized in Figure 5.2, is that the types of co-ordination represent types of decision process as an organization attempts to cope with the uncertainties of co-ordination. Admittedly the descriptions are very abbreviated but they provide a useful shorthand for attempting to understand the ways in which decision-making capacity needs to vary with variations in interdependence.

*Figure 5.2* Thompson's types of interdependence, co-ordination, and technology.

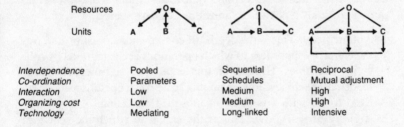

| Interdependence | Pooled | Sequential | Reciprocal |
|---|---|---|---|
| Co-ordination | Parameters | Schedules | Mutual adjustment |
| Interaction | Low | Medium | High |
| Organizing cost | Low | Medium | High |
| Technology | Mediating | Long-linked | Intensive |

*Source*: Thompson, J.D. (1967) *Organizations in Action*, New York: McGraw-Hill.

## The proposed additive nature of co-ordination methods

Co-ordination methods are likely to be additive rather than mutually exclusive. If we imagine an organization starting with the simplest pooled type of interdependence it will introduce parametric co-ordination. If interdependence shifts to the more complex sequential type, schedules would be needed but these would tend to be added to the already existing parameters. Similarly, if interdependence shifts to the reciprocal type, mutual adjustment would be needed but this would tend to be in addition to the need for parameters and schedules. Some evidence for this proposition comes from Van de Ven *et al.*'s (1976) study of interdependence and co-ordination in US employment agencies. Many of these agencies used team structures with reciprocal interdependence and mutual adjustment co-ordination in order to cope with the variations in problems confronted. But they also used a high degree of parametric and scheduled co-ordination methods (Miles 1980: 74–8). This would seem to be fairly typical of team working whereby a team is a way of providing sufficient decision-making capacity to cope with uncertainty but the team operates within a framework of rules.

## Workflow integration

The Aston group of researchers included in their study of a wide range of fifty-two organizations (already discussed in chapter 4) a scale of workflow integration for classifying technologies (Hickson *et al.* 1969, Pugh and Hickson 1976a) to include both manufacturing and service sectors.

The scale of technology was based upon the identification of three characteristics that seemed appropriate to describing workflow operations across all types of organizations. These were:

1 Automaticity. This is the degree of equipment automation and was measured by the extent to which operations are performed by self-acting machines. Highest on this scale were self-measuring and feedback machines; lowest on this scale were operations done by hand tools, with a number of intermediate points.
2 Rigidity of workflow. This is the extent to which the sequence of operations is interdependent.
3 Specificity of evaluation. This is the extent to which workflow activity can be evaluated using precise quantitative measurements as opposed to the use of non-quantitative, personal opinions of managers. The lowest point on this scale was personal evaluation only possible, whilst the highest point was measurement possible against a precise specification.

The results of the study showed that the three technology variables were highly associated with one another and could be formed into one scale called workflow integration which is, in effect, the sum of automaticity, workflow rigidity, and specificity of evaluation. Each organization could now be given a workflow integration score. The high scoring workflow integration organizations were those firms whose technology is characterized by greater automation of equipment, rigidity of workflow, and precision of operations measurement. The maximum score on the workflow integration scale is 21, based on 7 points each for the 3 measures contained in workflow integration (see Table 5.1).

*Table 5.1* Measurement of workflow integration

| Workflow integration is sum of: | | |
|---|---|---|
| 1 AUTOMATICITY | | |
| Degree of automation | | |
| | High | Self-measuring and adjusting machines |
| | | Automatic repeat cycles |
| | | Single cycle automatic and self-feeding machines |
| | | Powered machines and tools |
| | Low | Hand tools and manual machines |
| 2. RIGIDITY | | |
| Interdependence and unalterability of operations | | |
| | High | Outputs activities are direct inputs of other activities |
| | | Some activities are not inputs of other activities |
| | Low | Duplication of activities |
| 3. SPECIFICITY | | |
| Existence of precise standards of work measurement | | |
| | High | Specifications available over whole output |
| | | Partial specifications |
| | Low | Personal evaluation |

*Source*: Hickson, D.J., Pugh, D.S., and Pheysey, D.C. (1969) 'Operations technology and organizational structure: an empirical reappraisal', *Administrative Science Quarterly*, 14, 3 (September): 378–97.

The results showed that there were major differences between manufacturing and service firms. The manufacturing organizations generally had higher scores on workflow integration than the service ones. Service industries appear to be characterized by less automation, workflow rigidity, and specificity than manufacturing organizations.

Another finding is that workflow integration is related to the

bureaucratic dimension of structuring of activities. More specifically, as workflow integration increased so too did the need for
standardized procedures, formalization, and the use of various
specialists to plan and ensure the technology is kept running efficiently. As operations are more tightly linked together, the synchron-
ization of activities becomes more critical and the organizational
structure needs to be more crisp. The Aston findings are therefore
supporting the general ideas on interdependence and co-ordination
mechanisms put forward by Thompson and discussed above.

Another way in which the Aston research reinforces other research
is that it generally supports the findings of Woodward (1965) already
described. However, the Aston group found that technology affected
structure to a greater extent in the smaller organizations indicating
that technology will affect that part of an organization which is closest
to the technical core. In very large organizations so much of the
management structure is remote from the actual process of transforming inputs into outputs. We can expect the management of a small
firm to be much closer to the technical core than the management
of large firms. In large diverse organizations, size, ownership, or
environment may be more important to structural design because
upper-management activities are several levels removed from the
transformation process.

*Table 5.2* Unit technology and workflow integration

| ROUTINE | MODULAR |
|---|---|
| *High Integration* | *Medium Integration* |
| due to | |
| high automaticity | high automaticity |
| high rigidity | medium rigidity |
| high specificity | medium specificity |
| leading to | |
| High structuring | Medium structuring |
| CRAFT | NON-ROUTINE |
| *Medium Integration* | *Low Integration* |
| due to | |
| low automaticity | low automaticity |
| medium rigidity | low rigidity |
| medium specificity | low specificity |
| leading to | |
| Medium structuring | Low structuring |

Comparisons with Perrow's typology are also revealing (see Table 5.2). Routine technology will clearly tend to exhibit high workflow integration with a high degree of automation, linking together of work processes, and precise measurement (automaticity, rigidity, and specificity variables, respectively). Conversely, non-routine technology tends to score low on these variables. Craft technology might be assumed to be particularly low on automaticity whereas modular tends to be high on this. As modular operations are based upon the notion of putting together standard sub-assemblies in different configurations we might hypothesize that workflow rigidity is of a lowish amount (perhaps not as low as for non-routine). Craft work on the other hand can be quite rigid in its workflow; the essence is the handwork aspect but each handmade stage can require precise co-ordination with another. Both craft and modular types can be said to have intermediate specificity.

## ORGANIZATIONAL CHOICE: SOCIO-TECHNICAL SYSTEMS

One important approach to the study of organizational technology which shows technology as a man–machine relationship is that of socio-technical systems. This term is associated with the now classic studies conducted by researchers at the Tavistock Institute in the late 1940s and 1950s. Of particular interest is an investigation of the technical changes that were occurring in coal mines at that time due to the introduction of the longwall method of mining (Trist *et al.* 1963).

### The case of coal mining

Initially, Trist and Bamforth (1951) were interested in the social and psychological consequences of the technical changes taking place in British coal mining after the Second World War. The researchers were able to generalize from this study and introduce the notion of 'organizational choice' (Trist *et al.* 1963) pointing out that, even though the physical equipment in a production system is changed to a more routinized type, there is still considerable scope for varying the surrounding social organization. Equipment does not automatically cause social organization although it will impose constraints as to what the organization can be.

Traditionally coal had been mined by a craft system, the hand-got method, in which small groups of reciprocally interdependent miners would work at the coal face adjusting as necessary to changing seam conditions. Autonomous work groups of this nature are found in a number of occupations including other types of mining but also in research and surgical work. It is a form of organization particularly suited to ambiguous and variable tasks carried out remote from a centralized organization involving adaptation to local conditions. Decision-making capacity needs to be fairly high in these technical units.

Cohesive work teams emerged from the technical problems of mining coal, reinforced by the sharing of hardship and danger underground, the often isolated mining villages above ground, and by a uniform antagonism towards the management and owners. The mining groups would be essentially self-regulating within certain constraints set by the organization of the mine. They would contract with management for a price, and competition between groups would often be intense. Internally, groups were more or less undifferentiated with every miner capable of doing every job within these groups although an informal leadership would develop.

Mining was accomplished over a three shift cycle. Transition from one shift to the next was usually smooth. A subsequent shift was able to pick up jobs at the point left by the earlier shift because there was little differentiation of tasks between shifts.

The 'conventional' longwall method introduced the logic of the assembly line into mining. The new machinery had mechanical cutters and conveyor belts for removing the coal which could now be done much faster than with the hand-got method. With this came a socially differentiated organization. No longer were small autonomous undifferentiated groups working at the coal face but there was specialization and a forced pace of working. The three shifts were divided into separate phases – preparing, getting, and advancing – and there were now frequent co-ordination problems between the shifts with later shifts complaining that poor work on the previous shift held them up; that is, sequentially rather than reciprocally inter-dependent workflow predominated.

As there were now fourteen specialist jobs the experience of the work for an individual miner changed. Worker autonomy was now replaced by close supervision to co-ordinate the different tasks; the overall variation of tasks encountered by a miner was reduced, however, since each miner was more specialized and routinized.

The move from the reciprocal interdependence of the hand-got method to a sequential interdependence of the longwall method represented a change in beliefs about ends/means relationships – that is, the task was now treated as analysable and clear. It was a change from the logic of craft production to the logic of mass and routine production. The machinery of mass production undeniably had the potential to achieve great gains in productivity but this potential was hampered by an unsuitable social organization. Not only was productivity lower than expected but absenteeism was high.

The 'composite' longwall method developed as a result of the disappointing performance of the conventional longwall method. Managers and researchers came to devise a compromise form of organization which attempted to capitalize upon the cohesive and adaptable social organization of the hand-got method but kept the productive potential of the new machinery. This was achieved by creating a group of about forty miners who would rotate their work over the three shifts, thereby assisting inter-shift co-ordination, but still maintaining some degree of specialization. The researchers

*Table 5.3* Conventional and composite longwall methods of coal-getting compared

| Characteristic | Conventional | Composite |
|---|---|---|
| Number of miners | 41 | 41 |
| Number of completely segregated task groups | 14 | 1 |
| Mean job variation | | |
| task groups worked within | 1.0 | 5.5 |
| number of main tasks worked | 1.0 | 3.6 |
| number of different shifts worked | 2.0 | 2.9 |
| Production and Costs | | |
| productive achievement* | 78 | 95 |
| ancillary work at face, hours per man shift | 1.32 | 0.03 |
| average reinforcement of labour, % of total face force | 6 | 0 |
| % shifts with cycle lag | 69 | 5 |
| number of consecutive weeks without losing a cycle | 12 | 65 |
| Stress Indices | | |
| absenteeism, % of possible shifts | 4.3 | 0.4 |
| sickness | 8.9 | 4.6 |
| accidents | 6.8 | 3.2 |

Adapted from Trist, E.L., Higgin, G.W., Murray, H., and Pollock, A.B. (1963) *Organizational Choice*, London: Tavistock.
*Note*: * average % coal from each cut daily corrected for differences in seam transport.

showed that, from the perspective of the individual miner, mean job variation increased in moving from the longwall to the composite method as assessed by various indicators; the average number of task groups worked within by each miner increased by 1 to 5.5, tasks worked increased from 1 to 3.6, and number of shifts worked increased from 2.0 to 2.9. Hence, a certain amount of the job variety and autonomy found in the hand-got method was restored although pay differentials and an incentive scheme still existed (see Table 5.3).

Measures of efficiency also improved with the composite method. For example, production increased from 78 per cent to 95 per cent of its maximum potential, ancillary face work decreased from 1.32 hours per man shift to 0.03 hours, and absenteeism as a percentage of all possible time decreased from 20 per cent to 8 per cent.

The development of the composite longwall method shows how it is possible to have alternative social arrangements surrounding a given piece of equipment; there is organizational choice. Although a given piece of equipment imposes constraints on the form of organization in the surrounding technical core, choices are still available. This applies to a number of organizational variables such as degree and type of specialization, the method of co-ordination, and centralization of decision making.

## LEVELS OF ANALYSIS AND HIERARCHICAL PRIORITY

Large organizations can have multiple technologies, or technology zones (Miles 1980). Small operating units need to be linked together into some overall organizational order. From an organizational design viewpoint what basis is there for deciding about the hierarchical priority to be given to particular units?

Thompson gives us some ideas about this. As reciprocal interdependencies are the most costly to co-ordinate these should first of all be identified and units organized around these. This means that zones of non-routine activities (intensive technology) should be formed where areas of high decision-making capacity are needed; this would mean creating fuzzy structures through team-working conditions so that mutual adjustment co-ordination and interaction can take place. These teams have to be linked into a larger unit so the next step is to identify sequential interdependencies between zones. Scheduling mechanisms can now be used to link these units together. Finally, as the least costly, pooled interdependencies are the highest priority ordering. Units in which there is first reciprocal interdependence then sequential interdependence can be linked by pooled interdependence and parametric co-ordination (see chapter 2).

For the multidivisional firm there may be a whole variety of technologies in the divisions. These are linked to the central hub of the organization through pooled interdependence. The technology of the divisionalized company, especially in its pure M-Form type (see chapter 7), becomes similar to that of a venture capitalist balancing the risks of different investments in different parts of the portfolio; at this level it needs to operate a mediating technology (Thompson 1967) and the theory presented here would suggest that corporate management need to understand the skills associated with this type of technology. Decision making needs to be made upon the basis of hard rule-based facts gleaned from a widely spread information system giving data about different portfolio opportunities. On top of this, however, would also be the notion that softer internally-gleaned information concerning the track records of the divisional managements needs to be taken into account.

## EFFECT OF TECHNOLOGY UPON PEOPLE

Consideration of technology in terms of the dimensions of technology outlined can make us lose sight of the impact of technology upon individuals in an organization. Concern for individuals was a major motivation behind the socio-technical system approach outlined and we have seen some of the harmful effects of the mass-production logic in mining reflected by increased absenteeism and low productivity which are often taken as indicators of dissatisfaction.

Trist and Bamforth (1951), in their paper 'Some Social and Psychological Consequences of the Longwall Method of Coal-getting', emphasized how the craft groups of the hand-got method provided psychological support for difficult and dangerous working conditions. We must not romanticize such a system since it was still hard work, dangerous, and damaging to health, but the social organization provided support for the miners who had to work in these conditions. The social structure was also a support against an exploitive management which not only applied to coal mining but also to many other occupations.

Studies have examined the impact of technology upon individual workers. These studies generally have a common theme indicating the deleterious effect of routine machine-paced work upon factors such as job satisfaction and absenteeism or, conversely, the beneficial effect of jobs in which the technology allows discretion. Blauner

(1964) investigated four firms covering a craft firm, a machine tending operation, a car plant assembly line, and a continuous-process plant. It was found that alienation of the workers was greatest in the assembly-line work, where workers had least discretion; alienation was least in the craft and continuous-process production. Form (1972) examined four car plants, one each in four countries – the United States, Italy, Argentina, and India – representing decreasing stages of industrial development, and found that 'anomie' or lack of belongingness, was related to the lack of scope for social contact within the plant. This illustrates the point again that equipment or machinery (the assembly line in this case), does not completely determine the social format and that, according to the state of a country's development, the physical plant could be used in different ways. The plant allowing most interaction and giving lowest anomie was in India.

The notion of organizational choice suggests that the technical context is not the only factor leading to structure. Other factors can be environment and ideology, although these factors were not measured in the studies quoted. The institutional model of organization would suggest that such variables need to be investigated.

The effect of technology upon people has not only been noted in manufacturing organizations. Champion (1967) noted loss of job satisfaction and an increased anxiety amongst American bank employees as a result of the introduction of electronic data processing equipment. The equipment gave rise to a depersonalization of the work and a reduction in communication between people. However, automation need not lead to reduction in worker satisfaction as Mann and Hoffman (1960) showed through a study in power plants. Automation, as they point out, can increase responsibility and interest, and reduce isolation and centralization.

In an automobile plant, Walker and Guest (1952) associated the low job satisfaction of the assembly-line workers with the pacing, repetitiveness, low skill level, pre-determination of tools and tasks, and sub-division of work; Palm (1977) shows that repetitive work had the same effect upon Swedish workers twenty-five years later. Palm (1977) in Sweden and Roy (1952, 1954) in the United States and separated by twenty-five years, both noted that some extra-competent and individualistic workers (rate busters) manage to break out of this pattern and use the factory quite instrumentally, caring little for social relationships and earning as much as possible from the bonus system. Goldthorpe (1968), in a study of a British car factory, also noted that workers seemed to view the factory in this quite instrumental way, not worrying particularly about the wider social or political issues or about job satisfaction.

Concern with deskilling of work has been revived particularly through the interest in Japanese working methods where there is a reputation for greater harmony and greater use of team working than is general in the west; note here the limitations of this image of Japanese methods already given in chapter 2. Nevertheless, as Wood (1989) reports, there does appear to be a trend towards greater use of flexible working methods in the West although he questions the extent to which this is really transforming the nature of work.

## ADVANCED MANUFACTURING TECHNOLOGY (AMT)

Technical developments of the last fifteen years or so have wrought changes in the organization of manufacturing production but the same principles of organization would seem to apply. These changes have generally gone under the heading of Advanced Manufacturing Technology (AMT) (Child 1987) and are based upon the increasing power of computer-aided control systems which have allowed many manufacturing systems to move towards increasing integration between the different phases of production and even backwards into the design phase. Child (1987: 104) identifies a number of aspects of AMT through the increasing use of particular types of technology:

1 Robotics and programmed manipulation.
2 Numerically-controlled (NC) machines which can be controlled by tape. More advanced installations would allow re-programming via a built-in computer leading naturally onto:
3 Flexible manufacturing systems (FMS).
4 Computer-aided design (CAD) linked to computer-aided manu-facture (CAM), leading onto:
5 Computer-integrated manufacture (CIM), which denotes an overall and systematic computer control and integration of the manu-facturing system.

Hence, it becomes technically possible to imagine product designs – through information fed into a computer – automatically initiating manufacturing. Further, the developments in computer-controlled ordering and warehousing also raises the possibility of automatic-ally ordering from suppliers and the automatic storage and subse-quent distribution of finished goods. AMT provides scope for internal operating-efficiency improvements due to reduction in labour, improved productivity, reduction in manufacturing lead times, reduction in inventories, and work in progress. According to this view, and perhaps in the longer term more importantly, AMT provides scope for reduced design to production lead times, better design and engineering analysis, and increased responsiveness and flexibility of production. It is the latter features that in particular will permit companies to acquire a competitive advantage if greater responsiveness to market changes can be achieved.

## Effect of AMT on organizational design

If we return to Perrow's outline of the relationships between the two dimensions of technology and organizational structure – namely, ambiguity and variability – the same principles of organization should apply. The main point about AMT will be that for programming to to take place, the clarity and analysability of processes has to be very high indeed since all the knowledge and experience that would be contained in the heads and hands of operators under a craft or non-routine production system is now effectively codified. This is a pre-condition of effective AMT. Thus, in terms of our interpretation of Perrow's rather broad technical categories, AMT will result in a shift towards routine or modular production types and the associated organizational characteristics.

There is, then, a strategic choice for organizations as regards technology. A company can either go for the highly-efficient mass production of a small variety of products through a dedicated system (Child 1987: 115), or it can go for the more flexible market-sensitive modular production system. Under both options blue-collar unskilled or semi-skilled operators virtually disappear and we move towards Woodward's process production type where the processes are minded by relatively highly-qualified technicians who need the technical knowledge of how to deal with breakdowns, re-setting machines, carrying out routine maintenance, and the like.

Another dimension of technology is introduced by Child, that of the quantity of items produced (see Table 5.4). Here we see the existence of two other conditions, called the adapted (cell C) and the flexible (cell D) types. This latter shows a shift to some of the characteristics of the non-routine technology in that the organization will tend towards a fuzzier structure. Quantities are not large enough to warrant setting up crisp functional groupings since the product changes will tend to be *ad hoc* and unplanned. In the case of the adapted condition high investment in AMT is likely to be least attractive and there will be a tendency to 'make do' by adapting existing machines (see Table 5.4).

Table 5.4 The implications of production contingencies for appropriate new manufacturing technology and organizational design

| Quantity produced | Level of product variability | |
|---|---|---|
| | Low | High |
| | A. Dedicated production plant and systems | B. Use of CAD with computer-controlled machines possibly linked to FMC/FMS equipment able to manufacture families of products or items |
| LARGE | Crisp organization, specialized, formalized, centralized | Range of central functional departments. Design, production planning and control decentralized to teams or product groups |
| | C. Conventional machines possibly specially adapted | D. Fuzzy manufacturing centres and CNC machines |
| SMALL | Probably a small plant with largely semi-skilled labour. Simple structure with centralized planning by plant manager or small management group. Detailed shop-floor control, machine adjustment, and handling of operational contingencies by first line supervisors | Fuzzy organization. Close integration between marketing, design, machine programming, and operations. Trend towards role integration. Decentralized production planning and operational decisions |

Source: Child, J. (1987) 'Organizational design for advanced manufacturing technology', in T.D. Wall, C.W. Clegg, and N.J. Kemp (eds), *The Human Side of Advanced Manufacturing Technology*, ch. 6, Chichester: Wiley.
Notes: A = mass production white goods; B = clothing manufacturer supplying one or more monopsonistic retailers; C = small specialist parts makers, e.g., brass fittings; D = jobbing engineering firm.

Jurgens (1989) notes the changing support role of industrial engineers under the shift to flexible production. Under a traditional or purely routine production system the industrial engineers' function becomes that of controlling the production quite directly through job planning, time and motion study, and other techniques of Scientific Management. This often leads to considerable conflict with operators with comments like 'they walk around here with their damned papers and do not understand a thing' (Jurgens 1989: 199). This is traditional conflict between production and staff personnel that has been previously reported (Dalton 1959, Gouldner 1957). However, this changes with team work organization; the decision-making capacity is now located with operators as the teams now do the detailed planning; the industrial engineers now tend to come into conflict with design rather than production since their function is to ensure that design standards are met.

## BOUNDARY SPANNING: COPING WITH ENVIRONMENTAL FLUCTUATIONS

The logic of the technical core of an organization is towards increasing routinization. In this way the organization becomes more efficient but this efficiency can only be achieved if the technical core is permitted to operate continuously requiring the continuous supply of inputs side supplies and the continuous demand for products and services in the marketplace. Only in this way can management proceed with the detailed incremental improvements that will edge the technical core towards this ideal state of routine operations in which computational decision making becomes dominant. Above we have considered one way of coping with environmental fluctuations – that is, to permit the technical core structure to become fuzzier, but then some efficiencies of routinization have been lost (Thompson 1967).

An alternative is to use various forms of boundary spanning activity to protect the technical core as far as possible from these fluctuations. There are various techniques available for buffering; any number of these techniques may be used but there are three factors that might determine the most effective from the viewpoint of a particular organization:

1 The power that an organization has in the market, either as a buyer or as a seller. If it is small in relation to the market either on the input or output side and is in competition with other buyers or sellers then its power is low and its ability to enforce terms on the market is limited. High market power is achieved with the reverse of these conditions.

2 The managerial costs of each method; as we have asserted, increasing the decision-making capacity is likely to lead to an increased organizing cost.
3 The inventory costs of each method.

Table 5.5 gives a suggested rating of each method according to these three conditions.

*Table 5.5* Boundary spanning methods for input and output transactions

| Boundary spanning method | Needed power | Trans- action costs | Inven- tory costs | Problems |
|---|---|---|---|---|
| Stockpiling | low | low | high | Obsolescence |
| Forecasting | low | medium | low | Customer unpredictability |
| Smoothing | low | medium | low | Customer unresponsiveness |
| Specifying | medium | high | low | Technical analysability |
| Monitoring | high | high | low | Needs proximity |
| Batching | v. high | low | low | May not fit customer needs |
| Rationing | v. high | low | low | Customers do not like |

*Note*: JIT refers to boundary spanning methods likely to be used under Just-in-Time.

**Stockpiling** Inventories may be held on the input side for raw materials, or bought-in components stores created, and similarly on the output side in finished product stores. This would appear to be particularly suitable for sequentially interdependent technologies where waiting-time costs can outstrip the costs of inventories. However, in holding extra inventories the organization not only runs the risk of these becoming obsolescent but also faces delay in introducing product changes – factors which go some way towards negating any advantages of simplicity in terms of managerial costs. It is probably most appropriate for weak organizations and is often the only technique available to small firms.

**Forecasting** Predicting environmental fluctuations can allow an organization time to adapt to foreseen changes. Forecasting of peaks and troughs in demand or availability of supplies can give production time to respond. Weather may be forecast for outdoor events so that contingency plans can be made or economic forecasting made for planning future product and service changes. Forecasting imposes a managerial cost on the organization (rated medium), is low on inventory costs and needed power, but it depends upon being able to predict the behaviour of customers and/or suppliers or any other relevant conditions.

**Smoothing**   Environmental fluctuations may be smoothed by retailers offering cut-price sales inducements to shop during off-peak periods, or by bus, train, and airline companies in a similar way. Smoothing is also appropriate for relatively low power organizations, can be a way of reducing inventory costs, but imposes some managerial costs (rated medium). Its efficacy depends upon the sensitivity of customers to respond to incentives to adjust their habits: to what extent will people respond to travel agents' discounts to book their vacations early, for instance? The price reduction cannot go below marginal costs to any substantial degree.

**Specifying**   This means the detailing of specifications for components bought or products sold in such a way that the transactions can be conducted with the minimum of mutual adjustment. A firm might develop very precise specifications as regards the materials used in components and the method of manufacture so that the quality is controlled where any variation in components might cause problems for production or assembly. Specifying requires rather more power on the part of an organization since a supplier is only likely to be interested in responding to specific requirements if the orders are big enough and likely to continue. This is a technique used by Marks and Spencer in relation to its suppliers but it can impose high managerial costs since a great deal of work needs to go into drawing up detailed specifications. This method may also include specifying the manufacturing methods of a supplier.

**Monitoring**   It is possible for an organization to become quite directly involved in the management of the production of a supplier and to specify not only the product but also the production methods used and to demand some degree of control over that production. This becomes especially necessary if the quality of the finished product can only be assured in this way and complete reliance cannot be placed upon specifying. Monitoring within the supplier's premises can save quality control effort within the buyer's premises. Monitoring requires high power, since only large buyers are likely to gain access to supplier's premises, and is likely to involve high managerial costs but low inventory costs; this method will be greatly assisted by physical proximity. This is also done by powerful buying organizations such as Marks and Spencer and has been mentioned as a technique used by large Japanese corporations in controlling their suppliers.

**Batching**    Inputs may come in cohorts or batches as we see in the case of universities where students may enter only at specified times (say the beginning of an academic year or term). If students could enter at any time this would make the problem of timetabling difficult due to the uncertainty of numbers for particular classes. Batching enables economies of scale but generally may be seen as requiring very high power since it imposes conditions upon customers; on the other hand it is low on managerial and inventory costs.

**Rationing**    Simple queuing on a first come, first served basis is a form of rationing but this can develop into more sophisticated techniques in which rules and priorities are set to inject a degree of bureaucratic rationality. In hospitals emergency cases are dealt with before less urgent cases, and in the post office first-class mail is given priority over second-class mail. Rationing is a very cheap method of boundary spanning since most of the cost is borne by the customer (or supplier). It tends, therefore, to be found in cases where the consumer is relatively weak as in many public service organizations where the supplier has monopoly power, and when demand outstrips supply.

## Just-in-Time management (JIT) or the 'Kan-ban' technique

When a number of these techniques are put together into a deliberate strategy to reduce inventory costs and improve quality, they are sometimes known as Just-in-Time management (JIT) or, in Japanese terminology, 'Kan-ban'. As with most of the techniques discussed there is nothing new about the procedure; a greater emphasis has been given to JIT recently partly due to technical changes demanding ever-larger quantities of output and partly to competitive forces in particular industries (the automobile industry for example).

The aim of the ideal JIT would be to reduce the input stocks of a manufacturer to zero by very precisely detailing the time and place at which a supply would turn up, sometimes not just by the day of the week but also the hour of the day so that the supply can be fed into the factory, without inspection, for further processing or for assembly without having to go through an intermediate store (Wood

1989: 16). What applies on the input side can, in principle, apply on the output side but in a competitive market the scope to JIT is likely to be less.

The package of techniques will include, in particular, forecasting, smoothing, specifying, and monitoring in order to achieve this. The managerial costs, therefore, are high in terms of an institutional investment to set up JIT and it is only likely to be worthwhile if the cost of inventory or wastage is high since the extra managerial costs have to be accounted for by reduction in inventory costs. Physical proximity can be of a great help in JIT and it is noteworthy that Nissan (UK) designed its greenfield Tyneside plant with the facility to accommodate suppliers' factories alongside (Wickens 1987). Hence, the site will appear to work as one physical unit but organizationally the suppliers will remain separate, linked by a managed market (Butler and Carney 1983).

Savings however can also come through reduction in other overheads within the buying organization. Jurgens (1989) emphasizes that the JIT philosophy needs to permeate the whole production sequence and not just the input/output sides. If supplies are to turn up precisely on time the ensuing production processes must also be ready and waiting, implying a tight co-ordination of different technical stages and associated crisp structures. This does not only mean that production planning has to be good but so too does the quality control at each stage since any irregularity can reverberate up and down stream.

The Japanese way to cope with this problem is to expose the operators at each stage of the process to the consequences of any irregularities that their process causes. There is a constant pressure on the work teams to solve problems; once solved, however, pressure is maintained by further reducing inventories (Jurgens 1989: 208–9). The pattern becomes one of continuous process improvement. The old ways of Taylorism would leave the sorting of such problems to functional foremen (support people), removing discretion from the operator and treating him or her as a machine incapable of problem solving. The production lines at Toyota will not provide standby men, not even for personal necessities. Work stations may have warning lights which show when a worker or a team are having a problem. However, it is those places that do not show warning lights that become the object of management's attention since they now appear to have surplus capacity. Therefore, workers may be moved to those areas where problems are evident. This, however, requires a very flexible workforce with few demarcations between jobs. When we get down to such detail we see a rather different image of the myth of Japanese management.

## DESIGN IMPLICATIONS AND SUMMARY

Assess ambiguity and variability of technology and relate unit structure to this. In general, a shift towards less ambiguity and variability suggests a crisper structure, while a shift towards more ambiguity and variability suggests a fuzzier structure. From the viewpoint of efficiency a shift towards routinization is suggested; from the viewpoint of adaptability a shift towards intensive technology is suggested.

There is organizational choice; a given set of equipment does not completely determine structure although it sets constraints. Within these constraints structures should be designed in order to minimize job demarcations and maximize cycle times.

Boundary spanning techniques can be used to protect the technical core from environmental fluctuations. The Just-in-Time management (JIT) provides a way of reducing inventory costs and support costs. JIT management may be carried through the total production process to reduce waiting time and improve quality control. The principle is for operators, either individually or in teams, to solve technical core problems by removing inventories and support people as much as possible. This must be seen as a process of steady incremental improvement towards increasing clarity of technology.

Where multiple technologies are involved hierarchical prioritizing can be used. First, this involves identifying zones where the highest decision-making capacity is needed – namely, around reciprocal interdependencies and mutual adjustment co-ordination. Team structures are needed here in order to develop moral norms. Second, sequential interdependencies and co-ordination by planning are identified for the next level above; here the norms will tend to the instrumental. Finally, the pooled interdependencies are identified to be placed at the highest level.

The salient variables of the institutional model of organization discussed in this chapter are given in Figure 5.3.

Overall, we have argued that the intensive technology requires the fuzziest unit structure with high expertise and differentiation (but in a fluid-generalized way minimizing job demarcations), interaction, decentralization, collective rewards, and support in the sense that it is accepted that mistakes will occur because experimentation is

*Figure 5.3* The contingent institutional model of organization: salient variable relationships discussed in this chapter

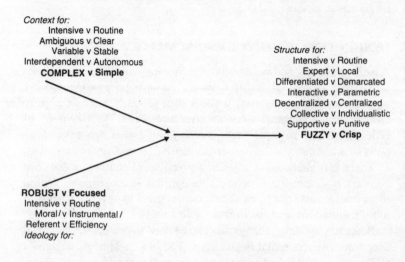

Context for:
Intensive v Routine
Ambiguous v Clear
Variable v Stable
Interdependent v Autonomous
**COMPLEX v Simple**

Structure for:
Intensive v Routine
Expert v Local
Differentiated v Demarcated
Interactive v Parametric
Decentralized v Centralized
Collective v Individualistic
Supportive v Punitive
**FUZZY v Crisp**

**ROBUST v Focused**
Intensive v Routine
Moral / v Instrumental /
Referent v Efficiency
*Ideology for:*

encouraged. The context for the intensive technology is that of high ambiguity, variability, and interdependence. The ideology for the intensive technology emphasizes moral and referent norms.

The routine technology, in contrast, will have a structure based on local skills and experience which is demarcated, centralized, individualistic, and punitive in so far as individual rather than team performance is rewarded, with mistakes tending to result in lower rewards. The context for the routine technology is clear and stable, while the ideology emphasizes efficiency and instrumental goals.

# Chapter six

# Strategy, environment, and structure

## STRATEGIC CHOICE

The institutional model of organization tells us of the need for an organization to exchange resources in its task environment and of its need to respond to performance norms set in the institutional environment. If an organization is perfectly determined it has no choice but to accept the overriding institutional norms on the assumption that they are immutable; such an organization is paralysed (Butler *et al*. 1977/8), has no choice, can make no decisions, and the structure, once set, remains in place.

In practice, organizations have degrees of strategic choice (Child 1972), they are not just passive recipients of a given environment any more than they are passive in relation to their technologies. In making strategic choices an organization is selecting a combination of normative, task environmental, and technological variables. While this chapter concentrates upon the task environmental determinants of structure we will see that the normative and technological variables cannot be separated from these.

### Coping with dependence and uncertainty

The key questions concern how an organization handles its major dependencies and the major uncertainties within its task environment.

An organization is dependent upon elements in the task environment for resources to the extent that there is a need for a particular supporter, that there is lack of an alternative supporter (Emerson 1962), and that there are barriers, such as regulatory barriers, preventing exit (Hirschman 1970) to an alternative supporter. The organization that is dependent in the above sense lacks both power over its task environment and room to manoeuvre: it is these dependencies that make up the source of determinateness; these are the relationships that the organization has to attend to, either by finding alternatives or by managing them.

Uncertainty in the task environment of an organization arises particularly from the unanticipated actions of outside elements, both supporters and rivals, whether this be the changing tastes of customers, competitors entering the market, unreliability of suppliers, or from unexpected regulatory action of governments and other bodies in the institutional environment. The broad thrust of the argument concerning the relationship between environment and strategic choice is given by Butler and Carney (1985) and helps us think about a complex issue. The task environment can be seen in terms of two dimensions: the concentrated versus open and the ambiguous versus clear.

Concentration is a major variable used by economists to measure organizational environments (Pfeffer and Salancik 1978) and refers to the density of actors within a task environment. Here we do not elaborate upon the technicalities of concentration measurements but point to the notion that high concentration occurs when there are few actors chasing a small pool of customers on the output side, or a small shared pool of suppliers on the input side. In terms of the institutional model an environment is concentrated when there are few actors, both rivals and supporters. Aero-engine manufacturing provides an example of a concentrated industry where there are only three major manufacturers world-wide and where there are only a small number of airframe manufacturer customers. Barriers to entry are generally high in this condition, perhaps because of high capital investment or because of regulatory barriers detailing a great many safety requirements. Low concentration occurs when there are many actors; grocery retailing is an example of such an industry where there are many supermarket groups in addition to many smaller grocery shops chasing a huge pool of independent customers and, on the buying side, facing a large pool of independent suppliers. This is where the environment is open to potential newcomers and barriers to entry are relatively low.

Concentration, therefore, can apply to both output and input sides of an organization, a point that is particularly important in the case of voluntary organizations (Butler and Wilson 1990); organizations have to develop strategies in both directions although the extent to which one direction is more important than the other is a resultant of the relative dependence upon the two segments of the environment. Voluntary organizations tend to be more dependent on their input sides, businesses in a competitive market tend to be more dependent on their output sides. There is obviously a connection between the notion of concentration and uniqueness of the organization; the more concentrated the environment, the more unique the organization is believed to be by the organization's major supporters.

When task environments have low concentrations and are open to new actors competitive strategies are appropriate (Thompson 1967, Pfeffer and Salancik 1978). The basis of a competitive strategy is alternative maintenance. As concentration increases, the number of actors decreases; alternative maintenance becomes less viable and an organization will tend to develop negotiated strategies. The basis of a negotiated strategy is the exchange of mutual commitments; for example, aero-engine manufacturers may form a joint venture to develop a new engine thereby suspending competition as regards certain areas of activity for the mutual benefits of sharing research and developmnent expertise and costs.

The other dimension relevant to a consideration of strategy is that of ambiguity versus clarity. Ambiguity refers to the extent to which beliefs about ends/means relations within the technical core are unclear; clarity is the extent to which the technology is analysable. This is an important dimension in strategic choice since it determines the extent to which the technical knowledge of the organization is transferable by means of standard procedures and other formalized

*Figure 6.1* Broad strategic types

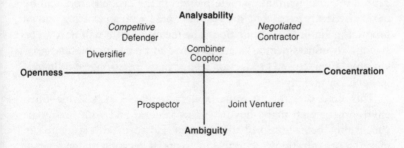

*Source*: Adapted from Butler, R.J. and Carney, M.G. (1985) 'Strategy and strategic choice: the case of telecommunications', *Strategic Management Journal*, 7: 161–77.

means (clear) or not (ambiguous). The concept was met in chapter 5 when discussing technology, where we were concerned with its effect upon the organization of the technical core, whereas here we are concerned with its effect upon an organization's ability to negotiate terms with environmental elements.

If we combine these two dimensions we see two broad strategic types – the competitive and the negotiated – and the approximate conditions under which each might be appropriate is depicted in Figure 6.1. Each of these strategic types has a number of distinctive aspects concerning the environmental and technological choices made.

## COMPETITIVE STRATEGIES

Competitive strategies have received most attention in the strategic management literature where the major thrust is to develop methods to encourage top management systematically to review their task environments for ways of improving their competitive position (Porter 1985). A number of typologies of business strategy exist (Daft 1989). Miles and Snow's (1978) outline is unusual and especially relevant to organizational design in that it suggests a link between strategy and organizational structure and we borrow from this typology.

### Defender

Here the emphasis is upon defending a patch through a narrow target market, aggressive pricing, advertising, cost-efficient production, and a crisp structure with internal control systems to ensure adherence to targets and detailed planning. The whole logic of the strategy is geared towards maintaining alternatives in the task environment by more efficiently expanding the customer base with an existing known product/technology combination. The technical core will need to be strongly routine since tasks are assumed to be analysable and non-variable. Finance and production tend to have the strongest influence in decision making.

This kind of strategy is particularly suitable in a stable–open environment with many buyers, many sellers, and with few goals concerning the institutional environment. However, this strategy can make an organization susceptible to errors of decision undercapacity since new opportunities can be overlooked through an obsession with competition within an existing product/customer framework.

## Prospector

Here priority is given to competing by staying ahead in the technological game, producing new products, drawing upon changing technology to be a step ahead of the competition, and putting price efficiency as a secondary objective. The logic is to maintain alternatives by ensuring that the organization has a flow of new products to capture the attention of customers. Research and development and marketing tend to have the most influence in decision making, and indicative planning acts as a guide to future action rather than providing hard and fast targets. The technical core will tend towards the intensive or non-routine type; in a sense, the organization is in a state of perpetual prototype production. The important thing is to keep ahead of the competition. The organization has to be restless, always on the move. There is a strong bias towards fuzziness.

The prospector strategy will be suitable in a task environment where there are many buyers and many sellers but, paradoxically, the goal is to try and steal a temporary monopoly by creating a protective niche before competitors follow. However, the niche can only be temporary and the problem is always to keep a step ahead of the competition. The prospector strategy both uses and creates

Table 6.1 Competitive strategies: defender and prospector

| Characteristic | Strategic type | |
| | DEFENDER | PROSPECTOR |
| --- | --- | --- |
| Strategy | Aggressive pricing | Keeping ahead |
| | Advertising | Price secondary |
| | Expanding customers for existing products | Tapping new customer opportunities |
| | Narrow surveillance | Wide surveillance |
| Technology | Routine | Intensive |
| | Large scale | Proto-typical |
| Structure | Crisp | Fuzzy |
| | Detailed planning | Broad planning |
| | Finance and production dominant | Marketing and R&D dominant |
| Ideology | Efficiency/instrumental norms | Referent/moral norms |
| Environment | Stable | Variable |
| | Open | Open |

Adapted from Miles, R.E. and Snow, C.C. (1978) *Organizational Strategy, Structure and Process*, New York: McGraw-Hill, International edition.

environmental variability. There will also tend to be little concern with institutional goals other than to develop a reputation for innovation.

Research by Peters and Waterman (1982), and Peters and Austin (1985) has pointed to a number of features of companies that become successful by pursuing policies of achieving excellence. Some of these features are specifically related to the issue of innovation. Hence such companies exhibit a bias towards action rather than analysis, simple organization with the minimum of staff, autonomy to encourage entrepreneurship, and a climate of trust and consensus building. In terms of the institutional model this would mean the development of moral norms.

A prospecting organization will be susceptible to errors of decision overcapacity. If the competition manages to catch up, the unique advantage of this strategy has gone yet the organization proceeds upon the assumption that the world outside is fuzzy; it runs the risk of rejecting the true hypothesis, as demonstrated by the competition, that the task environment is crisper than assumed.

## Mixed competitive strategies

Mixed types of strategy are, of course, possible. Miles and Snow (1978) describe the analyser type which is in-between the defender and the prospector. This becomes possible if an organization is developing new products whose production over their natural life cycle becomes more efficient. As a product loses its newness it will come to be sold upon the basis of price rather than its innovativeness. By the time this has happened new products can be introduced whose appeal is that of innovativeness. From an organization's viewpoint there can be a portfolio of products in different stages of development shifting from prospector to defender products.

An organization now has the problem of managing the life cycles of a number of products in different stages of development each potentially competing for managerial attention and organizational resources. One major structure for managing this problem is that of the divisional structure whereby product divisions are created around relatively self-contained technology/product/market combinations; over the corporation as a whole there will be divisions in various stages of the life cycle. Alternatively, the research of Peters and Waterman (1982) suggests that simultaneously fuzzy and crisp structures can be adopted; fuzzy in the areas of innovation and crisp in the areas of more routine production where efficiency and price consciousness become more important.

Diversification occurs when an organization attempts to expand its market by adding product or service lines (Glueck 1980: 209–10). If the diversification adds lines sharing a common or similar technology this is concentric diversification. Conglomerate diversification occurs when quite dissimilar lines are added; this will involve learning about new technologies and markets, and will tend to put a greater decision-making load onto management.

In addition to the defender, analyser, and prospector strategies Miles and Snow (1978) also outline the reactor strategy. As the term implies the reactor responds to events in the environment with little premeditation. It appears to drift and not be concerned with linking strategy to structure or technology. It has been generally considered that to be a reactor is not advisable since such an organization is blown about according to the whims and fancies of outside interests.

## Prestige seeking

Competitive strategies place an organization in an inherently unstable position; for the defender, a small deviation from the ideal cost curve will lose market share, and dependence upon a single or small product range opens the organization to obsolescence. Prospecting also has an inherent instability due to its cash hungriness for research and development, and the risk of being overtaken in technical development. The mixed strategies provide a way of balancing risks in different parts of the environment.

Thompson (1967: 33) suggests that prestige seeking is another way of trying to gain stability within a competitive environment. Prestige involves establishing a favourable image in the eyes of major supporters in the task environment. The underlying aim is to establish uniqueness. It is an approach more obviously available to, say, voluntary or educational organizations where the inherent ambiguity of the organization's task makes assessment difficult. However, many business organizations do succeed in establishing an aura of prestige; Rolls–Royce is an example of a prestige-seeking manufacturer.

If successful, prestige seeking makes elements in the environment seek out and want to acquire and maintain contact with the 'prestigeful' organization. Students seek out a prestigeful university because they know they will gain kudos when job hunting and in social standing generally. Similarly, a supplier may seek out a prestigeful company as a customer. For a manufacturer of clothing to be able to state that they supply, say, Marks and Spencer, may give an edge over a competitor; or for a business school to develop links with a large international corporation can give considerable prestige over its competitors.

In order to create an image of prestige an organization needs to develop an aura of quality and excellence (Peters and Waterman 1982, Peters and Austin 1985). This entails a number of specific goals whereby the overall objective is not to compete in terms of price on the one hand or in terms of innovation on the other, but in terms of quality of product and service and to broadcast this message to the various supporters of the organization. Some specific steps towards this end suggested by Peters and Waterman are:

1 Get close to the customer. Here the dominant concern must be to listen to the needs and concerns of customers to the extent of the chief executive of a company personally reading the customer complaints cards.
2 Clear business focus. Excellent companies, however, do not move too far outside their area of expertise; that is, they recognize the constraints upon decision-making capacity.
3 Leadership vision. Excellent companies have leaders with a clear vision of where they are going and what the company stands for.

However, other factors would also need to be emphasized for a prestige strategy. The stress is not on innovation but on producing a solid long-lasting impression of being the best in the field. Time horizons tend to be long and patience required to build up the image of excellence step by step. Some specific factors can help in this process; maybe to get patronage from prestigious people, either as customers or through patronage. Voluntary organizations may make an association with royalty or other well-known people; Band Aid in the mid-1980s successfully raised large sums of money internationally as a result of the activities of pop star Bob Geldorf (Butler and Wilson 1990).

Prestige seeking has its dangers. It can lead to fossilization of the organization through association with a past prestigious image or person. This has been the case for some voluntary organizations. When the image becomes associated with a particular person it becomes dependent upon the fame and fortune of that person and this may decline.

# THE NEGOTIATED ENVIRONMENT: CO-OPERATIVE STRATEGIES

Competition is an inherently unstable process. There may be little that any one organization can do about this other than to accept the situation. Others may be able to acquire power within their task environment by drawing upon the possibility that other organizations also face complementary contingencies of dependence and uncertainty (Thompson 1967: 34, Pfeffer and Salancik 1978). If this is the case they have the basis of creating greater security for themselves by negotiating mutually beneficial terms between them. Some specific types of negotiated strategy can be seen.

## Contracting

Organizations can come to an arrangement whereby a contract is made by organization A to supply organization B with specific goods or services in certain quantities and at certain times in exchange for a consideration. This is typified by a large firm such as Marks and Spencer in the kinds of arrangements it makes with its suppliers. It is a form of boundary management that is most suitable when the organization initiating the contracts is in a powerful position in relation to the contractee and when the terms of the contract are sufficiently tangible to be specified in a written contract. Such contracts tend to based upon areas of technological clarity.

## Coalescing

The most prominent example of coalescing is a joint venture; this is less formal than contracting and is common in aerospace and other high-technology industries where the obligations to be exchanged cannot be so precisely defined as in contracting. The joint venture requires a sharing of expertise and resources, and is probably most successful when the two organizations are of roughly equal power, can offer complementary skills, have similar outlooks on the way to operate in their industry, and each of them finds that they cannot go it alone. Therefore, there needs to be a mutuality of ideology. Joint ventures tend to be based upon areas of technological ambiguity.

Project Mercury, the alternative telecommunications network to British Telecommunications, was based upon the relatively unknown technology of optical fibres and fulfilled all these conditions quite well. By drawing together Barclays Merchant Bank (to provide finance), British Petroleum (to provide experience in coping with the regulatory environment), and Cable and Wireless (to provide technical expertise) this joint venture provided complementarity, equal power, and size focused onto a task involving relatively unknown technical and political problems (Carney 1984).

Joint ventures are often made with direct competitors thereby reducing competition in the area over which co-operation is occurring but usually only for a specific duration. This phenomenon is particularly noticeable in the aerospace industry. For example, Rolls-Royce competes with Pratt and Whitney and America's General Electric for the aero-engine market but often co-operates through joint ventures in the very expensive design, development, and prototype testing needed for a new engine; each co-operating company does not have enough resources to go it alone on such major projects.

## Co-opting

Co-opting is the absorbing of outside elements into the management of an organization as is seen when outside directors are appointed onto the board of a company (Pfeffer and Salancik 1978) or, as is often the case in charities, prominent people act as patrons or presidents to increase prestige in anticipation of certain future benefits such as presenting a favourable image of the organization in the environment, or by providing expertise or favoured access to resources. A director of a bank may be appointed to the board of a company to give advice on financial matters or a politician may likewise be appointed in anticipation of contacts in, and advice on, the workings of government.

The problem with co-opting from the perspective of a focal organization is that co-opted individuals may become more involved in the management of the organization than was originally intended and autonomy can thereby be lost (Pfeffer and Salancik 1978: 164). Co-opting tends to put an obligation on the focal organization to accept any advice given and hence an organization tends to lose autonomy through such a device. As a method of managing the environment, co-opting tends to be particularly appropriate for an organization that is relatively weak (Thompson 1967: 36) or vulnerable, or wishes to strengthen itself in a particular segment of the environment.

Pfeffer and Salancik (1978) investigated the composition of the boards of eighty randomly selected non-financial companies. They argued that co-opting appropriate members onto the board is an alternative way of managing important dependencies and uncertainties when merging or buying are not viable options, perhaps because the other organization is too big or where there are regulatory constraints preventing this (such as monopolies legislation). They present data to suggest that the proportion of outside directors on company boards increases with size of company, debt ratio, and regulatory constraints. As companies grow they tend to generate more heterogeneous environments with a greater range of dependencies and uncertainties needing management; debt ratio is a measure of the dependence of the organization upon financial institutions; regulatory constraints are, in effect, government-imposed dependencies also requiring management.

## ENVIRONMENT AND STRUCTURE

The environment of an organization is both selected for that organization and selected by that organization. There is strategic choice but that choice is limited by the major dependencies and normative factors. Two important dimensions of context have already been discussed; these are the open–concentrated dimension, a measure relating to the number of actors in the task environment, and the clear–ambiguous dimension, a measure relating to the technology of the organization. In this way we have already established that strategy involves a linking of task environmental and technical factors.

We now need to consider more specifically the relationship between the selected environment and the kinds of structures that an organization will use in managing that environment. The principle remains that of developing the requisite decision-making capacity. In general, an organization would need to develop its boundary spanning structures to match decision-making capacity to the overall uncertainty of the environmental action.

Three primary dimensions of the environment chosen are considered as especially relevant to boundary structures: the heterogeneity–homogeneity, the variability–stability, and the interdependent–autonomous dimensions. As heterogeneity, variability, and interdependence increase we can see that the problem of managing boundary transactions increases. With three variables of the environment there are eight possible conditions to describe; this is too many to give separate treatment to each condition. The ensuing discussion details how an organization might cope with an increase in any one of the variables taken individually and from this we can deduce what might happen in particular combinations of values on the variables according to our organizing principle.

## Heterogeneity versus homogeneity

An organization operating in a simple homogeneous environment will only have to deal with a small number of similar environmental elements. The single product firm approaches this image where there is only one group of customers, all with similar tastes and demands, and a very small number of suppliers.

A heterogeneous environment can be seen in the case of a local council social services department providing services to many different constituencies and has many other interested parties, such as professional associations, and local and national political parties (Thompson 1967, Duncan 1972). In the business sphere a firm may start as a single product firm but then diversify its products thereby creating a more heterogeneous environment for itself as the number of product/market segments increases. There is now a need for greater decision-making capacity since the variety of problems facing the organization increases. The appropriate structural response to this would be to increase internal differentiation by creating separate units to cope with relatively identifiable and independent segments of the environment. Each unit would now have discretion to make decisions concerning problems met within its own task environment. The typical example of this would be a multidivisional company where each division operates as a semi-autonomous unit. Similarly, hospitals create units to serve distinct types of patients, such as paediatrics, geriatrics, outpatients, heart cases, and the like. Units may also be established on the basis of geographical contiguity, a particular hospital serving a particular catchment area. A textile manufacturer, such as Briggs (see pp. 137–9), may create separate divisions to make and sell cord for tyres, industrial webbing, and spun yarn. The key problem is to establish self-contained units around a set of core decisions which are then delegated to these units to be made within certain parameters.

We need to make a distinction between differentiation and specialization. Differentiation refers to the extent to which the internal structure shows variety in procedures (Lawrence and Lorsch 1967) for problem solving. Specialization refers to the extent to which the internal structure is broken down into well-defined categories occupied by participants who do that job and no other (Pugh and Hickson 1976a). Differentiation brings with it the attendant problem of achieving integration and this is where the ideology will be particularly important. Since differentiation means the variety of approaches in solving problems it needs to be accompanied by a plural and moral ideology – plural because there will be a variety of ideas concerning problem solving, moral because an overarching agreement over what the organization is trying to do is also needed.

## Variability versus stability

Some environments consist of elements liable to sudden changes in their demands or where new dominant elements may quickly replace or supplement existing ones. A local government social services department is liable to possible quite sudden changes in demands upon its resources. These changes may emanate from variability in the political climate, the tastes of the clientele, or ideas concerning appropriate technologies of care (Didrickson 1989).

Variability can be coped with by means of decentralization (Thompson 1967: 70–2). Decentralization can lead to a problem of lack of control in an organization unless accompanied by an overarching agreement as to what the organization is trying to achieve – that is, by a moral ideology.

## Interdependence versus autonomy

A change in one part of the task environment might have an impact upon another part of the task environment. A social services department well exemplifies this situation. A scare concerning, say, child abuse in one council in a different part of the country, can impact upon other councils and requires them to review their policies as regards the care of young children (Didrickson 1989). The single product firm is likely to be relatively immune from such interdependence.

Interdependence requires an interaction with environmental actors as a means of co-ordinating an organization's activities with the environment. An example of this can be seen in the case of United Kingdom universities where a committee, the Committee of Vice-Chancellors and Principals (CVCP), was created to try and co-ordinate certain aspects of university policy. Matters might cover agreements over fees, student numbers, examination policy, co-ordination of public relations, and the like. An even more striking instance is the case of local governments where, over specific issues such as rail transport, a considerable amount of co-ordination with environmental elements is developed encompassing a number of bordering local authorities, British Rail, and various local community groups. These interests are brought together into a local Rail Executive which has responsibility for planning and timetabling of rail services.

These examples show how increases in interdependence require an increase in decision-making capacity. Increases in environmental interdependencies can occur unexpectedly through links that have not previously been considered relevant. Emery and Trist (1965) indicated that the most dangerous linkages in the environment of an organization come from what they call a second-order environment, that is, those elements which are not directly in contact with the organization but which have the potential to affect the organization in the future.

## The combined effect of environmental variables upon structure

The above discussion has separately treated the likely impact of each of the three environmental dimensions upon structure. In order to establish the combined effect of these variables we suggest an additive relationship. Hence, the most complex context occurs with heterogeneity, variability, and interdependence; under this condition we would, according to the Principle of Requisite Decision-Making

*Figure 6.2* Boundary spanning structures and environmental complexity

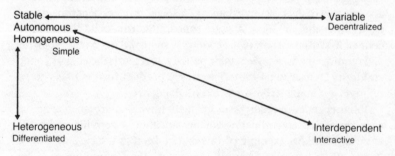

Heterogeneity + Variability + Interdependence = Fuzziness

*Source*: Adapted from Thompson, J.D. (1967) *Organizations in Action*, New York: McGraw-Hill

Capacity, expect to see a boundary structure that is decentralized, differentiated, and interactive (see Figure 6.2). In general, we can say that as the environmental context shifts in this direction the structure needs to become fuzzier.

The structure outlined is obviously a very demanding one. In chapter 7 we examine the matrix organization as a specific structure to handle this condition. The extent to which an organization achieves the match between context and structure indicated by the above application of the Principle of Requisite Decision-Making Capacity will depend, however, upon the extent to which it is having to compete for resources. Hence, we suggest that openness is likely to lead to a greater propensity for an organization to match structure to context.

## Insight: failure to recognize interdependence

Although the use of the single product firm already discussed illustrates an apparently simple environment it should not be assumed that such environments cannot erupt into sudden complexity. When this happens the problems confronting an organization can be far greater than those experienced by an organization used to complexity because of the unfamiliarity of the management to such conditions and the lack of ability to introduce more appropriate decision-making structures quickly enough. The case of Briggs, a textile company, illustrates this problem.

Briggs was a well-established North of England textile company, proud of its history as witnessed by the line of portraits exhibited in the board room of the family dynasty that had dominated the firm for ninety years. It was organized into three divisions representing fairly separate lines of activity, the Cord Division making textile cord for tyres, the Industrial Textile Division specializing in fabrics for conveyor belts, and the Spinning Division.

The company was faced with a worsening financial situation in the late 1970s and in the end decided to close unprofitable manufacturing plants. By the mid-1980s the company had been bought up by the Courtaulds company and later effectively closed down. A company with a proud history ceased to exist.

As an illustration of the problem of environmental interdependence it is worthwhile to examine one particular plant closure decision since it illustrates well the failure of the management to appreciate quickly enough the interconnectedness that had developed in their environment. Below are described a number of categories of links that developed over time of relevance to that particular decision. Some of these links had been unrecognized by management for a long time but then became forcefully apparent.

*Links 1* In the institutional environment, technical and scientific developments had taken place over a number of previous years which resulted in the move to long-life, steel-braced, radial-ply tyres; this resulted in a decrease in demand for textile cording. These technical changes occurred without the company taking action until late in the day.

*Links 2* The Cord Division was dependent upon a single supplier, Courtaulds, for its raw material and was not in a position to negotiate reduced prices.

*Links 3* While the company had not seen itself in a position to buy its own supplies from abroad, its main customer, Goodyear, had no such qualms in buying from foreign competitors. Further, Goodyear, as an international company, was in a position to transfer production out of the United Kingdom to other countries, a factor which made the demand for British-made textile cord more uncertain.

*Links 4* The main domestic competitor was in a better position since it was able to produce at lower cost.

*Links 5* There was, therefore, a triple pressure on the Cord Division: reduced demand for textile corded tyres, foreign competition, and the strength of the main domestic competitor. The company now went to the Department of Industry to try to raise a grant and to get the Government to put pressure on Goodyear to buy British cord (the Government was a major customer of Goodyear).

*Links 6* This move prompted a number of links especially from the institutional environment. The local member of Parliament became involved and, as various Government departments were big consumers of tyres, there was a move to put pressure on Goodyear to buy British cord. In a sense, therefore, Government departments can be seen as second-order customers of the company. The Member of Parliament in particular spearheaded this but in the end was only successful in gaining a small concession from the Government. There was still no guarantee that any such purchases would be from Briggs rather than from its British competitor. The main union was also involved, putting pressure on the Member of Parliament and threatening industrial action across all three divisions. This now brought in the other divisional directors. The director of the Industrial Textile Division had also been involved from an earlier date since he was concerned about the closure of a plant that supplied his division.

An apparently straightforward commercial decision had now become complex. In the end the plant was closed although this was delayed by a few months. The unfortunate outcome of this decision resulted from the failure of the company to appreciate the interdependencies in the environment, particularly the long-term technical trends. It is especially from the institutional environment that new connections can become significant to an organization's viability.

During the decision-making process intensive boundary-spanning activity was carried out by the director and management of the Cord Division. The increase in interdependence meant that these managers spent a considerable amount of time interacting with other elements in the environment and in discussions between themselves.

## EVIDENCE: STUDIES BY LAWRENCE AND LORSCH

One of the classic studies that illustrates the relationship between environmental characteristics and structure was carried out by Lawrence and Lorsch (1967). They selected three industries representing a range of environmental uncertainties. These were the plastics, container, and food industries.

Plastics was characterized by high competition, short product life cycles, and considerable process and product changes (heterogeneous, variable, and open environment combined with variable technology in terms of the institutional model). The container industry was relatively stable with no significant new products in the preceding decade; sales growth had kept pace with general economic growth but nothing more (homogeneous, stable, and fairly concentrated environment with a small number of large companies dominating the industry, and a stable technology). The food industry gave an intermediate type of environment as regards these variables, with some product and technology change and medium concentration.

Lawrence and Lorsch hypothesized that the more successful firms within each industry would match their organizational structures to the environmental variables obtaining within their own environments. A number of measures of the environment were made including features such as the rate of change, clarity of information that management had about the environment, and the length of time it takes for management to get feedback from the environment.

Organization structure was measured using two basic themes – those of differentiation and integration. Differentiation refers to the degree of specialization and the associated beliefs that managers held concerning goals, time horizons used in decision making, and interpersonal behaviour. A highly differentiated unit would be represented by one with many experts who hold different sets of beliefs. Differentiation is a way of providing the requisite decision-making capacity.

Integration refers to the various integrating devices that the organization introduces in an attempt to co-ordinate disparate activities. These include devices to achieve both horizontal and vertical co-ordination, such as rules, procedures, plans, committees, and the like. Integration is also, therefore, part of the attempt to provide the requisite decision-making capacity in the sense that the whole host of decisions made by various boundary and technical specialists have to be linked into an overall organizational plan.

Lawrence and Lorsch found evidence to support the basic hypothesis that the more successful firms in each industry tended to be those who match the degree of differentiation and integration to the uncertainty in the environment. Hence, they found that the successful plastics firms generally had more differentiation and integration than did the successful food firms which, in turn, had more differentiation and integration than the successful container firms which had the most stable and certain environment.

In addition to considering the overall structure of the firms, Lawrence and Lorsch investigated the structures of organizational sub-units. They noted that different departments in an organization deal with distinct sub-environments and that these sub-environments create distinct departmental structures. Some structural characteristics of departments in the more successful plastics firms can be seen in Table 6.2. What we notice from Table 6.2 is that each department has its own distinct structural profile reflecting its sub-environment. For production the sub-environment consists of buying stocks from suppliers, obtaining equipment (fairly infrequent decisions), and obtaining relatively unskilled labour. All these tasks can be interpreted as requiring routine decision making and hence high formality can be used to achieve efficiency. For sales departments, the environment consists of a number of fairly routine transactions in the administration of relationships with customers, but the actual selling function – and in particular the gaining of new customers – requires activities using high degrees of interpersonal and social skills. Time horizons tend to be short in sales as in production.

*Table 6.2* Departmental characteristics and sub-environments of successful plastics firms

| | Department | | | |
|---|---|---|---|---|
| | *Production* | *Sales* | *Applied research* | *Fundamental research* |
| SUB-ENVIRONMENT | Raw material transactions | Customer transactions | Testing equipment | Scientific journals |
| | Equipment purchase | Advertising agencies | Research centres | Professional associations |
| | Unskilled labour | Distribution | | Conferences |
| | | Competitors | | Universities |
| CHARACTERISTIC | | | | |
| Formalization | Highest | High | Low | Lowest |
| Interpersonal orientation | Task | Social | Task/social | Social/task |
| Time horizon | Short | Short | Medium | Long |
| | CRISPEST | | | FUZZIEST |

Adapted from Lawrence, P.R. and Lorsch, J.W. (1967) *Organization and Environment: Managing Differentiation and Integration*, Homewood, Ill.: Richard D. Irwin.

The two types of research department tend to have much in common in terms of their environments and structural characteristics. For the fundamental research department the environment consists of the scientific community as represented by universities, scientific journals, and professional associations. The structural emphasis now needs to be on long time horizons, low formality, and the need to use mutual adjustment as a means of communication. When we shift to applied research we see a shift towards slightly greater formality and shorter time horizons as the purpose of this kind of department is to transfer fundamental research into production.

## THE DESIGNED ENVIRONMENT

We have emphasized the negotiated nature of the environments of many organizations and the extent to which organizations can have strategic choice in selecting their task environments. Much of the established business policy and strategic management literature (Glueck 1980) does not take into account the designed nature of many organizational environments. Organizations are not passive receivers of a particular set of competitors, customers, suppliers, and regulations. Through their actions organizations create a domain for themselves; indeed, the implication of much of the above discussion has been to suggest that the best way to survive is to avoid competition and to move towards co-operative strategies where greater control can be achieved over the task environment.

This notion is undoubtedly gaining strength as environments become more complex. The increasing density of environmental connections led Emery and Trist (1965) to write in terms of the 'causal texture' of environments meaning that organizations need to look to the variety and multiplicity of environmental inter-dependencies as being the primary 'cause' of internal structures. This view made much more sense in the mid-1960s when organizations were perhaps studied more from a public service rather than from a business perspective. Business theory was not ready to embrace such ideas but Pfeffer and Salancik (1978) brought them to bear more upon the business sector when they wrote about the 'created environment', perhaps implying that businesses can set out to design environments much in the same way that internal structures are created.

Designing environments on a large scale necessarily requires action within the institutional environment of the organization and for the organization to become a political actor. But the designed environment means going further than lobbying from a perspective of self-interest which has often been the view taken in the past when, for instance, reference is made to the way in which large corporations attempt to wield power over national governments (Dunkerley *et al.* 1981). This has been well documented both in academic and popular literature. There is, to date, lack of systematic research on the method and the extent to which organizations design environments on a wider scale.

## Insight: collaboration in the aerospace industry

An example of the need to design environments comes from the aerospace industry. Airbus Industrie is a consortium of European aerospace companies, including companies such as British Aerospace. These companies form joint ventures for the development, manufacturing, and marketing of aircraft. One such aircraft is the long range A310 jet for which there is a large market in the Soviet Union and Eastern Europe where the airlines have for long complained about being forced to buy noisy, outdated Russian planes.

Because of a NATO ban on the export of high technology equipment to Warsaw Pact countries European aerospace companies have been severely restricted as to the planes that can be sold there. This ban has been controlled by the American-dominated Co-ordinating Committee for Multilateral Control (Cocom). Airbus Industrie, however, managed to acquire a £120 million order for the A310 aircraft from the East German airline Interflug. This was only achieved after obtaining agreement from the powerful Cocom.

Environmental design took place in a number of ways in this case in order to obtain that agreement. In the first place, individual aircraft manufacturers formed a joint venture which enables them to achieve greater power over their environments. Action was then required to design an agreement which was acceptable to a number of interested parties such as Cocom, Interflug, and various Warsaw Pact and NATO governments. One concern was that East Germany and other Soviet bloc countries did not learn the secrets of the plane's navigation system and of the American General Electric engines. In order to do this the agreement required that:

1  All sensitive units were to be in sealed containers which had to be returned to the West for maintenance.
2  Only day to day maintenance was to be carried out by Interflug and that more serious work was to be done by Lufthansa, the West German airline.
3  No engineers were to be trained in the East into the skills required for maintaining the equipment in question.
4  Interflug was only to hold the basic owner's manual and not any detailed drawings or specifications.

(*The Times* 1988)

This is only one example of the kind of action that is often needed by organizations pursuing their strategy. It is a process that has for long been familiar in the construction industry where large projects such as the Channel Tunnel require action by several contractors, financial institutions to provide finance, governments to provide political leverage and to clear the way through the complex of planning permissions, and a whole host of subcontractors.

Butler and Carney (1983) describe the process as taking place within a managed market where competition is the norm but where this norm is overlaid by a hierarchy and collective arrangements where trust and informal agreements play an important part. For example, the construction of a North Sea Oil Terminal (Halsey 1980) involved the setting up of a contract between the managing contractor and a number of contractors. At this stage political action was needed in the sense of gaining the necessary planning permission, and so was competitive action in the sense of awarding contracts following a process of competitive tendering. However, once the contract is under way, the power shifts increasingly to the contractors. Contractors often return to the main contractor and ask to renegotiate particular terms because unforeseen problems have arisen – soil conditions may be claimed as more difficult than expected or other new information come to light exposing difficulties, or surprise events may be said to have intervened. As far as possible, the main contractor will have written contingency clauses into the original contract but the inherent uncertainties in the technology for carrying out large-scale projects make it impossible to write all such contingencies into contracts. Hierarchy comes into play through the setting up of a joint venture company which has a contract as its basis; the legal system now becomes the ultimate arbiter in disputes instead of an internal hierarchy with top management as the arbiter.

The Principle of Requisite Decision-Making Capacity is still at work in designing environments. Contracts between many organizations cannot be written on a once and for all basis (Williamson 1985) when there is uncertainty surrounding the conditions of that contract. To force premature crispness would be to risk incurring errors of decision undercapacity when contractors would be tempted to hide deviations from specification in the hope that they would not come to light until some later date. To permit undue fuzziness would be to risk incurring errors of decision overcapacity when contractors would make excessive profits from the work.

## IDEOLOGY AND BOUNDARY STRUCTURES

The line of thought running throughout this book is that the organizational design problem can be reduced to three sets of variables contained within the broad categories of context, structure, and ideology linked together by the Principle of Requisite Decision-

Making Capacity. We have seen how the key environmental variables reflect those of the key technological variables. Hence the variables of ambiguity, variability, and interdependence have been met in considering both environment and technology. The variable of heterogeneity can be seen as appropriate to the description of technology, although not specifically discussed under that heading, in so far as a mixture of technologies can be used in an organization thereby increasing the range of decisions that have to be made.

In the discussion on environmental variables we have not given much attention to ideology. When discussing technology we noted that the intensive type of technology will need a robust ideology where primacy is given to an overarching morality but strong ideas are also needed about efficiency, instrumentality, and referents. If our reasoning is correct we should see a similar effect in boundary structures except that here the overriding source of organizational ideology will be the norms that derive from the institutional environment. Hence, for the firm in the competitive market where the norms require a profit to be shown (an efficiency norm) and the task environment is open to new rivals, the efficiency norms must predominate. If, however, we move to the most complex case where the predominant norms are moral, and the task environment variable, interdependent, and heterogeneous, the organization now gains support by means of exchanges of obligations; moral norms must predominate in the boundary structures of this organization.

This most complex example is difficult to find in practice since the pressures must surely be to try to simplify the structure by defining more homogeneous, stable, and autonomous spheres of operation. In general, however, we can argue that as the context provided by the environment gets more complex due to increases in openness, ambiguity, variability, interdependence, and heterogeneity so too does the need to develop fuzzy structures and robust ideologies. Whether an organization takes this organizational choice must, in the final analysis, depend upon the predominant performance norms deriving from the institutional environment; an organization is free to choose but within constraints. All the time decision makers need to be aware of how the organization is being assessed by its major supporters in relation to its rivals. Even an organization in an apparently unassailable position in its task environment is open to changes in regulations permitting new entrants, or to illegal entrants.

## DESIGN IMPLICATIONS AND SUMMARY

Organizations make strategic choices and in so doing select normative, task environmental, and technological variables for themselves. Two key dimensions of strategic choice are concentration (a measure of the dependence of the organization upon key supporters) and ambiguity (a measure of the technical uncertainties faced in conducting resource exchanges within the environment). This strategic choice is exercised within constraints set by the normative variables.

The underlying problem of strategic choice is to cope with dependence and uncertainty and to provide the requisite decision-making capacity to manage the boundary transactions associated with a particular strategy. When concentration and ambiguity are low the defender strategy is appropriate; this requires efficiency and instrumental norms. When concentration is low and ambiguity high the analyser strategy is appropriate; this requires internal referent and moral norms. When concentration is high an organization can attempt to control its environment by negotiated strategies involving exchanges of obligations with other organizations in the same field. As the exchange of obligations creates a more interdependent environment, ideology is likely to have to shift increasingly towards the robust type.

From the perspective of the Principle of Requisite Decision-Making Capacity, three dimensions of the selected environment are particularly appropriate in discovering the kinds of boundary spanning structures that are needed to manage boundary trans-actions. Starting from the homogeneous/stable/autonomous environment where boundary structures would emphasize centralization and a simple functional structure, if the environment now increases its complexity due to a shift towards greater heterogeneity, the main boundary spanning method. If the environment becomes interdependent, interaction becomes the appropriate device becomes that of differentiating positions and units to cope with relatively homogeneous parts of the environment. If variability occurs in the environment, decentralization becomes the most appropriate boundary spanning method. If the environment becomes inter-dependent, interaction becomes the appropriate device.

Environments can be designed and this becomes more important as the conditions for negotiated strategies strengthen. To design an environment means combining with other appropriate organiza-tions for the duration of particular projects, often across national boundaries, and involves action in institutional environments to obtain the appropriate regulatory regime.

We summarize the variables discussed in this chapter into the framework given by the institutional model of organization as shown in Figure 6.3.

*Figure 6.3* The contingent institutional model of organization: salient variable relationships discussed in this chapter

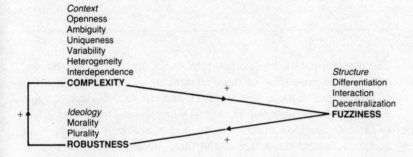

# Chapter seven

# Hierarchical profiles

The institutional model of organization sees structure as an outcome of a context consisting of three streams of action: the normative, technical, and resource streams. Each of these streams raises contingencies for an organization and to this point we have treated the effect of each stream upon structure more or less separately. The question now is to assess the effect of the three streams upon the overall resultant structure. We do this by means of the notion of a structural or hierarchical profile.

## APPROACHES TO PROFILES

Organizations often go to great lengths to detail their formal structure, usually in hierarchical form, in order to define a number of aspects of the behaviour expected from participants. Typically these aspects may cover the accountability of participants detailing who reports to whom, the responsibilities of participants defined through job descriptions and the like, and departmentalization specifying affiliation to sub-groupings within the organization; these aspects are often formalized into an organization chart (Daft 1989: 211). One object of such formalization is to communicate to participants what the organization is trying to achieve and how, and how they fit into this scheme. The aim is to communicate economically to participants, via a summary profile, the central ends/means beliefs of the organization. An organizational chart provides a kind of map to guide participants in their day to day work. It represents a broad hypothesis as to how decisions are to be made and as such it is open to errors of undercapacity or overcapacity in decision making.

A number of authors have used types or configurations to summarize organizational structure (Miller and Mintzberg 1983). Pugh and Hickson (1989: 23) outline a taxonomy of bureaucratic forms using the dimensions of centralization and structuring of activities. High centralization and high structuring provide what they call a 'full bureaucracy'; high centralization and low structuring provide a 'personnel bureaucracy' where the main control comes through determining the personnel policies as regards hiring and promotion; high structuring with low centralization provide a 'workflow bureaucracy' where the emphasis goes into controlling the work itself, and 'non-bureaucracies' have minimal control as found in small organizations.

Mintzberg (1983b) presents five configurations based upon the patterning of internal parts or sub-systems (similar to those outlined in chapter 1), and matching contextual conditions. Mintzberg's 'simple structure' is not dissimilar to the non-bureaucracy above where there is direct centralized control; it is suggested that this organization is best suited to simple, dynamic environments. The 'machine bureaucracy' is not dissimilar to the full bureaucracy above in that control is by standardization; the key part of the organization is the technostructure of technically-qualified support people and is most suited to old technologies and stable external conditions. The 'professional bureaucracy' uses standardization of skills (see chapter 4) and the key part is the technical core with the suitable context being a complex but stable environment. The 'divisionalized form' uses standardization of outputs with the key part of the organization being the middle level divisional management and is suited for diversified (heterogeneous, see chapter 6) environments. Finally, there is Mintzberg's 'adhocracy' where mutual adjustment is the prime control method and the key aspect of the organization is that support and operating people work closely together (as in the non-routine technology, see chapter 5); this configuration is suitable for complex dynamic environments.

## DEPARTMENTALIZATION: THE PROBLEM OF SELF-CONTAINMENT

The above, and the other configurational approaches to organizations, provide useful summaries of structures. Here we take an approach to organizational profiles based upon the departmentalization used and how these departments fit into an overall hierarchy.

Departmentalization refers to the method by which participants are allocated to particular types of activity. Two dimensions to the problem are suggested: departmentalization by process and departmentalization by product. The organizational design question now becomes: what is the appropriate criterion upon which departments may be defined within the constraints of the Principle of Requisite Decision-Making Capacity?

We can view departmentalization in terms of a two-dimensional matrix (see Table 7.1). The horizontal axis represents the technical knowledge used in converting inputs into outputs. The vertical axis represents the impact of the task environment in that inputs derive from segments of the environment which, following transformation in the technical core, are sent to output segments. These two dimensions give the basis for a process organization (alternatively known as a functional organization), and a product organization, respectively (Simon 1947).

*Table 7.1* The basic matrix of departmentalization

|  |  | Processes | | | | |
|---|---|---|---|---|---|---|
|  |  | 1 | 2 | 3 | 4 | 5 |
| Products | A | → | → | → | → | → |
|  | B | → | → | → | → | → |
|  | C | → | → | → | → | → |

As a simple example Table 7.1 shows a three-product firm with five basic processes. The products might be different versions of an engineering product, all of which need some of the five processes to be applied in order to make a final product. The model can be equally well applied to a service organization, such as a hospital, where the processes might be basic medical disciplines such as X-ray, various types of consultation, drug treatment, surgery, and physiotherapy, each of which has to be applied, in different ways, to three types of patient (the 'products') who might be categorized as paediatric, maternity, emergency, or by some other appropriate designation.

Whether an organization adopts a process or product departmentalization is a question of drawing boundaries horizontally or vertically around participants on this matrix. If the departmentalization is by process, vertical groupings will be created, that is, participants will belong to process 1, 2, 3, etc., but will work on a variety of products. If the departmentalization is by product, horizontal groupings will be created, that is, participants wil belong to product A, B, or C but will have to possess a variety of skills.

## Requisite decision-making capacity

Following the Principle of Requisite Decision-Making Capacity, we may draw up some rules as to which type of departmentalization should be followed. A department is a group of people who share an identity based upon the notion of a common task. That identity may be centred upon a skill or profession (process departmentalization) or upon a product/market combination (product departmentalization). In order to provide the requisite decision-making capacity it is suggested that departmentalization should attempt to do the following:

1  Minimize interdependencies and associated interactions between departments, maximize interdependencies and interactions within departments.
2  Make organizational and spatial locations contiguous.
3  Base departments upon similar identities or ideologies.

Thompson (1967) has suggested that departmentalization should proceed in the order of a hierarchical priority as discussed in chapter 5. First, the most complex interdependencies requiring mutual adjustment co-ordination and the greatest interactions are located within self-contained units. Above this, the next most complex interdependencies requiring scheduling would be placed within self-contained units. Finally, above these would be placed the least complex interdependencies requiring parametric co-ordination.

Occasions may arise where one or more of these rules are in conflict: for instance, minimizing interdependencies may mean cutting across existing ideologies and identities especially when an organization is in a state of change. Here a choice has to be made between letting the existing ideology take precedence over the technical requirements of minimizing transactions costs, or attempting to change the ideology (see chapter 10).

## PROCESS DEPARTMENTALIZATION

An example of a simple process-organized manufacturing firm is given by the firm Playskills as shown in Figure 7.1. The predominant grouping of participants is by skill and resource. These skills are allocated to essential activities needed in order to produce the final output. The firm manufactures a range of outdoor climbing frames and other outdoor toys which are sold to private and institutional customers for use in parks and school playgrounds. The basic technology is fairly routine, involving a number of operations such as cutting, galvanizing, bending, welding, and the like. All these processes are well understood. Many products are sold standard and off the shelf but some are custom-built to specification.

Production contains the greatest number of employees and is divided into departments each headed by a supervisor. Sales is headed by a marketing director with five salespersons who specialize by type of customer, the main distinction being made between retail and institutional sales. There is also a mail order department supplied with components from production. Finance consists of bookkeeping, invoicing, credit control, and payments activities. A simple budgeting and cost-control system operates with departmental estimates made annually; there tends to be some specialization amongst accounts people. Administration covers personnel, insurance, buildings, transport, and any other general administrative problems that arise.

*Figure 7.1* Typical process/functional organizations – a small manufacturer (Playskills)

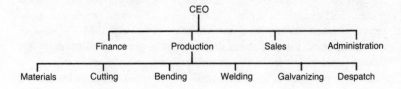

## Characteristics of the process organization

If we now put the characteristics of the process organization described above into the terms of the institutional model and its variables (see Table 7.2) we can say that such an organization will have a generally crisp structure which will be formal, centralized, and where parametric control rules abound. Control will be by costs and budgets.

The context for which the process organization is particularly suited is an environment and technology which is homogeneous, clear, and stable. Hence the number of product lines is likely to be small (maybe just one), technology routine (stable and clear), and size small to medium.

Ideology will be singular, concentrating upon a small number of goals and efficiency or instrumentally oriented as the internal goals are aimed towards reducing costs and improving control. Skill development can also be an important goal since the process organization can be effective at developing technical expertise.

*Table 7.2* Characteristics of the process organization

| | |
|---|---|
| *Structure*: | Departmentalization: by skills and resources |
| | Control: costs and budgets |
| | Crisp, formal, parametric, centralized |
| *Context*: | Environment: clear, stable, homogeneous |
| | Technology: clear, stable, homogeneous |
| | Size: small to medium |
| *Ideology*: | Instrumental (based on technical specialization) |
| | efficiency, singular |
| *Strengths*: | Economies of scale |
| | Skill development |
| *Failures*: | Top decision overload |
| | Excessive meetings |
| | Slow to change |
| | Professional/craft loyalty rather than customer |
| | orientation |

Adapted from Duncan, Robert (1979) 'What is the right organization structure? Decision tree analysis provides the answer', *Organizational Dynamics*, winter 1979: 59–80.

The strengths of the process organization are in achieving economies of scale and in depth skill development (Galbraith 1977, Daft 1989).

## Symptoms of failure

If the firm develops, the environment becoming more heterogeneous with different identified market segments, technology more variable, and size increasing but the structure remaining of the process type, some symptoms of tension and failure may now begin to emerge. Typically:

— Top decisions overload.  Whilst the structure remained small with a simple technology a few top managers could make the major decisions but as we saw in chapter 4 the simple hierarchy becomes overloaded as the context becomes more complex.
— Excessive bureaucracy.  One response to top management overload may be to introduce operating procedures and planning systems. While these can be helpful they have their limitations, especially as technological and environmental complexity increases.

— Excessive meetings. Another response might be to try and improve both vertical and horizontal co-ordination by the use of committees, task groups, or liaison roles. These linking mechanisms will be discussed in greater detail below but generally they are all designed to increase mutual adjustment and interaction in decision making. The problem arises when too much management time is spent in this type of activity rather than seeing to the basic goal of the organization. Writing reports and running committees can now become the *raison d'être* of management.
— Slow to change. Another problem may be a lack of ability to adapt to changes quickly enough.
— Remoteness from customer. The consequence of the above changes can be to divert management attention from satisfying customer needs and profitability to running the bureaucracy. Procedures and planning can become the objective.
— Politicking. A possible outcome of this escalation in organizational failures can be excessive conflict and politicking.

## PRODUCT DEPARTMENTALIZATION

When the failures of an existing process profile become strongly evident management might consider a move towards a product profile. This would allocate activities and participants by product thereby lining activities up more closely to environmental rather than technological requirements. Profit centres now become the primary focus for performance measurement. These profit centres operate as semi-autonomous organizations although internally they may display a process profile. Figure 7.2 shows an example of a product organization. Key positions are held by a comparatively small central headquarters staff whose main responsibility is for corporate planning, and by the product division management whose main responsibility is to ensure profitability of the divisions.

### Characteristics of the product organization

In terms of the variables of the institutional model the structure overall will be crisp in the sense that there will be formal analytical procedures for planning and assessing product division performance. However, the divisions will represent nodes of relative fuzziness in that they are decentralized, differentiated from one another, and internally interactive.

*Figure 7.2* Example of a product organization

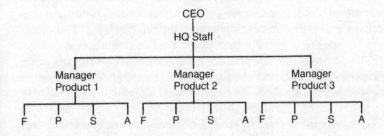

*Notes*: F = finance; P = production; S = sales; A = administration.
Production broken down into a number of specific operations.

The appropriate context of the product organization is more complex
than that for the process organization. It is heterogeneous due to multiple
product lines which form the basis of autonomous divisions; however,
there is comparability in that the performance of divisions can be
compared to other divisions within the same corporation and to other

*Table 7.3* Characteristics of product organization

| | |
|---|---|
| *Structure*: | Departmentalization: product/customer divisions |
| | Control: cost/profit centres |
| | Crisp overall, comparatively fuzzy in divisions: |
| |     formal, parametric, analytic, differentiated, |
| |     individualistic, decentralized |
| *Context*: | Environment: comparable, heterogeneous, open |
| | Technology: heterogeneous |
| | Size: large |
| *Ideology*: | Efficiency (product development, customer |
| |     satisfaction), plural |
| *Strengths*: | Can concentrate upon customers and products |
| | Adaptation to local conditions |
| | Economical on top management decision making |
| | Risk reduction across range of products |
| *Failures*: | Duplication |
| | Product standardization difficult |
| | Innovation flow incomplete |
| | Divisional rather than company loyalty |
| | Lose in-depth skill development |

Adapted from Duncan, Robert (1979) 'What is the right organization structure? Decision tree analysis provides the answer', *Organizational Dynamics*,
winter 1979: 59–80.

companies in the similar markets. This comparability and autonomy forms the basis of corporate control and enables the shifting of investments from less to more profitable businesses. Heterogeneous technologies will also develop around the product lines. This structure is especially suited to the larger kind of organization.

The ideology of the product organization will be based upon efficiency; it is assumed that product divisions are competing within their respective markets as semi-autonomous units. There will also be a degree of pluralism in that each division, while having to acknowledge the overriding need of efficiency, can represent a distinct business idea which will tend to have its own beliefs and values.

As summarized in Table 7.3 the particular strengths of the product organization are that it is easier to concentrate upon customer satisfaction and product development rather than upon technical expertise. It also permits greater adaptation to local conditions as each product division takes over responsibility for its own market development. In this way top management time is released for more strategic thinking covering the whole corporation.

### Symptoms of failure

Product organizations can also fail for a number of reasons:

— Duplication. The product organization requires that each operating division be relatively self-contained and hence there is the possibility of duplication of resources. This is the converse of the process organization's strength of being able to use economies of scale.
— Product standardization difficult. The pressures are towards product differentiation and hence the possibility of wasteful variety.
— Divisional rather than corporate loyalty. Participants may feel they belong to a division rather than to the corporation.
— Competitive rather than co-operative. Divisions come to compete for a common pool of resources. The competition is increased as the requirements for profitability increase.
— Divisional innovations not diffused. The product organization is designed to provide an incentive for divisional management to innovate but as divisions see themselves as competing they will tend to keep innovations to themselves.

One response to these failures, if they emerge, can be for an organization to develop an extensive headquarters staff to try to provide corporate skills and expertise. As this staff gets bigger, and more decisions are removed from the operating division, the organization is making a shift back towards the process structure.

## THE M-FORM FIRM

The market form or M-Form (Williamson 1975) organization can be seen as an extension of the product form of organization in that the primary groupings are based around product/market identities. In the M-Form, the central part of the organization consists of a minimal financial planning core. Each division operates as an autonomous organization, perhaps not even bearing the name of the parent corporation, looking to the centre essentially as an internal bank to which a division would go requesting funds to finance various capital investment projects.

It is this idea of the corporation as an internal capital market that is at the centre of the M-Form organization. The questions from the Requisite Decision-Making Capacity perspective are why – if the divisions are autonomous in the sense of being able to make their own product/market decisions – is it necessary to have the corporate headquarters, and why could each division not act as an independent company?

Williamson gives the answer to these questions in terms of transactions costs theory (see chapter 2). The internal bank, that is corporate headquarters, becomes privy to special inside information that is not available to an outside bank and hence is in a better position to evaluate the riskiness of projects. This inside knowledge derives from the various internal planning and management systems used to evaluate the performance of the divisions and assess individual project proposals, and from other less formal information concerning the track record of individuals. The purity of the M-Form is likely to decay if corporate management is tempted to intervene in the internal workings of the divisions. Temptation to do this will increase as the crossflows between divisions increase.

## CO-ORDINATING LINKAGES

Departmentalization and organizational profiles can only provide an approximate solution to the problem of organizational co-ordination (Simon 1947). There will always be participants at the boundary of a department who could, on the basis of the Principle of Requisite Decision-Making Capacity, be more suitably located elsewhere but, because an organization is always in a state of flux, changing location is not worthwhile in the short term.

This situation need not be a particular problem since an organization can draw upon other co-ordinating devices which do not involve changes in departmentalization. The organizational design problem is to co-ordinate participants in both vertical and horizontal dimensions (Galbraith 1977, Daft 1989); regardless of the particular type of departmentalization both kinds of linkages are needed. Linkages attempt to provide requisite decision-making capacity although they vary in the extent to which they can do this.

## Vertical linkages

We can rank vertical linkages in an approximate ascending order of the extent to which they can provide increased decision-making capacity (see Table 7.4):

*Table 7.4* Vertical linkages

In supposed ascending order of decision-making capacity and cost:
1. HIERARCHICAL REFERRAL
   Referring decisions up hierarchy for consideration. Increases centralization and can overload management.
2. STANDARD PROCEDURES
   Decision rules for familiar problems. Suitable for routine problems but fails under new problems.
3. PLANNING
   Periodically setting and changing targets. Suitable for familiar tasks but not where conditions change rapidly.
4. ADD LEVELS
   Overcomes management overload by reducing spans of control but slows down vertical communication and decision making.
5. MANAGEMENT INFORMATION SYSTEMS
   Can transmit much information but expensive to set up.

*Source*: Galbraith, J.R. (1977) *Organization Design*, Reading, Mass.: Addison-Wesley.

**Hierarchical referral**   One way of linking vertically is through hierarchical referral, that is, by passing a decision upwards for consideration. The more hierarchical referral takes place, the more centralized decision making becomes in an organization. Providing the superior can cope with the decision-making load this is a quick method of co-ordinating but there are severe limits to this as managers can get overloaded with routine problems. Hence, we can say that the capacity to convey large volumes of complex information is low and we see this linkage as providing the least ability to cope with decision complexity.

**Standard procedures**    Organizations can set up procedures and decision rules for the more familiar problems and thereby save direct decision-making effort on the part of managers. Tasks can be standardized and procedural rules created to cope with a whole range of problems. An example is the rules governing selection of students into a university. As far as possible these are defined in precise terms covering a number of aspects such as qualifications, experience, and the like. Similarly, procedures of capital investment appraisal in organizations can use highly involved calculations and algorithms.

Compared to hierarchical referral, standard procedures can cope with higher volumes of information although the capacity to cope with unfamiliar situations is limited. One of the dangers of standard procedures is that an organization may try to use established procedures which are unsuitable for a new problem. Standard procedures provides a way of decentralizing in that once procedural rules are set up subordinates are permitted to make decisions within the limits set by the rules.

Standard procedures ranks second on the scale of decision-making capacity and therefore the ability to cope with complex problems.

**Planning**    When new problems are likely to arise standard procedures cannot predetermine solutions to these and a planning cycle can be introduced to permit some degree of mutual adjustment and interaction. The most common plan is perhaps the annual budget which may be calculated according to a formula, but the actual amount and the range of activities covered can vary from year to year. The production schedule is another example of planning. Production targets for individual departments will be derived from the overall sales schedule but these targets are adjusted as the sales schedule changes.

Planning ranks third on our scale of decision-making capacity.

**Add levels**    As we have seen, adding a level to a hierarchy is a way of reducing the overload on a superior. This may start by creating an assistantship position. Adding levels ranks fourth on our scale of decision-making capacity (see also chapter 4 for limitations).

**Management information systems**    Management information systems provide a vertical flow of information that can be used in decision making. Flowing downwards, this information provides instructions or guidelines for decision making at lower levels in an organization. Flowing upwards, this information provides feedback to higher management as to progress and performance at the lower levels. The extent to which management information systems provide requisite decision-making capacity will depend upon the volume of relevant information that can be transmitted and upon its up-to-dateness. Well-designed systems can provide increased interaction and quite high decision-making capacity; we can rank this method of vertical linking fifth.

The precise way in which each of these linkage mechanisms gets used will vary but, at the risk of over-generalization, we can say that as we ascend this scale of decision-making capacity we increase the ability to cope with complex problems. At the same time, however, we also tend to increase the managerial cost involved.

## Lateral linkages

A number of mechanisms exist for the horizontal co-ordination of activities in an organization which do not require vertical referral or any of the other vertical linking mechanisms. As with the vertical linkages above we order the horizontal in approximate ascending order of ability to cope with decision-making complexity (see Table 7.5).

*Table 7.5* Lateral linkages

In supposed ascending order of decision-making capacity and cost:
1. REPORTS
   Periodic special exercises for informing about aspects of the task. Suitable for unfamiliar problems but slow and not providing much feedback.
2. DIRECT CONTACT
   Creating meetings between appropriate people. Good for feedback between the individuals involved but quite limited in diffusing information.
3. LIAISON ROLES
   Specially set up roles to co-ordinate activities. Similar but better than direct contact.
4. TASK FORCES
   Creation of specific groups to solve and report on specific problems. Good at providing mutual adjustment but slow and time consuming.
5. TEAMS
   Creation of long-term specific multidisciplinary groups to work on a task. Good at producing internal communication between team members but team identification may become more important than organizational.

*Source*: Galbraith, J.R. (1977) *Organization Design*, Reading, Mass.: Addison-Wesley.

**Reports**   Special reports on various aspects of an organization's activities are an often-used method of lateral linking. A research and development department may produce a one-off report describing its ideas for product innovation and circulate this widely throughout the organization requesting comments and discussion.

**Direct contact**   If the work of two departments or groups in an organization requires inter-communication, direct contact – whereby representatives from each department meet to discuss problems – provides a simple and relatively low-cost method of lateral linking. By removing the need to use hierarchical referral and by solving problems at a grass roots level, direct contact increases the inter-action during decision making.

Direct contact requires a high degree of spatial closeness, empha-sizing the notion of one-site solutions to organizational communica-tion problems. Another way in which direct contact can work is through the transfer of people from one department to another although it has been found that the impact of this tends to diminish with time (Galbraith 1977: 114).

**Liaison roles**   Direct contact has its limitations and as the amount of work flowing laterally between two or more points in an organiza-tion grows it becomes beneficial to set up a special linking or liaison role where the full-time job is to co-ordinate activities without the need for upward referral.

**Task forces**   A task force is a kind of liaison position but consisting of a group of individuals from a number of departments whose remit is to work on a special project or problem. This allows for more complex decisions to be made than would be possible with a single liaison role.

**Teams**   A team may be set up to permit co-ordination over an exten-ded time period and concerning a specific job.

As we ascend this scale of decision-making capacity we increase the ability to cope with complex problems. At the same time, however, we also tend to increase the managerial cost involved.

### Insight: a very large functional organization – The Ford Motor Company

Although it has been suggested above that process organizations are better suited to small-size conditions, the question of size needs to be related to the industry concerned. One of the advantages of process departmentalization is that there are greater opportunities for economies of scale. This becomes a particularly important factor when looking at highly capital-intensive industries such as the motor industry. The Ford Motor Company gives us an example of a very large and famous international corporation whose organization has a strong process form. Its worldwide structure is shown in Figure 7.3.

*Figure 7.3* Ford Motor Company organization

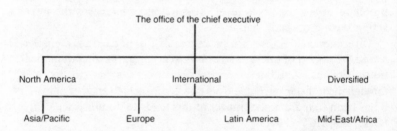

The automotive operations are split between North America and International Divisions. The International Division covers four areas: Asia/Pacific, Europe, Latin America, and Mid-East/Africa. Within the International Division, the European operations are a self-contained business but with close ties to other world activities of Ford. For example, there is a tendency for Europe to send precision components to Latin America to be introduced at a later date. Ford, in its European operations, presents a highly-integrated process structure. There are certain key aspects in its context overriding the logic that large size would push the organization to a product form, namely, the pressure to technical routinization through standardization and interchangeability of components, the presence of interdependence in that components are moved around the various European plants for assembly, and the goal of achieving the greatest economies of scale possible. This integrative requirement is strengthened by the desire to shift production from one country to another if there are labour or political difficulties or if costs in one country increase too much (see Figure 7.4).

Ford has a pan-European management system co-ordinating the activities of each of the national companies which retain their legal identity (a way of managing the institutional environment) but which can be considered as a gigantic functional or process organization. There are the principal functions of product development, manufacturing, sales, truck operations, and export. Under sales comes Ford of Britain, Ford of Germany, the European Sales Operation, and the Parts Operation.

*Figure 7.4* Ford organization in Europe

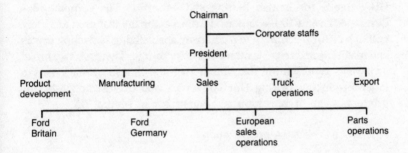

Ten vehicle lines (Fiesta, Escort, etc.) covering cars and trucks with different derivatives and options are offered. Each vehicle comprises several thousands of parts but certain parts and assemblies (engines for instance) are common to a number of product lines thereby permitting economies of scale in the production of these items. There are also seven major manufacturing plants throughout Europe, each supplying several assembly plants. There are approximately 15 markets in Europe and over 100 outside, each one of which takes finished products from more than one assembly plant.

The profit centre concept cannot be easily operated under this system since it is not possible to separate major pieces of manufacturing operations from the overall business of producing motor cars. Further, it is difficult to find competitive benchmarks to establish transfer prices. Ford do operate some profit centres where such competitive pricing can be done. Performance comparisons can be made between equivalent manufacturing units. Wherever possible competitive suppliers are found for components, such as between alternative manufacturers of door handles.

The system is sensitive to exchange rate fluctuations. Each national subsidiary has to produce accounts within its country but management information is on a pan-European basis. The finance function is strong since financial information is basic to the integration of the total system. There is a ten-year strategic plan from which flow corporate, financial, and business objectives. There is a five-year financial plan and budgets for a one-year operating plan.

### Insight: product organization – BBA

BBA stands for British Belting and Asbestos. The company has developed over a 100-year period from a company that used to supply belt drives for machinery to a company specializing in friction drives and materials and related automotive components. There are two broad groupings representing the Automotive and Industrial markets, the latter producing belting (for conveyors and drives) and asbestos products. The organization is summarized in Figure 7.5.

*Figure 7.5* The BBA organization

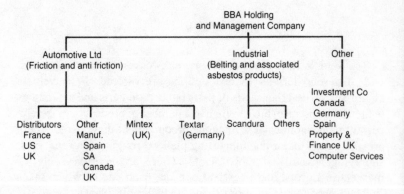

*Notes*: Employes 4,300 (UK 1,800, overseas 2,500). Financial planning at top.

Within the Automotive products group there are a number of manufacturing companies throughout Europe and the world. Mintex in the UK and Textar in Germany are the two biggest, each producing a wide range of automotive products such as brake linings and clutches. There are other manufacturers in Spain, South Africa, and Canada. There are also distribution companies in France, the US, and UK.

Within the Industrial Group, Scandura is the largest unit prod·icing the range of industrial products, including asbestos which is sold to the Automotive companies Mintex and Textar. There are also a number of other mainly investment companies in Canada, Germany, Spain, and the UK, and a computer services company which provides in-house services but is free to sell its services on the open market.

Overall is a holding company, located near to Mintex but occupying no more than a small country house. Headquarters staff are small, their main function being to provide financial planning. Subsidiary companies are given targets in the annual planning cycle and are left substantially to run their own affairs.

## MATRIX ORGANIZATION

As organizations differentiate both in terms of products and processes there is an increasing tension between the two dimensions of the matrix shown in Table 7.1. The desire for economies of scale and process expertise tends to push an organization towards the process type; the desire for accountability to markets and self-containment tends to push an organization towards the product type.

*Figure 7.6* An example of a matrix organization: a typical business school

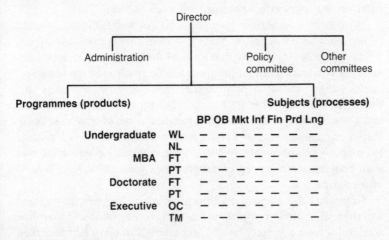

*Notes*: Subjects – BP = business policy; OB = organizational behaviour; Mkt = marketing; Inf = information systems; Fin = finance; Prd = production; Lng = language.
Programmes – WL = with language; NL = no language; FT = full time; PT = part time; OC = open courses; TM = tailor-made courses.

Although we have suggested the two primary forms of profile – the process and product profiles – some organizations have a formal structure explicitly recognizing the inherent product/process matrix and the tensions between these two dimensions. This is called a matrix organization (Knight 1976, Davis and Lawrence 1977, Daft 1989). It originated in the aerospace industry and other situations where technology is complex and rapidly changing, and the environment is differentiated into a number of distinct sectors of process and product. Figure 7.6 shows a business school as an example of a matrix organization.

## A business school as an example of a matrix organization

In the case of a typical business school we see the organizational problem of trying to develop identifiable academic programmes with which students and other supporters can identify from a number of subjects which are generally considered as necessary to management education. Typically, the subjects might be business policy, organizational behaviour, marketing, operations research, finance, and production. There might also be a language teaching requirement. Different schools may apply different labels and each subject grouping may exhibit a wide variation. For administrative purposes a subject head or chairperson is appointed for each subject.

Typically, programmes may range across undergraduate, master of business administration (MBA), doctoral, and executive types. There might be variants within each of these categories: let us say there are two undergraduate programmes, one with a foreign language, one without; two MBA programmes, one full time, the other part time; two doctoral programmes, one full time, the other part time; and a whole range of executive programmes, some of which are open-entry programmes repeated fairly frequently, the others tailor-made to company requirements. Whatever the particular programme mix each programme or group of programmes would also have a head or a chairperson.

To produce this range of teaching programmes requires the meshing together of different mixes of subject contributions. Individual academics have a subject loyalty and interest and will be concerned with developing research in their field. At the same time the organization also requires their contribution to the teaching programmes. In order to co-ordinate these dual sets of activities an overarching hierarchy or directorate is needed. This hierarchy may typically consist of a dean or a director who will have an administrative staff; there would usually be a policy committee and various other committees to achieve co-ordination on more specific problem areas.

## Characteristics of the matrix organization in general

In general terms the matrix has a dual hierarchy. One dimension represents processes and resources with each process group headed by a process manager; the other dimension represents products (outputs), each product line headed by product managers. Within the matrix are individuals or managers of groups/departments who report to both heads. Most participants in a matrix structure report to two bosses – a product and a process head. Over the whole organization is a directorate whose main function is to ensure that the power is balanced between the two dimensions of the matrix. Internally, control is by a mixture of profit centres and cost centres as applied to the product dimension, and budgets as applied to the process dimension.

The overriding problem of the matrix organization is to manage the dual logics of the technology and the environment. As a matrix organization is most appropriate in conditions of high uncertainty it has to manage the tension between trying to pursue both competitive and referent norms at the same time.

Key positions of the matrix organization are:

— Director. He or she has to balance the power of the two axes.
— Directorate staff. They report to the director and will assist in overall planning and co-ordination.
— Process head. Here the responsibility is to ensure that the necessary skills and resources are available and ensure that people are up to date in their skill.
— Product head. This position may be better known as product manager in manufacturing; this person has to ensure that the output gets made to the satisfaction of its user.
— Operations. The cells of the matrix are occupied by operators or operational managers. They have a dual accountability.
— Planning committee. This is usually needed to develop overall strategy and would probably consist of the director, some key directorate staff, all functional and output heads.

If we interpret the matrix organization into the variables of the institutional model we see that structure is primarily fuzzy and secondarily crisp. There is fuzziness because of reliance upon expertise, a differentiated knowledge and product base, and decentralized operation; a high degree of symbolism will help to hold this together, an aspect of organizations elaborated in chapter 8. There is crispness because parametric measures are used particularly in the form of cost centres and budgets in order to maintain control; there also tends to be a fairly high degree of individualism in the sense that such organizations are full of professional workers who tend to be highly competitive, especially relative to reference groups outside the organization.

This is clearly an organizational profile providing a high decision-making capacity and for this capacity to be necessary the context needs to be complex. The knowledge and product base would be variable. We would also expect to see a heterogeneous context in terms of task environment and technology, and essentially ambiguous and interdependent technology. Due to the complexity of the organizational context it cannot be particularly large, but on the other hand if it is too small it cannot achieve sufficient economies of scale.

Because of the difficulty in co-ordinating such an organization the ideological variables are particularly important. The ideology needs to provide a body of ideas for decision making which reflect the structural differentiation and general fuzziness. Hence ideology needs to be plural and tolerant in the sense that there needs to be a wide range of ideas and an acceptance of new ones, and persistent in the sense that the ideology needs to persist through difficult decisions. Above all, however, the ideology must be moral in the sense that there needs to be an overall understanding as to the rightness of the ends and means of the organization.

The main strengths of the matrix structure are that it permits flexibility in the use of resources while at the same time developing skills and products. The aim is to get a commitment to both customer requirements and technical expertise.

## Failures of the matrix organization

The matrix structure highlights a number of behavioural failures of formal structures which, although often present in other kinds of structure, are amplified by this profile.

**Role conflict**    The matrix structure is not a place for an easy time although people with the right attitude can find it exciting and enjoyable (Knight 1976). Operators in particular tend to experience a lack of definition in their jobs and tend to get pulled in two directions. They have output managers demanding conformity to schedules and quality standards and they have process managers demanding that they should be at the forefront of their disciplines.

**Decision making**   Because of the need to represent a large number of interests (process and product heads, directorate staff, and maybe operational managers), the decision-making coalition tends to be large and complex.

**Power and politics**   The consequence of this enlarged coalition will be to increase the propensity for politicking and hence for bargaining in decision making.

**Ideological conflict**   Underlying the above problems in a matrix organization is the problem of conflict between the efficiency ideology of the product dimension and the referent ideology of the process dimension. The first expresses the need to respond to customer/client needs, the second to develop the subject disciplines or processes to

*Table 7.6*  Characteristics of matrix organization

| | |
|---|---|
| *Structure*: | Departmentalization: process and product |
| | Control: cost centres and budgets |
| | Fuzzy: expert, interactive, differentiated, decentralized, symbolic |
| | Crisp: parametric, individualistic |
| *Context*: | Environment: variable, heterogeneous, open |
| | Technology: variable, ambiguous, heterogeneous, interdependent |
| | Size: moderate |
| *Ideology*: | Plural (product and technical development), tolerant, moral |
| *Strengths*: | Achieves product and skill development |
| | Flexible use of resources |
| *Failures*: | Decision making complex |
| | Power can shift to one axis of matrix |
| | Directorate may not achieve power balance |
| | Politicking due to multiple interests |
| | Role conflict due to dual loyalty |
| | Requires high degree of interpersonal skills which may not be available |

Adapted from Duncan, Robert (1979) 'What is the right organization structure? Decision tree analysis provides the answer', *Organizational Dynamics*, winter 1979: 59–80.

which participants belong. The directorate has a key role to play in resolving this kind of tension through developing an overarching moral ideology representing the overall goals of the organization. The central planning process will play a part in this but the process of planning, the way in which different people participate, the way in which the outcomes are communicated, will be as important as the plan itself. In this process the directorate needs to play a symbolic role as much as anything, not getting too actively involved in either the process or the product dimension and favouring neither (see chapter 8).

The characteristics of the matrix organization are summarized in Table 7.6.

## Project organization

A project organization has many of the features of the matrix organization except that the product dimension of the matrix now becomes a project dimension. The distinction is that projects are, in a sense, products of a limited but definite duration; once the project is completed the project group is dismantled and its members reassigned to other projects (Knight 1976).

Projects are seen particularly in the construction industry where the project may be to construct a building, a bridge, a tunnel, and the like. During the project's life project managers act rather as do programme managers in the matrix organization. Project organizations need to have well-developed planning and costing procedures in order to keep control over progress and the cost of a given project.

## DESIGN IMPLICATIONS AND SUMMARY

Profiles provide a communicable summary of an organization's ends/means beliefs for its participants. Three principal profiles, the process, the product, and the matrix types, have been developed.

A process profile is seen to be most appropriate when the environment and technology are clear, stable, and homogeneous. Under these conditions participants can be departmentalized by means of skill and process, and structures are relatively formal and centralized. Ideology stresses efficiency and instrumental norms; the process organization is particularly adept at developing skills but to the possible detriment of product/customer development.

A product profile is seen to be most appropriate when the

environment is comparable and open, and technology heterogeneous. The basis for an effective product organization is to group participants into relatively autonomous units related to product/market boundaries and to allow comparative performance measurement both within and without the corporation. Structures are formal, decentralized, differentiated, and individualistic; product division heads are rewarded according to the performance of their unit. The ideology is of the efficiency type. However, there is also room for a degree of pluralism in that the divisions can develop different norms. Product/customer development takes priority over technical development.

A matrix profile is seen to be most appropriate when the environment is heterogeneous and variable as regards both processes and products, and technology is also ambiguous and interdependent. Structure is expert based, decentralized, differentiated, interactive, and symbolic – that is, a highly fuzzy structure. Ideology under these conditions is plural and tolerant in the sense that different ideas and norms are needed but there also has to be an overarching morality. Technological and product/customer development are of equal importance.

*Table 7.7* The contingent institutional model of organization: salient variable relationships discussed in this chapter

|  | *Process* | *Product* | *Matrix* |
|---|---|---|---|
| Context: | clear<br>stable<br>homogeneous<br><br>SIMPLE ⟵————⟶ | comparable<br>autonomous<br>heterogeneous<br>open | ambiguous<br>interdependent<br>heterogeneous<br>variable<br>COMPLEX |
| Structure: | formal<br>centralized<br><br><br>CRISP ⟵————⟶ | formal<br>decentralized<br>differentiated<br>individualistic | expert<br>decentralized<br>differentiated<br>interactive<br>symbolic<br>FUZZY |
| Ideology: | efficiency/<br>instrumental<br>singular<br>FOCUSED ⟵————⟶ | efficiency<br>plural | plural<br>tolerant<br>moral<br>ROBUST |

A summary of the application of the variables of the institutional model to a comparison of the salient features of the process, product, and matrix profiles is given in Table 7.7. We can see that as we move from process, through the product to the matrix organization the context shifts from simple to complex, the structure from crisp to fuzzy, and the ideology from focused to robust. Any fuzziness that occurs in the process organization will tend to be resolved within process groups, any fuzziness in the product organization is resolved either within product groups or at the central headquarters. Fuzziness in the matrix is resolved at the nodes of activity where processes and products meet.

# Ideology

Ideology is a way by which an organization proclaims itself to its supporters (Brunsson 1989: 4). In the crisp structure there are precise rules about the resolution of uncertainty when decisions arise. At the limit, all the organization asks from its participants on these occasions is to follow the rules; this is the essence of instrumental norms and decisions get made by computation. Under this condition an organization proclaims itself as crisp and with a focused ideology.

In the fuzzy structure there are elastic rules about the resolution of uncertainty when decisions arise. At the limit, the organization has no rules to offer and on these occasions participants have nothing more to guide their actions other than that which is implied in their mutual understandings; this is the essence of moral norms and decisions get made by inspiration. Under this condition an organization proclaims itself as fuzzy and with a robust ideology.

## ROBUST AND FOCUSED IDEOLOGIES

There is more to ideology than just the presence of a dominant norm; this is best illustrated by reference to the fuzzy structure. In our discussion of workers' co-operatives we indicated that such an organization is not likely to get very far on morality alone. We suggest that a robust ideology needs normative plurality, that is, the existence of all four types of norm. In addition to understandings about the rightness of what is being done (the essence of the moral norm), there also needs to be views on efficiency, instrumentalities, and appropriate referents. Further, there needs to be a tolerance of new and different views as new conditions unfold. Overarching the plurality and tolerance, however, must be beliefs about the morality of action in the organization which we would take as the dominant norm in a robust ideology.

Robustness prepares an organization ideologically for many varied conditions. The essence is to provide a body of ideas that can be applied to many types of decisions. It is an ideology that is only likely to come about as a result of long practice amongst a given cohort of organizational participants. The aim is not to get consistency of views, but to get diversity of views to ensure that decisions are made in accordance with the overarching morality. Such an ideology is likely to be political (Brunsson 1989) but politicality must be tempered by morality.

Where the fuzzy organization needs robust ideology, the crisp needs a strong (Brunsson 1985) or focused ideology. Where the robust is plural the focused is singular, concentrating upon a narrow set of ideas. Where the robust is tolerant the focused is particular, taking care to filter out inappropriate ideas. Where the robust is moral the focused is instrumental, requiring only that portion of participants' abilities which is relevant to a particular decision.

## STRUCTURE AND IDEOLOGY

We have suggested a relationship between structure and ideology resting upon the notion that certain kinds of structure foster certain kinds of ideology. A number of contrasting dimensions have been suggested as distinguishing between crisp and fuzzy structures. For instance, we are suggesting that implicit, differentiated, interactive, collective, supportive, and symbolic structures encourage robust ideologies. The argument for this can perhaps be illustrated by considering what would happen to robustness if structure drifted towards the crisp.

Instead of implicitness we would see formality, instead of interaction we would see parameters defining decision making, instead of collectivism we would see individualism, instead of supportiveness for errors we would see punishment, and instead of symbolism we would see literal translations of rules. All these, we suggest, would drive out the processes needed to develop plurality, tolerance, and morality.

The link between structure and ideology is formed by a secondary or outer learning loop. By adopting appropriate structures an organization can learn to be focused or robust in its ideology. We suggest that this outer learning loop operates upon a longer time cycle than the inner learning loop. We also accept that less is known about the outer learning process than about the inner learning loop; most of organizational theory has concerned itself with the inner rather than with the outer loop.

## THE REWARD/CONTRIBUTION BALANCE

The above sets the general thrust of the argument to be pursued. There are many gaps to be filled. The more specific question now concerns how ideology may be developed within an organization. As ideology comprises the underlying norms, values, and beliefs within an organization and provides the basis for a social contract between participants and the organization, it is the nature of this contract and how it might be nurtured within an organization that we now examine in more detail.

As organizations attempt to cope with uncertainty, the exercise of discretion is a crucial element in organizational action. If we assume that individuals join organizations in order to gain certain rewards they could not otherwise gain and that, in return, organizations demand certain contributions from participants, the design of the reward/contribution balance is crucial to developing organizational ideology.

An organization is solvent only insofar as the rewards are sufficient to draw forth the required contributions (March and Simon 1958). The reward/contribution balance is the foundation of the contract, part formal, part informal, whereby the expected contributions from participants and the expected rewards provided by an organization are specified. Rewards are inducements made by an organization to participants and include wages to employees, goods or services to customers, dividends to investors, and various non-monetary benefits that an organization provides. Contributions are the benefits that the organization expects to accrue in return for its investment in inducements and may include goods or services received, money, information, manual power, and dexterity or decision-making ability.

The essential question from the perspective of the Principle of Requisite Decision-Making Capacity concerns the nature of the contract needed to provide the appropriate ideology.

### Pay

Pay is probably the most basic of rewards given out in organizations yet few systematic attempts have been made to categorize such systems. An exception to this observation is provided by Lupton and Gowler (1969), and Lupton and Bowey (1976), who classify rewards on two dimensions. The reciprocity dimension refers to the directness with which rewards are provided following a measured performance, as opposed to deferred rewards which are provided after some time lag. The effort dimension refers to how participants' contributions are measured; output measurement assesses the contribution of the direct good provided to the organization, while input measurement assesses investments made by the participant with these investments being taken as surrogates for expected outputs; academic qualifications is an example of an input contribution and some payment schemes allow for extra increments according to qualifications gained.

Another aspect of reward systems concerns the method by which the standard is set. Here we can think of four ways, reflecting the four types of performance norm already outlined. Some standards are set by bargaining (efficiency/competitive norms), some by hierarchical dictate (instrumental norms), some by peer group review (referent norms), and others by collective review (moral norms). These represent theoretical extreme conditions but provide benchmarks against which other types of payment systems can be compared.

We can now fit the three aspects of a payment system together as shown in Table 8.1. We consider, first, the purer types and hence we can see that profit based pay fits the condition of reciprocity and output measurement; for example, payments to self-employed business people or to company directors whose pay is closely related to the profit of their company. We count this as standard setting by bargaining on the premise that all prices in a competitive market are ultimately set by bargaining. Other kinds of contracts in the labour market can be set this way, such as for certain kinds of casual work. When bargaining is done by a union on behalf of a group of workers it becomes collective bargaining. This payment method is appropriate when a competitive or efficiency ideology is desired.

*Table 8.1* Reward systems and norms

| Effort measurement | Reciprocity | |
|---|---|---|
| | Reciprocal | Deferred |
| | **Competitive norms** | **Instrumental norms** |
| Output | profit based | hierarchical review |
| | incentive bonus | |
| | hourly paid | |
| | incremental scales | |
| | payment by session | salaried with tenure |
| Input | | |
| | **Referent norms** | **Moral norms** |

When effort is measured by output but payment is deferred, pay is determined by periodic hierarchical review. This is a typical situation for the employee working on a more or less fixed pay scale but where there is a procedure, perhaps annually applied, for pay awards settled according to some assessment of performance. Pay may be received monthly or weekly but the rate of pay is determined less frequently. Under these conditions the organization will have moved away from a mainly market-based reward system because of the difficulty of measuring performance in a sufficiently precise way. This payment method is appropriate where the norms are essentially instrumental.

When input measures are combined with reciprocal payment we have a situation that is typical of the payment given to professional workers who are paid by the session; here we might think of medical consultants whose pay is determined by their level of training and seniority but are paid for a unit of work. Ultimately, however, the rate for the job will be determined by a system of peer group review; here referent norms would be the underlying ideology.

Finally, is the situation where payment is deferred and effort is measured by input as found in cases where participants are paid a stipend and more or less have job tenure; judges are an illustration of this case, but the case can also apply to academics in universities or to priests in a church. The essential ideology would be based upon moral norms; the individual has now to be trusted to deliver the promised contributions. In the case of a co-operative, pay will be determined as a result of a meeting of the collective.

These are, in a sense, pure cases but most payment systems are in-between and mixed types as denoted on Table 8.1. Incentive bonus schemes which pay a basic wage, usually determined by means of collective bargaining plus an amount determined by output, are an attempt to introduce a competitive ideology; hourly paid workers could be said to occupy an intermediate position on reciprocity but their pay is rather less linked to output. Workers on incremental pay scales (civil servants) score rather less on reciprocity and have an intermediate position on the output–input dimension.

## Interdependence

The above discussion has tended to assume payment schemes for individuals but there is always some degree of interdependence between individuals within an organization. In general, a shift away from the moral norms corner of Table 8.1 towards the competitive corner requires a reduction in the degree of interdependence until, as we have seen in chapter 2, we reach a market condition requiring pooled interdependence and large numbers. A shift in the reward system towards the moral corner will encourage co-operation and commitment to the organization or to the unit in question.

Overall, the reciprocal/output payment method is suitable for the technical conditions of clarity, autonomy, and large numbers. Such a contract is likely to foster competitive norms. At the other extreme, the deferred/input payment method is suitable for conditions of ambiguity, interdependence, and uniqueness. Such a contract is likely to foster moral norms.

## THE DYSFUNCTIONS OF INAPPROPRIATE REWARD SYSTEMS

### Incentive bonus schemes

A vivid account of the dysfunctions of the competitive element of incentive bonus schemes is given by Roy (1952, 1954). Although devised as an economic system by management to encourage workers to respond to opportunities to earn more, Roy observed that a great deal of the behaviour of workers was not directed towards maximizing earnings.

Two aspects of the behaviour can be discerned. First, was a considerable component explicable in terms of economic rationality. Workers were by no means disinterested in their earnings; for some ratebusters – those who consistently set out to break the prevailing output norm – this was the prime motivation. But there was a considerable component of non-economic behaviour in that workers appeared more motivated by playing a game with management.

Through intensive participant observation Roy noted that quota or output restrictions could be explained partly by economic self-interest. Because workers were given times on jobs their bonus depended upon their ability to improve on this time. They also knew that if they 'made out' too well management would find a reason for retiming an easy job thereby reducing bonuses. Workers in the machine shop would collude to keep knowledge of such 'gravy' jobs from management.

Quota restriction involved a complex social system that went beyond the machine operators themselves. Various service people, set-up men (those who set up the machines), inspectors, tool-crib men who gave out tools to operators, and time checkers who recorded the completion of jobs, were all involved in beating the system. Foremen were also an accessory to this arrangement in that they largely turned a blind eye to many happenings which went on against management rules.

Methods of beating the system involved checking off non-piece-work items after starting on a piece-work item, a procedure which involved time checkers and foremen, changing the methods of working, going in and out of the tool crib to obtain tools, and speeding up the machine which wore out tools more quickly.

The intensity with which this system was pursued and the closely knit social structure heightened the sense of playing a game against management. Management had attempted to create an economic competitive system in which workers were supposed, in part, to compete with each other but instead chose to see it as a competition with management. In the front line of this game was the time-fixer – the person who was primarily responsible for rates on jobs. It became a game in which, almost as a matter of principle, the aim was not to do things the management way.

## The difficulty of measuring performance

The problems of trying to develop appropriate output measures for professional work that is inherently ambiguous are shown by Blau's (1955) study of an employment agency. The task of the agency was to place applicants in unskilled garment industry jobs, a task that involved obtaining some basic information about experience and qualifications of applicants and trying to match these to available jobs. Initially, only one performance measurement was used to assess an interviewer's performance: the number of interviews conducted during a specific time.

The consequence of the single performance measure applied to interviewers was that, in the words of one interviewer describing the behaviour of her colleagues, 'they used to throw them out . . . they tried to get rid of them as fast as possible' (Blau 1955: 30), whether they were appropriately placed or not. The rewards were for throughput rather than for long-term placement. No note was taken of how long a person stayed in a job.

However, when the labour market became more complex due to labour shortages and differentiation of skill requirements applicants could no longer be treated as an undifferentiated mass of people. A new agency head introduced multiple measures of performance, namely: number of interviews conducted, number of clients referred to a job, number of placements following referrals, proportion of interviews resulting in placement, number of notifications sent to the unemployment insurance office, and the number of application forms made out (a service sometimes required by clients). These multiple measures were aimed at capturing the standards of performance required by a more complex job market.

An overall job performance improvement took place in terms of number of placements, and overall there was now a greater concern with placement. However, dysfunctions of the new system also became apparent. Supervisors came to rely increasingly upon statistical data to the neglect of developing co-operation with subordinates. The mixture of measures was still not an adequate representation of the required performance. For instance, interviewers could increase their performance index by placing temporarily laid off workers, or by placing workers in jobs for which they were not particularly suited and which they left after a short time. Another side effect of the new measurement system was that the measures themselves became the basis of the relationship between interviewers and supervisors giving rise to an impersonal relationship which was not satisfactory for the increasingly complex job.

## Implications

Reward systems involve measuring performance and relating the reward to performance. According to the Principle of Requisite Decision-Making Capacity the dysfunctions described above are errors of decision undercapacity. In the machine shop example described by Roy, management were assuming that all appropriate expected contributions from workers could be summarized into simple output parameters and that workers would be motivated to maximize these output parameters; the result was too crisp a structure since it ignored the requirement for innovation and co-operative behaviour. Similarly, in the case of the employment agency even the introduction of multiple performance measures produced distortions in actual behaviour since the relative weightings of the measures could not be specified. Didrickson (1989) has noted the great difficulty of evaluating performance in a social services department where social work is essentially ambiguous. The theory presented in this book would suggest that under the conditions of ambiguity and interdependence co-operative team structures need to be the unit of analysis for performance measurement; this is an aspect of Japanese management that has been stressed (Wickens 1987). Teams can be located within a hierarchy whereby group performance norms can be set up.

## THE CONTENT OF REWARDS

### A hierarchy of needs

We have assumed so far that rewards are almost synonymous with pay but the total package of inducements that participants receive covers many other factors. Maslow (1943, 1965) suggested that there are five types of needs that an individual tries to satisfy. When applied to jobs these five needs can be arranged in hierarchical order in such a way that once a lower-order need is satisfied the individual becomes concerned with the next level, and so on, until the highest level is reached (Maslow 1965, Luthans 1981: 179). The five needs are:

1  Basic needs.  In organizations the most basic needs will usually be pay, which in western society is a means of satisfying physiological needs, and working conditions which must provide the minimum level of safety to ensure physical survival and health.
2  Security needs.  Once the basic physiological needs have been satisfied, people tend to want to ensure longer-term security. In organizations this amounts to participants becoming concerned with job security, pensions, and the like. According to the hierarchy of needs, basic needs will no longer be at the forefront of consciousness but, if they cease to be satisfied, they would take over again and dominate the drives of the individual.
3  Belonging needs.  This category of needs derives from the notion that people seek affiliation and identification with their immediate peer group. According to the hierarchy principle once security has been satisfied the belonging needs come to dominate.
4  Esteem needs.  The second from highest level of needs, esteem needs, refers to the requirement to be recognized by others in terms, say, of professional recognition, and also to have self-esteem.
5  Self-actualization needs.  The highest level is the need for people to be self-fulfilled and to 'transform perception of self into reality' (Luthans 1981: 178). This is the need that is typically satisfied in organizations by creative activities but, as with the other needs,

Maslow's theory insists that as soon as any lower-level need is no longer satisfied self-actualization is no longer a motivator.

Theoretically, the hierarchy of needs has a number of weaknesses. For example, whether a given level of need is satisfied will vary widely between individuals. For one person, a physiological need may include what another person sees as a luxury non-basic need. One person may include the requirement to have a separate office as a basic need while another may consider this unnecessary. In determining what is important we are likely to have to extend our theory to include factors such as the particular social group to which a person belongs and uses as a comparison. Although there is little empirical support for the hierarchy principle (Luthans 1981: 180), Maslow's theory has a forceful intuitive feel about it and from our viewpoint it serves to alert us to the ranges of rewards that participants may seek from an organization.

## The reward package

The above discussion emphasizes that the reward system of an organization needs to be seen as a total package with a number of components. These components can be defined as: pay (already discussed), fringe benefits, career prospects, and social needs. We also need to consider the extent to which rewards are provided on an individual, group, or organizational scale, the extent to which there might be problems of equity, and the way in which the rewards might vary between different organizational functions.

### Fringe benefits

In addition to pay, organizations give other kinds of benefits which may be approximately grouped as tangible and intangible. Tangible fringe benefits are those to which some market value may be assigned and cover aspects such as company cars, medical insurance, share options, a company pension scheme, or discounts on company products. The intangible fringe benefits are those for which assigning a market value is more difficult and include aspects such as access to company sports and social facilities, or vacation and holiday entitlement. These are often known as fringe benefits, so called because they are not seen as central to the pay package although they can have an extremely important effect upon inducements and the overall reward/contribution balance.

In terms of the above contingency theory of pay, fringe benefits are low in reciprocity since they are not generally conditional upon performance. The most that can usually be done is to increase their value with service or seniority. As part of the inducement/contribution package, fringe benefits are a way of tying the individual to the organization and are therefore most appropriate for trying to inculcate a degree of commitment to the organization, that is, of increasing the moral dimension of ideology, and form a particularly important dimension to the reward/contribution balance in co-operatives and other types of collective organizations. For instance, in the Mondragon co-operative it is noted that wage levels and differentials are less than found in an equivalent capitalist enterprise (Bradley and Gelb 1982) but membership of the co-operative gives a person access to a whole range of fringe benefits available from the Mondragon community, such as education, health, social facilities, or discounts in the super-market (BBC 1980).

## Career structure

Another important aspect of the reward package is expectations concerning career. Relevant to this point are a number of aspects of a job:

1  The extent to which the job offers potential for learning and potential for valued experience.
2  The extent to which the job offers visibility and hence opportunities for promotion or mobility outside the organization.
3  The extent to which the job offers prospects of increased future earnings.

Organizations differ in the degree to which they provide career opportunities. For managerial staff an important aspect is the extent to which staff are transferred within the company. Galbraith and Nathanson (1978) report that managerial transfer in European multinational firms is a way of ensuring technology transfer and tends to lead to a decentralized structure. Such a policy on the part of a firm encourages commitment to the organization and is a way of developing moral ideology. Other organizations may take a different approach and buy-in new talent as and when required on the basis that it leads to greater flexibility. This would be more appropriate for the organization trying to develop a competitive ideology and managers would accept as part of the rules of the game that they are disposable; the implications for them would be to ensure that they maintain their marketability.

Organizations may design special jobs in order to keep valued people and to provide channels for promotion. Thus, the formal structure may not represent what might be expected in terms of the purely technical aspect of organizational design. An extra level may have been inserted to provide promotion opportunities, for instance.

## Social inducements

Research has shown (Roethlisberger and Dickson 1939, Roy 1952, 1954) that important work inducements derive from the social aspects of the job, the ability to make friends, to chat, organize out-of-work activities, and the like. Generally, the social inducements become more important in a routine technology where other aspects of the reward package are lower and where employees are not expected to develop a great commitment to the organization.

## Job satisfaction

Although research concerning the connection between job satisfaction and productivity is inconclusive the intrinsic nature of the work and the pleasure that it gives can be an important part of the reward package (Luthans 1981: 190–1).

## Equity

One problem organizations have in setting reward systems is to deal with the question of relativity of rewards. If one individual or group feels under- or over-rewarded they may feel that a principle of equity has been breached and motivation suffers accordingly (Adams 1965). Equity theory starts from the assumption that a person will compare himself or herself to another appropriate person in terms of the ratio of the outcomes (rewards) obtained from a job to the effort put in (contributions or inputs) as compared to the other person's outcomes/inputs ratio. In this theory a high ratio of outcomes to inputs is to be valued by the individual since this means a big reward for a small effort.

Equity theory states that individuals try to maintain equality of this ratio in comparison to the relevant others. Hence, for balance:

$$\frac{\text{person's outcomes}}{\text{person's inputs}} \text{ equals } \frac{\text{other's outcomes}}{\text{other's inputs}}$$

Outcomes are all the rewards obtained from a job including pay, fringe benefits, and job satisfaction. Inputs are all the contributions an individual considers to have been made to the job; these may include the direct time spent on the job and any investment already made in training, gaining qualifications, and experience. The other person(s) selected for comparison could be an individual in the same line of work, same profession, or same community. The theory does not directly give us any guidance as to how the relevant other is selected but assumes that a perceived unequal ratio requires a person to make an effort to reduce the inequity. Two cases can be seen, one when a person's ratio is lower than other's ratio and feels under-rewarded, that is:

$$\frac{\text{person's outcomes}}{\text{person's inputs}} \text{ is less than } \frac{\text{other's outcomes}}{\text{other's inputs}}$$

In the second case the person feels over-rewarded, that is:

$$\frac{\text{person's outcomes}}{\text{person's inputs}} \text{ is greater than } \frac{\text{other's outcomes}}{\text{other's inputs}}$$

In both cases the theory stresses that action will be taken to restore equity. This can come about, Adams (1965) suggests, by a person altering inputs or outcomes, cognitively distorting inputs or outcomes by inflating their inputs, or deflating the other's outputs, for example, or by leaving the situation. Alternatively, a person can act on the other's outcomes and inputs to restore balance.

A considerable amount of laboratory research has been conducted on this theory and reviews of this research are quite supportive of its main tenets (Luthans 1981), although field research is less supportive (Carrell and Dittrich 1978). Nevertheless, we seem fairly safe in concluding the following (Goodman and Friedman 1971, Luthans 1981: 198):

1 Overpaid hourly or salaried employees are likely to increase their contribution by producing more. Studies provide some support for this finding.
2 Overpaid piece-rate employees will increase quality rather than quantity. Studies strongly support this finding.
3 Underpaid hourly or salaried employees reduce quantity. Studies provide some support for this finding.

4 Underpaid piece-rate employees will increase quantity and reduce quality. This finding is strongly supported amongst the small number conducted. A person can increase earnings without substantially increasing inputs in this way.

If we take these findings as given, equity theory clearly gives some guidelines as to the possible interaction effects of changing rewards for one group of workers and takes motivation theory out of an over-individualistic stance by providing some kind of social context. But it also begs a number of important questions. In particular there is the question of how the relevant other for comparison purposes is selected. If employees feel themselves overpaid one way of coping with this is to select another reference group against which they appear to be equitably paid. Although the theory allows for this to happen there is no way of predicting whether this will happen and which relevant other will be selected.

## Variations with function

The preceding discussion derives some general aspects of reward packages offered to participants. The composition of this package will need to vary with the nature of the work and the general situation in the organization. One way of examining this question is to see how rewards might vary with sub-system function (see chapter 1 for definition of sub-systems).

As we have seen in chapter 5 the ideology in the technical core of an organization tends towards instrumental/efficiency norms and interdependence tends to be high, although there are exceptions to this. The package of rewards, therefore, will need to reflect this; generally, individual incentive bonus schemes are unsuitable if team work is high. If the technology is routine there will be little scope for intrinsic job satisfaction or little meaning to be attached to the concept of career progression. Hence, the other parts of the reward package will need to compensate for this. In the non-routine technology, rewards need to match the ability of participants to cope with technical problems.

In the boundary spanning function participants will need to be rewarded according to their ability to cope with the contingencies deriving from the environment. Individual rather than collective decisions are more usual than in the case of the technical core as seen, for example, in the selling function and hence individual incentives are more feasible. Salespersons can have rewards based upon their ability to acquire sales, purchasing people upon their ability to gain discounts. Even here, however, caution needs to be exercised since these boundary roles also interface with the technical core and rewards simply for gaining sales may conflict with the technical logic of requiring predictability in the production schedule.

The concern of the institutional function will be to ensure that rewards reflect the fitness of the organization as a whole to prepare for future action. It is at this level that rewards need to be most strongly linked overall to organizational performance norms; for the market organization directors' rewards can be linked to profitability, to share options and the like; for the agency rewards can be linked to the ability to meet output targets; for the mutual benefit organization rewards will tend to be assessed on the ability of the leader to meet the organization's moral objectives; for the charity the leader's rewards will tend to reflect the ability of the organization successfully to expand its constituency of givers and receivers.

## INSTITUTIONALIZATION OF THE INDIVIDUAL THROUGH CULTURE

The discussion of the reward/contribution balance has emphasized the purposiveness of human action and the variation this can exhibit amongst individuals. In specific situations, however, the range of knowable ways of behaving can be severely limited due to the homogenizing effect of culture and existing social structures (Thompson 1967: 102); individuals by no means consistently exhibit the restless searching behaviour that some of the above theories suggest. Culture can be seen as a set of beliefs that are held amongst people and sets the pattern of common understandings about a correct way of behaving (Smircich 1983, Schein 1984) and carrying out tasks. The concept obviously bears a close affinity to that of ideology. At the societal level culture helps to determine the basic norms that are carried into organizations to evaluate those organizations and their participants.

It is only quite recently in history that it has been more or less universally accepted that all humans are fundamentally alike (Beattie 1964). The universality of human nature, although implicit in most of the world's major religions became particularly apparent to western man with travel, trade, exploration, and colonization. Anthropology developed the study of remote tribes and nations through, in particular, the concept of culture and its comparative nature across tribes and societies. Culture is essentially about the values and beliefs held by the members of a society and hence is an important aspect of understanding ideology in organizations.

## Societal views of culture

We can usefully make a distinction between the study of culture at a societal level and at an organizational level. Over a number of years Hofstede (1980) conducted research on culture in the world-wide IBM corporation covering over 66 different countries. His intention was to discover the vital dimensions that could be used to describe societal cultural differences as they affected organizational operation. From his survey work four main dimensions emerged as significant:

1 Power distance. This dimension describes the extent to which managers and subordinates feel separated by the authority relationship between them.
2 Uncertainty avoidance. This is the extent to which individuals belonging to a culture try to control the future and generally avoid uncertainty. This dimension is associated with traditionalism, superstition, dogmatism, and authoritarianism.
3 Individualism. This dimension describes the extent to which the members of the culture wish to act on their own, or in conjunction with others (perhaps colleagues, friends, or family) in making decisions and problem solving.
4 Masculinity. The masculinity dimension highlights cultures where money, material standards, and overall 'machismo' is important. In contrast feminine cultures are supposed to put a value upon the quality of life, interpersonal relations, and a sense of service.

The scores obtained for each IBM subsidiary were taken as representative of the culture of each host country and Hofstede plots out patterns for groups of countries on these four dimensions as shown in Table 8.2.

The English-speaking group of countries (UK, US, Australia, Canada, New Zealand) displayed a profile which was very high on individualism, low on power distance, medium on uncertainty avoidance, and fairly high on masculinity. Japan was a contrast to this pattern, showing a low individualism combined with high masculinity, a low tolerance for uncertainty, and a fairly high power distance. Compared to the other nation groups the Japanese stand out as well to the right of the diagram especially in contrast to the Scandinavians who are almost an exact opposite of the Japanese on all dimensions. Germany shows a profile not dissimilar to the English-speakers but scoring rather less on individualism.

*Table 8.2* Hofstede's national cultures

| | | | | | | | |
|---|---|---|---|---|---|---|---|
| low collectivism | a | s | g | | j | | high collectivism |
| low power distance | | s | a g | | j | | high power distance |
| low uncert. avoid. | | | s | a g | | j | high uncert. avoid. |
| low masculinity | s | | | | a g | j | high masculinity |
| scale | 1 | 2 | 3 | 4 | 5 | | |

Adapted from Hofstede, G. (1980) *Culture's Consequences: International Differences in Work Related Values*, London: Sage.
*Note*: Nation groupings - a = English-speakers (US, UK, Australia); g = Germany; j = Japan; s = Scandinavia (Sweden, Denmark, Norway).
Uncert. avoid. = uncertainty avoidance.

Organizations are embedded in their nations and cannot be divorced from the wider culture. Individuals will bring with them their beliefs and values and this will affect the operation of an organization as, in particular, the discussion of the Japanese corporation shows in chapter 2.

## Organizational views of culture

As already indicated, use of the term culture has its origin in anthropological studies of organization whereby an organization is investigated in a manner similar to remote tribes in terms of ritualism and ceremonies, and other aspects of social structures. Comparing organizations to tribes has validity; anyone entering an organization for the first time can often detect an atmosphere that appears special to that organization. This uniqueness might cover a number of features – the way people dress, the manner of speech, the physical appearance of the premises, and even the smell.

Smircich (1983) defines culture as the key values and guiding beliefs shared by organizational participants. According to this definition culture obviously has an affinity to the notion of ideology as particularly demonstrated by Sathe's (1983) suggested six major aspects of organizational culture which follow.

**Shared values** These are the fundamental goals of the organization.

**Guiding beliefs** These are the fundamental understandings about how tasks should be carried out.

Shared values and guiding beliefs are seen by Sathe as the underlying culture. At the same time a more overt culture is serving the function of reinforcing and implementing the underlying values and beliefs. These two variables may also be directly compared to the two dimensions of performance norms outlined in chapter 2, namely, that norms are about the values to be pursued and about the means to achieve them.

**Ceremonies** These are rites which provide dramatic examples of beliefs and values. For example, a national day ceremony in a country (say July 4 in the United States or Bastille Day in France) reminds citizens of what the country stands for. In a firm, a ceremony may be held to launch a new product, mark a particular success, or open a new building.

**Legends and myths** These often centre upon stories of great exploits and heroism exemplifying underlying values and beliefs. National heroes (Mao Tse Tung and the Long March in China, Gandhi in India) and associated stories of great deeds can reinforce a feeling of strength or of overcoming problems against great odds. Business organizations also have their heroes.

**Language** National languages serve to reinforce values and beliefs by excluding non-speakers and by assisting communication internally. Rulers often try to impose a language upon a conquered nation, such as the Normans through the introduction of Norman French into the island of Britain. Conversely, nations asserting their independence deliberately try to preserve their language, such as the Welsh or Basques. Organizations also develop special languages which serve to unite the participants and exclude outsiders.

**Symbols** Flags, anthems, and totems also serve to reinforce values and beliefs. Every four years the Olympic flag and flame become symbols of international sportsmanship. Conversely, symbols may be ceremonially removed as a sign of a change in regime, such as the removal of statues of Queen Victoria in India which served as a reminder of British rule, or the more recent burning of Communist Party membership cards in Romania. Organizations have symbols; mottoes or creeds are used (Daft 1989: 92) to communicate the values and beliefs of the organization.

Symbolism is central to the study of culture. A symbol is something which carries information, or carries out some practical function, but is at the same time expressive (Beattie 1964: 71). Thus the wearing of certain types of dress in a business organization, while having the obvious function of protection and warmth, may carry information about rank or type of work and also take on an expressive meaning beyond the function. Ceremonial robes, which have lost any original function they may have had, are used in many types of organization – in universities for example where they are now expressive of the solemnity of certain occasions such as when students or honorary graduates undergo what Glaser and Strauss (1967) call a status change at the conferment of degrees. An increase in status is associated with the permission to wear a particular type of dress. Conversely, the use of a uniform dress is also symbolic of a desire to show that everyone is equal where the intention is to develop harmony.

A symbol may also be seen as 'something that represents another thing' (Daft 1989: 509); in practice this means that organizations can attempt to develop an ideology of commitment to common goals by directing attention to symbols that represent the fundamental values of the organization. A decision by Jaguar to re-enter motor racing at the Le Mans 24-hour race goes deeper than the desire to gain technical knowledge about the operation of high performance cars under arduous conditions; it is symbolic of the values for which management would like the company to be recognized in the eyes of the public at large, potential customers, and employees.

*Table 8.3* Ideology: norms and culture

| Culture | Norms | | | |
|---|---|---|---|---|
| | Efficiency | Instrumental | Referent | Moral |
| Values: | Non-unique | Unique | Non-unique | Unique |
| Beliefs: | Non-ambiguous | Non-ambig-uous | Ambiguous | Ambiguous |
| Legends re: | Salespeople | Administrators | Scientists | Founders |
| Language: | Price, money | Procedures | Technical | Shared meanings |
| Symbols: | Pay, bonuses | Orderly office | Accolades | Founder's shrine |
| Ceremonies: | Winners | Tidy department | Nobel prize | Service awards |

Cultures vary between organizations and within organizations. What is now particularly appropriate to our discussion is to translate these ideas into an organizational setting by suggesting a relationship to the types of performance norms as summarized in Table 8.3.

Efficiency or competitive norms are typified by attempting to perform the best from among a number of competitors. Legends may include stories of great salesmen who brought off a tricky deal; the language of salespeople covers money factors, myths about high prices sold-at, low prices bought-at, great discounts, and the like. Pay and bonuses can be key symbols; ceremonies may include a salesman of the month award or some similar award for outstanding competitive behaviour. Mintzberg (1983a) suggests that ideologies are incorporated into organizations but that such incorporation is weakest in the case of calculative norms.

Instrumental norms are typified by the reaching of a known goal and may get reinforced by means of stories about a great administrator who was able to improve the functioning of an administrative system. The language becomes that of developing new procedures, symbols might be the gaining of a larger office or better equipment, and ceremonies may emphasize the tidiest office of the year competition.

Referent norms are typified by striving to develop expertise and status within the professional peer group. Legends may be about great scientists or engineers, the language will be mainly technical, while ceremonies might centre around the presentation of accolades and meritorious awards given by an external peer group – the award of a Nobel prize to a scientist is a good example of this.

Moral norms are concerned with the unity and common values of a group stressing its own uniqueness. Legends will tend to be about great leaders who have sacrificed themselves for the good of a cause; here, religious leaders provide prominent examples although a similar effect may be found in business organizations where the founder of a company has devoted his or her life to the business. The language used becomes that of shared meanings and there may be a symbolic shrine to the founder, maybe a statue or portrait, which is the focus for periodic ceremonies. Incorporation of ideology by means of moral norms gives rise to identification (Mintzberg 1983a) with a cause whereby there is an evoked set of norms (Mills 1956) derived especially from a process of socialization, indoctrination, and inspirational stories (Bendix 1956).

## Culture and ideology

We are suggesting here the notion that organizational culture is part of organizational ideology. As we have stressed, culture has a wider environmental aspect to it in the sense that participants bring the external culture of their society or nation with them into an organization and the organization develops a sub-variety of that wider culture. As Gouldner (1954) shows, an organization which is tightly embedded in a local community comes to be dominated by the values and beliefs of that community, that is, through a local cultural orientation. Conflicts arise when a manager from a more cosmopolitan world who does not appreciate or accept that culture as relevant to a business organization intervenes to make changes.

Filby and Wilmott (1988) interpret organizational culture in terms of the way in which myths reinforce an organizational ideology, especially as regards power relationships. This notion is illustrated through the case of a public relations department within a large public bureaucracy. The ideology of public relations work emphasizes its ambiguous nature and the ex-journalists, who largely staffed this department, made it clear that their ideology did not fit with that of a bureaucracy. Following bureaucratic (instrumental) norms the personnel department did not accept a high job grading given by a manager in the public relations department to an assistant, on the basis that jobs should be scaled according to the number of people supervised and that this assistant did not supervise anyone. The manager giving the grading thought that the concept of accountability was meaningless in that particular context since people within the unit would carry out any job according to the need of the moment. However, rather than face a battle with the bureaucracy the manager rewrote the job description stating that the assistant would be in charge of the department upon the manager's absence. Personnel then accepted the grading.

The myth in this case is a bureaucratic one concerning account- ability and the notion that the more subordinates reporting to a manager the more that manager is worth to the organization. Due to the ambiguity of the work (at least in the eyes of the public relations staff) it is an idea that is difficult to apply in this context but, on the other hand, a public bureaucracy is held accountable by external assessors and therefore has to carry this myth into the organization. Participants acting informally in this way reinforce the myth but at the same time create a dual structure (Meyer and Rowan 1977) of 'double talk' (Brunsson 1989) loosely coupled to one another (Weick 1976), one for external consumption, the other informal, internal, for day-to-day use, enabling participants to get on with their jobs. As Brunsson (1989) points out, a major output of a large political organization is the structure developed; in the absence of concrete outputs such organizations take care to conform to the expectations of dominant supporters as to the structures they adopt. Hence, an organization may form an equal opportunities committee to show that they are doing something about racial and gender discrimination. The reality of the extent to which policies are effected may show little change.

Culture, and myths as part of culture, we suggest, can be most usefully viewed as reinforcing a particular organizational ideology. The public relations example emphasizes that there can be inconsistencies between the official (formal) norms in an organization and the actual (informal) norms which guide participants, especially those at a lower level in an organization. In this sense, the kinds of implicit bargaining between machine operators, foremen, and ratefixers reported by Roy (1952, 1954) is comparable to the kinds of implicit bargaining related by Filby and Wilmott (1988) previously. In both cases lower-level participants conspire to push the rules to the limit during the day-to-day negotiation of the reward/contribution balance; in both cases the result has to be interpreted into a language acceptable to the organization but that takes on a symbolic nature. In the case of incentive bonus schemes the myth that real productivity is being measured has to be preserved for symbolic reasons; in the case of the public relations department the myth that numbers supervised is a measure of worth also has to be preserved. It is a myth that can suit both management and the lower-level participants since it allows the organization to continue functioning.

## IDEOLOGY AND CONTEXT

The discussion to this point has concentrated upon the concept of ideology, how individuals are institutionalized by ideology, and how ideology is related to structure. The other key aspect of ideology within the institutional model of organization concerns the connection between ideology and context.

Our earlier discussion of context included environmental and technological factors. These factors have perhaps been presented as rather hard and fast, as aspects which an organization has to accept as the objective reality. Thus, competition may be seen as something which can be counted as real and objective. But environments have to be interpreted (Johnson 1987) as can be shown by a simple experiment. In a study of non-profit organizations (there is no significance in the non-profit aspect since a similar experiment could equally as well have been conducted on for-profit organizations) chief executives were asked to name the 'significant other' organizations against which they compared their organization's performance (Butler and Wilson 1990). The answers showed that different chief executives facing similar objective realities could give quite different interpretations of their environments. Of particular interest were the answers given by the chief executives of two major Third World agencies, both roughly the same size and involved in many similar projects throughout the world. One chief executive saw his organization as facing five significant others while the other chief executive gave only one other organization as significant.

What we are seeing here are the different interpretations put upon an environment; environments are, in a sense, creations of the minds of key individuals. It is not only that context sets the scene within which organizational participants act out their parts (Mangham 1987) but that context is set by the ideology brought by organizational participants to a particular situation.

As explained, ideology consists of the values and beliefs that social actors bring with them to a situation. For convenience we have summed up the values and beliefs of particular relevance to the question of ideology in organizations by the polar extremes of robustness and focus. Going back to the example of the chief executives of the non-profit organizations defining their contexts, we would propose that one chief executive was displaying a robust ideology in seeing many significant others, the other a focused ideology in selecting few. Robustness leads to a complex context, focus to a simple context.

## Ideology and strategic choice

An important aspect of context concerns the strategic choices made by an organization and how these are affected by ideology. Whittington (1989) argues that organizational decision makers are located within a social structure and that the nature of this social structure will affect the kinds of strategic choices made; it is not just a matter of environment in the objective sense of that word that determines strategy. In line with the argument of the institutional model, ideology plays a key role in shaping strategic choice. Thus, the relevant local ideologies concern the beliefs and values held by the powerful organizational decision makers concerning how the organization sees its environment and lines itself up to this environment. These beliefs provide both constraints and opportunities for action. It is in this sense that Simon (1964) notes that organizations do not have objectives, merely that participating individuals have constraints within which they can act. The crisp organization sets tight constraints, the fuzzy sets elastic ones.

In addition to the notions of focus and robustness there are a number of other aspects to local ideologies that appear relevant to the definition of strategic choice (Fox 1971). First, ideology has an evaluative component meaning that there are beliefs about the objectives for which it is appropriate to strive; some firms, for instance, may place market share above profitability through pursuing a growth-first strategy. Second, there is a cognitive component to ideology defining what is possible; for the firm pursuing a growth strategy there would be associated instrumentalities as to how this could be achieved, perhaps stressing ever-increasing economies of scale in production. Third, ideology provides ways of legitimizing the actions of the organization to the wider institutional environment; hence the firm pursuing growth and market share might stress the public service through cutting costs and contributing to the country's exports.

## The sources of ideology

The question now becomes: if ideology is the values and beliefs brought by participants to organizational decisions what is the origin of these values and beliefs? One source has been suggested above, namely, the rules of the game written into the structures of the organization. But, as Whittington (1989) points out, participants are also located within a wider social structure; ideas do not just originate in the individual alone (Mannheim 1936) but also from various group memberships. Here the notion of 'the web of group affiliation' put forward by Simmel (1955), whereby individuals are simultaneously members of a number of different groups with these overlapping memberships providing referents and sources of values and beliefs, is relevant to considering how social structure affects ideology.

Whittington (1989: 295) has suggested four such group memberships as important in considering strategic choice, namely: class, generation, gender, and ethnicity. Other group memberships could be thought of but if we stick to Whittington's, he attempts to show how top managers in the firms he studied, who were exclusively male, belonging to a capitalist class, and many of whom were Jewish, brought their ideologies to bear upon choosing strategy. For instance Jewish family life provides a close-knit web of affiliation and it was from this external referent that these particular managers drew ideas about the kinds of strategy the business should pursue, the kinds of technology to be used, and the kinds of appropriate structures.

Other types of external affiliations can also provide important referents for ideology. Educational institutions attended, religious convictions, or professional memberships can be major sources of ideological beliefs. Strong group affiliations provide filters and stimuli for interpreting the environment; the context becomes, in part, socially constructed (Berger and Luckmann 1966) rather than an objective reality although, as mentioned, there will be externally-imposed constraints upon available strategic choices.

## The affiliative web

Group affiliations can overlap one another to such an extent that a 'power elite' (Mills 1956) results. Such a power elite, Mills suggests, comes about through managers coming from a limited range of owning families, attending a limited range of schools, attending particular business schools, belonging to the same golf club, and so on. This is essentially a class-based theory of the control of major business corporations and of other major institutions which, Mills indicates, is not simply restricted to class-ridden 'old' Europe but also applies in the 'new' world of the United States.

The significant aspect of such a power elite is that strategic choices would be made within a limited range of 'recipes' (Grinyer and Spender 1979). Whatever theory of class is applied to a particular society the complex web of group affiliations provides a source of the ideas and constraints that are brought to bear in defining strategic choice.

We might at this point make the following proposition: the greater the diversity of the web of the group affiliations (or the affiliative web) of the management of an organization the greater the ideological robustness. Conversely, the more restricted the affiliative web the more focused the ideology. The recipe, then, for an organization trying to expand its degrees of freedom in relation to its environment – that is, to increase the range of strategic choices – lies in the seeking out of management with a diverse affiliative web. In Whittington's (1989) terms, this would mean expanding gender, ethnicity, class, and generation and not constricting these variables. In Simon's (1964) terms it would mean loosening the constraints upon decision makers. In terms of the actual actions taken in an organization in order to increase the degrees of freedom it is easier to define some of the things that should not be done rather than the things that should be done; it would mean not recruiting managers who went to similar schools, who live in the same area, who are of the same religion or ethnicity, who went to the same business school, and so on.

A word of warning. To create a robust ideology in this way without also allowing context, structure, and decision-making strategies to change would cause a misfit in the model. In practice the misfit would be evidenced by the presence of a diverse, able management team all raring to go but who are constrained by existing structures and prevented from exerting due influence over decisions. The organization would exhibit errors of decision undercapacity, setting the scene for great frustration and wasting of managerial talent.

## DESIGN IMPLICATIONS AND SUMMARY

Ideologies concern the underlying norms that are used in making decisions. A focused ideology is singular, particular, and efficiency oriented and is appropriate for a crisp organization. A robust ideology is plural, tolerant, and moral and is appropriate for a fuzzy organization.

A fuzzy structure emphasizes implicitness, symbolism, supportiveness, collectivism, and decentralization all of which foster a robust ideology. Conversely, a crisp structure emphasizes formality, centralization, individualism, punishment, and literalism all of which foster a focused ideology. The principle variables of the institutional model discussed in this chapter are given in Figure 8.1.

Participants form a contract with an organization in which there are expectations about the reward/contribution balance. Each contract communicates certain information concerning the ideology of the organization through giving indicators as to the type of performances that will be rewarded, and which will be punished. Some contracts are fuzzy, others crisp. The requisite decision-making capacity is likely to be achieved when the nature of the reward/contribution contract matches the ideology.

*Figure 8.1* The contingent institutional model of organization: salient variable relationships discussed in this chapter

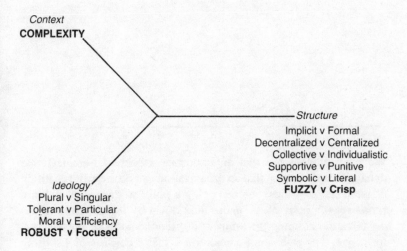

*Context*
**COMPLEXITY**

Structure
Implicit v Formal
Decentralized v Centralized
Collective v Individualistic
Supportive v Punitive
Symbolic v Literal
**FUZZY v Crisp**

*Ideology*
Plural v Singular
Tolerant v Particular
Moral v Efficiency
**ROBUST v Focused**

Total rewards consist of pay, fringe benefits, social factors, and career opportunities. The reward/contribution balance can be classified on a reciprocal-deferred dimension and an input/output dimension. Hence, the reciprocal/output condition is most appropriate for competitive/efficiency norms; in practice this means rewarding participants on incentive bonus schemes or profit sharing and the like. Conversely, when a moral ideology is required rewards need to tend towards the deferred/input condition.

As ideology consists of the underlying values and beliefs held in an organization, culture is a major factor in the fostering of ideology. Organizations are influenced by the culture of their host societies but also develop specific internal cultures which can also vary internally. The importance of symbolism in developing ideology has been pointed to.

# Chapter nine

# Coalition management

We have emphasized that an important aspect of organizational dynamics is the notion that an organization can be seen as a coalition of interests, that these interests play a political game but within a broad set of 'rules of the game' laid down by the structure of the organization defining the limits of discretion and of acceptable performance. The essence of a coalition is that it consists of a shifting alliance of interests in which, while having to take note of the rules of the game, individuals and groups will manoeuvre to improve their position within the organization. The rules set constraints but are flexible and, to varying degrees, open to negotiation; the fuzzier the organization, the greater the flexibility.

We do not wish to imply that this kind of political action is necessarily detrimental to an organization or immoral. Rather, that individuals will take note of their reward/contribution balance and take action to acquire what they consider their due within an acceptable bargaining zone (Abell 1975). The organization that can demonstrate its fitness for future action will be one that is able to manage this process of organizational flux.

## ORGANIZATIONAL POWER

As political behaviour is a key dimension in coalition management it is important to understand the origins of power and how power affects, and is affected by, the political structure of an organization.

There are a number of terms in the English language related to the notion of power: power itself may be said to be the ability to get other people to do things they might not otherwise do (Dahl 1957), influence (Wrong 1968) is the process of exerting power, and authority (Weber 1968) is the voluntary compliance of people with the power that another has. These definitions highlight the distinction between three terms that are in everyday use. Power is a potential to act; whether action is taken depends upon a number of other factors such as the motivation to act. Influence is a process of getting others to do things. Authority is vested within the rules surrounding a position and in the voluntary acceptance of those rules; in formal organizations this tends to flow down a hierarchy. There is also another aspect of power, which we call rule power (Lukes 1974; Clegg 1979), deriving from the institutionalized rules of an organization (or, on a wider scale, a society) whereby people are powerful because of the position they inhabit within a social structure and/or the ability that the structure gives them to bias decisions in the way they wish. An organizational example of rule power is the ability that the chairperson of a committee has to set the agenda of meetings whereby it is possible to filter out items for discussion that are not wanted by the chair.

## Vertical power

The design of an organization lays down a system of control and authority outlining tasks and the decision-making discretion available to participants in different positions (Pfeffer 1978). An underlying source of vertical power is that of formal position. As soon as a person is promoted upwards in a hierarchy certain rights accrue to that person which were previously not available and, in general, the extent of these rights increases as a hierarchy is ascended. Formal power may be seen as equivalent to legitimate power (French and Raven 1959) deriving from the rational–legal authority (Weber 1968).

Some major rights that flow from a position in a hierarchy can provide the ability to:

- Control resources, e.g., access to a budget which may be used to reward people (French and Raven 1959).
- Control decision premises, e.g., due to formal position a manager may have a greater ability than others to set decision premises by writing the agenda for a meeting thereby circumscribing the topics of discussion to those of interest to that manager (Pfeffer 1981).
- Network centrality, e.g., a manager who has a central place within an information network and access to other top people (Pettigrew 1973) can come to gain power over those without these factors.

## Upward and horizontal power

Although the above factors are generally assumed to increase with higher formal position this need not always be the case. Lower-level participants are not powerless (Mechanic 1962); in fact it is not desirable that they should be so but they have to go about acquiring power in different ways from more senior people. In particular they will not have the same automatic fund of organizational rules, resources, and access to information and other top people that senior managers have. They have to work harder to acquire power and to rely more upon the sources of power such as expertise, persuasion, manipulation, reputation for reliability built up over time, or chance access to information or to the corridors of power acquired during their work. The case of Kenny, the computer specialist who swayed a computer purchase decision in a particular direction using his access to senior management (Pettigrew 1973) is a good example of how more junior people can come to influence more senior people.

Participants at a given level may not have the same power although formally the organization may consider them equal. For example, the production and personnel directors in a manufacturing firm may be at the same level in an organizational hierarchy but one may come to exert considerably more influence over decision making than another.

## Bases of interpersonal power

Because of the importance of non-formal sources of power in an organization the question of how one individual can come to influence another, regardless of formal authority, takes on a particular significance. This is the question of interpersonal power. French and Raven (1959) discuss how one person (P) can influence another person (O). They see the problem as the extent to which a person can draw upon certain social resources, or bases of power, which can then be used to influence the other person. Five such bases of power are now outlined:

**Legitimate or formal power**  Already discussed in this chapter, this base of power derives from the 'oughtness' of O following P's wishes because of P's office or position and is closely related to Weber's (1968) rational–legal authority.

**Reward power**    This is based upon the ability to provide the other person with valued objects, which may be money, promotions in an organization, or recognition. These valued possessions may be under P's control and O therefore will respond to the expectation of a reward from P. This expectation will usually be based upon O's experience of receiving rewards and will also depend upon an accurate perception on the part of P as to what O counts as a reward. Over time, the utilization of rewards (instead of merely promises of rewards) by P is likely to increase the attraction of O for him or her, and hence begin to develop moral power as described below.

**Moral power**    Power of this nature derives from a 'feeling of oneness' of one person with another (what French and Raven call referent power). Moral power is essentially a power in which one person identifies with the values held by another. This identification can occur because one person is a member of a reference group or because of identification with a common set of values or ideology. Thus, moral power is a power base that we might particularly expect to find at work in religious or voluntary organizations. It can, though, operate effectively in small units or groups within economic organizations, especially under conditions in which a group is singled out as special, such as when a project group has been formed to develop a new material, or product, or some project requiring the close working together of a group of specially picked members.

**Expert power**    If O attributes to P special knowledge which O values but does not possess then P can be said to have expert power over O. One aspect of expert power is that its range is limited to the specific area or discipline in which P is an acknowledged expert. It is also a power base that can erode as O learns P's skills.

**Coercive power**    This is based upon P's ability to manipulate the withdrawal of objects desired by O. In addition to the removal of desired objects, coercion can involve inflicting punishment which may be physical or involve loss of face, humiliation, damaging of reputation, and the like. The consistent use of coercion is likely to reduce the mutual attraction between O and P.

There is clearly a link between these bases of power and organizational ideology and norms already outlined. Reward power is likely to be a predominant power base in an organization where competitive/

efficiency norms predominate; legitimate power is appropriate to the bureaucracy where instrumental norms predominate; expert power belongs to the referent ideology and professional organization. Coercive power we reserve for a special category to be seen as the negative of the other four power bases; what counts as coercion will also depend upon the ideology of that organization. In general, we see the exercise of coercive power as an unusual and last resort act in modern organizations. Coercion in a market is used to reduce the earnings of an individual, in a hierarchy to demote or fire, in professional work to remove specially interesting work, and within a collective to ridicule and ostracize (Butler 1980b, 1983). The power base and the act of using it cannot be divorced from the prevailing system of norms; as with the discussion of norms we have to accept that few situations offer a pure case and mixed types are practised.

## THE STRATEGIC CONTINGENCIES OF POWER

In addition to the power that derives from the overall rules of the game and ideology of an organization, power also derives from the strategic position of individuals within the workflow of an organization. Individuals are located within the structure of an organization. They belong to functional groupings which can gain or lose power as the contingencies facing the organization change over time. The strategic contingencies approach to power sees the power of managers as emanating from the location of their department or sub-unit within a social structure and upon their ability to draw upon a functional position which the sub-unit possesses within the overall workflow and problem-solving activities of the organization (Hickson *et al.* 1971).

The outcomes of power can be assessed by the influence that individual managers have over a range of decisions in an organization through:

1 Weight. This is the amount of influence wielded by each manager on a particular decision issue, and
2 Scope. This is the number of decision issues over which influence is exerted.

According to this theory the variables leading to power are seen to be:

— Centrality. The extent to which a particular sub-unit's activities are interdependent with the activities of other sub-units in the organizational workflow.

— Immediacy. The extent to which stoppage of a unit would affect operation of the whole organization.
— Non-substitutability. The extent to which it is difficult to replace a particular unit.

High centrality, immediacy, and non-substitutability together create a condition of high dependence of the organization upon a unit. This is typically the position of a production department within a manufacturing firm. Additionally there is:

— Coping with uncertainty. The extent to which a unit deals with uncertainties critical to organization and the final variable seen to lead to power (see Table 9.1).

*Table 9.1* Strategic contingencies leading to power

| | | |
|---|---|---|
| CENTRALITY | | |
| interdependence in workflow | | |
| IMMEDIACY | | |
| speed with which workflow can be stopped | all lead to | POWER |
| NON-SUBSTITUTABILITY | | influence over decisions |
| difficulty of replacing | | |
| COPING WITH UNCERTAINTY | | |
| ability to resolve critical problems | | |

*Source*: Hickson, D.J., Hinings, C.R., Lee, C.A., Schneck, R.E., and Pennings, J.M. (1971) 'A strategic contingencies theory of intraorganizational power', *Administrative Science Quarterly*, 16 (2): 216–29.

Coping with uncertainty is a particularly important variable in explaining the power of managers; it assesses the extent to which a manager's department is dealing with new problems and key issues in the organization and is especially representative of an organization as an open system responding to environmental problems. It is possible to consider a unit (such as a production department) scoring high on immediacy, centrality, and non-substitutability but achieving a relatively small influence over decisions because its task is so routinized that it deals with almost no new problems. The question now is whether it is possible to consider a unit which does not have much in the way of immediacy, centrality, and non-substitutability factors but which achieves power because it is dealing with perceived new problems emanating from the environment?

Such an instance was found in a study conducted to examine power relationships of managers in brewing and packaging companies (Hinings *et al.* 1974). These organizations had a simple functional structure. The relative influence of the managers of production, sales, personnel, and accounting departments in each of seven organizations was assessed by all managers rating the influence of all other managers over a range of seventeen decision issues covering the following categories:

— Sales. For example: marketing strategies, new products, product packaging, price, interpretation of the alcohol licensing laws.
— Engineering. For example: obtaining equipment, operation of equipment.
— Production. For example: obtaining raw materials, product quality, production efficiency, overall production plan.
— Finance. For example: overall capital budget, overall non-capital budget, reviews of the non-capital budget.
— Personnel. For example: salary revision, training and development, labour relations.

From this it was possible to compute an overall perceived power rating of each department head in each firm. The researchers also assessed the extent to which each department controlled the strategic contingencies within their organizations. That is, departments were assessed as to the degree of immediacy, centrality, non-substitutability, and coping with uncertainty they possessed. From this data it was possible to assess the effect of the strategic factors upon the power of sub-unit heads as shown in the results in Table 9.2.

Table 9.2 The strategic contingencies of sub-unit power: the case of breweries and packaging companies

| Power Rank | Strategic contingency variables | | | | |
|---|---|---|---|---|---|
| | Coping | Immed | Non-sub | Cent | |
| first 1 | h | h | h | h | 7 production depts |
| 2 | h | m | l | l | 5 marketing depts |
| 3 | l | m | h | m | 3 engineering, 2 marketing, 2 accounting depts |
| last 4 | l | l | l | h | 5 accounting depts |

Source: Hinings, C.R., Hickson, D.J., Pennings, J.M., and Schneck, R.E. (1974) 'Structural conditions of intraorganizational power', Administrative Science Quarterly 19 (1): 22–43.
Notes: Coping is coping with uncertainty; Immed is immediacy; Non-sub is non-substitutability; Cent is centrality, h = high, m = medium, l = low scores on these variables.

The results confirmed that those departments which have high scores on all the strategic variables are ranked first in terms of influence over a broad range of decisions. Without exception these were production departments. There is nothing particularly startling in this finding; what is the most interesting aspect of the results are the second rank departments which are five marketing departments. These all score low on non-substitutability and centrality, medium on immediacy, but high on coping with uncertainty thereby showing the particular importance of coping with uncertainty as a source of power within an organization.

At the time of the study these organizations were operating in relatively stable markets. They were production oriented. The uncertainties that did exist were coped with by marketing through gathering and interpreting environmental data but these departments were not seen as at all central in the workflow and were substitutable in the sense that some of the work could be done by an outside agency or perhaps by other internal people.

The last departments in order of influence were five accounting departments which were seen as very central – since accounting information affects most corners of these organizations – but are very low on coping with uncertainty, immediacy, and non-substitutability.

Some implications of the strategic contingency theory of power can be drawn. First, department heads can increase their power by their departments becoming more central, more immediate, less substitutable, and through coping with uncertainty. This is the obvious implication and generally confirms the theory. What is less obvious is that coping with uncertainty was shown to be more important than the other variables but that it is not enough on its own. Third, high centrality is not enough to achieve influence as shown by the accounting departments.

This conclusion is not limited to manufacturing organizations but can also be applied to very different organizations such as universities. In universities a key aspect of workflow leading to centrality and non-substitutability is the ability to bring in research funding, and Pfeffer and Salancik (1974) found this ability to be a strong determinant of the influence that department heads exerted over university decision making and, in particular, over their ability to gain a favourable budget. The specific context of the university differs from that of a simple functional manufacturing organization in that departmental representation upon university committees is a visible way in which a department influences decision making. Once a department has acquired this position, however, its power becomes a self-reinforcing process since it is now in a position to further influence the budgetary decision in its favour.

## The dynamic

An important aspect of the strategic contingencies theory is not that it is indicating that one particular type of department or function is automatically more powerful than another but that power depends upon the contingencies obtaining at any time. The theory allows us to predict the kinds of changes in power balance that may take place in an organization which is facing some change in its context. For instance, a firm in a stable task environment may have been producing the same product for many years with a stable technology. During this period the major decisions will most likely have been most heavily affected by production and then finance, but the firm finds that the market is changing. The major problems are now seen to be assessing changing market needs and producing new designs to match these. We could predict a shift in power to marketing and research and development.

At one level the strategic contingencies theory of power can be seen as a functional theory stating that those sub-units and their managers which are the most critical to the organization gain power. In general and across a large number of organizations this accords with everyday experience. If a firm did not allow this to happen an open systems perspective of organization would predict that it would not survive over the long term.

However, a notable part of the theory concerns the dynamic by which power relationships might resist these contingent changes in an organization, or alternatively, how internal units can use opportunities to change the power balance in their favour. The variable of coping with uncertainty emphasizes the importance of a rare and specialized expertise in gaining power. An example of this comes from an investigation in a French tobacco monopoly (Crozier 1964) of the manner by which maintenance engineers were able to cling to a degree of power that their formal position in the organization would not suggest they possessed. Their power base was the possession of a unique knowledge of how to run and maintain old and decrepit machinery which kept on breaking down and which, without their expertise, would not operate.

This is not an unusual situation in organizations and may be related to the discussion of the ways in which lower-order members of a hierarchy can gain power. We also see this phenomenon when personal assistants to high-level managers gain information which gives them power over other high-level managers, or when other kinds of technical experts such as information systems analysts have an expertise which is of special value in the organization. In the case of the maintenance engineers they had acquired their expertise through long experience and intimate knowledge of the idiosyncrasies of the equipment. It was essentially a local rather than cosmopolitan knowledge (Gouldner 1957) and therefore not available outside the organization. Machine stoppages were the only major happenings which could not be predicted in an organization in which most activities were highly routinized and for which standard procedures had not been developed.

There were three important aspects to the strategy employed by the maintenance engineers to keep their position. First, was a strategy towards the operators of the equipment who were mainly women. The maintenance men were insistent that they were the only ones with the necessary skill to keep the machines going and took every opportunity to reinforce this by pointing to the bad consequences following those rare occasions when an 'unqualified' operator had interferred.

Second, was a strategy which strongly resisted any formalization of their activities. Any blueprints that had existed disappeared. Everything was done by rule of thumb without written instructions. They emphasized that the only way in which the skill could be learned was by on-the-job learning.

Third, was a strategy towards their bosses, the technical engineers. Since their bosses had no access to the relevant information there was no way in which the maintenance engineers could be closely supervised.

It is now possible to lay down some general rules as to how participants can exploit positions of discretion to increase their power and to examine possible routes to greater power. Hinings *et al.* (1974) give two such routes. First, is a route where there is already a fair degree of immediacy. Here the technique is to foresee areas of forthcoming high uncertainty and to move into one of these. This can be seen when someone perhaps makes a sideways move to a new position in a hierarchy which may appear inexplicable to many others in the organization since others have not yet understood how this area might develop; but some positive action to cope with uncertainty has to be taken requiring the acquisition of new skills which no one else has and from this extend activities (increase centrality) to more areas of the organization.

The second route starts from a lower existing power position but still requires the prediction of an area of high uncertainty. This person has got to work harder since skills still have to be acquired to reduce substitutability, immediacy has to be increased and so does centrality. Further, the risk of failure is higher since if an incorrect prediction has been made there is no fall back position. Route two, so to speak, puts all eggs into one basket.

## COALITION MANAGEMENT: THE BRADFORD STUDIES

To this point we have noted the manner by which individuals may gain power within an organization. The managerial problem, however, is to be able to contain political behaviour within manageable bounds by a process of coalition management.

One approach to the study of coalition behaviour and its management has been to investigate the processes of top level decision making. It is only recently that a systematic attempt has been made to observe the processes of strategic decision making across a large number of decision issues in many different types of organization (Hickson *et al*. 1986).

The Bradford Studies examined 150 strategic decisions in 30 organizations of many different types ranging across a spectrum of manufacturing and service, and public and private organizations. Detailed observations and interviews were carried out concerning the processes used in a range of decisions within each organization and covering a number of topics. Generally, these were high level or 'top decisions', involving the long-term strategy of the organization covering a range of issues dealing with matters such as the introduction of new products, closing down facilities and factories, reorganizations, mergers or acquisitions, personnel matters, or investment in new equipment. Observations were made concerning a number of specific variables of the processes as follows:

**Scrutiny** This is the basic process of searching, designing, and evaluating solutions and includes the following sub-processes:

— Sources. In an organization participants search for information beyond that which is contained within themselves and an important

aspect of this search is the number of different sources and experts that are called upon.
— Information variability. This is the extent to which the information collected is considered to be of doubtful reliability.
— Information externality. This is the extent to which information is sought from outside the organization.
— Effort. Some information is more readily available in organizations than other information. Effort is a measure of the work that has to go into collecting, collating, and generating that information. Effort may range from information available from personal knowledge or opinions (low effort), through information readily obtained from records, to information synthesized by integrating diverse sources of information (high effort) in order to design optional solutions and to evaluate them.

**Interaction**   Decision making within an organization involves social interaction between participants of various kinds. Two types of interaction seemed particularly important:

— Formal. Organizations may try to channel a decision formally through committees or any number of formal procedures that may exist.
— Informal. A great deal of interaction in organizations is informal involving discussions over lunch, in corridors, or elsewhere.

**Negotiation**   When decisions involve more than one participant, negotiation is liable to occur in all except the most simple cases. A number of possibilities can be seen ranging from the decision being not open to negotiation, through to negotiation occurring only in the final stages, to negotiation resulting in limited consensus.

**Delays**   Impediments, or 'interrupts' (Mintzberg *et al*. 1976), in the smooth flow of a decision may occur for a number of reasons ranging from problems of sequencing, through awaiting priority in the order of attention, solving and awaiting further investigations, to awaiting to overcome resistance to change.

**Duration**   Some decisions are made more quickly than others as measured by the time between an issue being deliberately considered in the organization and final authorization.

**Level**   The extent to which a decision is centralized or decentralized is usually considered to be a major variable of decision making in an organization.

The general assumptions behind the research were those of the decision-making model already outlined in chapter 3 whereby it was proposed that, as uncertainty about means and uncertainty about ends increase so too would there be a tendency for the activities under the process variable headings to increase as the organization attempts to cope with the uncertainties associated with a decision.

However, the Bradford Studies used the term 'complexity' to capture the notion of means uncertainty, and the term 'politicality' to capture the notion of ends uncertainty. Hence, it would be expected that, for example, the various forms of interaction and information search increase as complexity and politicality increase.

One aim of the research was to discover what happened in organizations as they struggled to make major decisions. The data were subjected to a cluster analysis to establish patterns of decision making. Three distinct patterns or clusters emerged as shown in Table 9.3. The first, the sporadic cluster, consists of a group of fifty-three decisions with more delays, impediments, scrutiny (on all sub-variables), informal interaction, and duration, and were authorized at the highest level in the organization following some negotiation.

*Table 9.3* Three ways of making top decisions

| Decision process cluster | | |
|---|---|---|
| CONSTRICTED (narrowly channelled) | FLUID (steadily paced, quick, formally channelled) | SPORADIC (informally spasmodic and protracted) |
| Less: Scrutiny, effort Interaction, formal | Less: Scrutiny Delays Impediments Duration | Some: Negotiation More: Delays Impediments Scrutiny Interaction, informal Duration |
| More: Scrutiny, sources | Some: Negotiation More: Interaction, formal | |
| Lower level | Highest level | Highest level |

Adapted from Hickson, D.J., Butler, R.J., Cray, D., Mallory, G.R., and Wilson, D.C. (1986) *Top Decisions: Strategic Decision-Making in Organizations*, Oxford: Basil Blackwell; San Francisco: Jossey-Bass.

Overall these decisions may be described as informally spasmodic and protracted.

As a means of managing the coalition of a very wide range of British organizations, the sporadic method was used in about one-third of the decisions studied. This sporadic cluster may be contrasted to the fluid cluster (consisting of forty-two decisions) where it can be seen that these decisions experienced less delays, impediments, scrutiny (all constituent sub-variables), and duration, sone negotiation and more formal interaction, but were still authorized at the highest level. Overall, these decisions may be described as steadily paced, quick, and formally channelled.

The third group, the constricted decision cluster (forty-one decisions), is characterized by less scrutiny effort, negotiation, and formal interaction than the other decision types, is authorized below the highest level but, paradoxically, uses more scrutiny sources than does the fluid. Overall these may be seen as narrowly-channelled decisions.

## Which method of coalition management?

Is there some guidance we can now give to managers as to the method of coalition management to use when a decision issues arises? To answer this question the Bradford Studies also assessed the associated complexity and politicality of the various decision issues. In general,

*Table 9.4* Decision modes and topic issues

| | | Complexity | |
| | Low | | High |
| --- | --- | --- | --- |
| Politicality — Low | | rare non-contentious FLUID | |
| | familiar non-serious non-contentious CONSTRICTED | | unusual serious interest diversity contentious external influence |
| Politicality — High | | | SPORADIC |

Adapted from Hickson, D.J., Butler, R.J., Cray, D., Mallory, G.R., and Wilson, D.C. (1986) *Top Decisions: Strategic Decision-Making in Organizations*, Oxford: Basil Blackwell; San Francisco: Jossey-Bass.

those decisions displaying the most complexity and politicality were treated in a sporadic way and hence the sporadic issues were found to be those involving many diverse interests, were serious in their potential consequences, contentious, and externally influenced (see Table 9.4).

Those decisions which were slightly less on complexity but least of all on politicality tended to be treated in a fluid manner. The really distinguishing feature here over the sporadically treated issues is that the fluid issues were less serious but rarer (more unusual). Hence, it appears that top management wanted to hold these decisions in their hands permitting only that degree of delegation that can be formally managed.

Decision issues with the least complexity and politicality were handled by the fluid process. The distinguishing feature here is that they were familiar (programmed) issues involving internal interests only and were non-contentious.

## Dynamics of the coalition

The Bradford group found that organizational type had little effect upon the top decision-making processes. In other words, any one organization was, with some exceptions, equally likely to experience sporadic, fluid, or constricted decision processes. The important determinant was the nature of the issue topic. Organizations, therefore, appear to adjust their dynamics of coalition management to the issue in hand.

**Sporadic dynamics** The most difficult instance of coalition management occurs when complexity and politicality are high and the sporadic mode is the appropriate way to provide the requisite decision-making capacity. The sporadic mode bears comparison to the garbage can model of decision making described by Cohen *et al*. (1972) and outlined in chapter 3 – a large number of interests have the potential to become involved and there are solutions waiting to be matched up to choices. However, this image overstates the anarchic nature of the process.

The Insight, 'Reorganization of Pathology Services' (chapter 3), is an example of a sporadic decision. Here the coalition was very large, with many medical disciplines and outlying hospitals with an interest in the issue. The issue, however, was only defined over time as it was realized that the best possible technical performance was not being achieved and the cost factor became more critical; the issue needed the bringing together of these two aspects, aspects which were highlighted by the preceding organizational changes in the health service. Solutions had to be designed and carefully analysed in terms of cost and technical feasibility and advantages, but there were minimum performance standards which acted as constraints. Politicality and complexity were high. However, the organization could survive and continue to operate without the reorganization; in the end, action had to be authorized at the highest level in the organization.

**Fluid dynamics**   A different situation can arise when an issue presents little disparity over the ends desired, but the means present some uncertainties. As we have seen, this is the situation in which the fluid process is most appropriate.

An example of the fluid process occurred in a finance company, Probity, which had the opportunity to purchase an ailing insurance company. For Probity, the decision marked a deliberate growth strategy and the first venture into insurance; hence it was a fairly rare decision but essentially non-contentious in the sense that it was seen to be a matter of doing the calculations and negotiating a price. Time was short and presented a major performance constraint. This decision was taken quickly, with the minimum of delays and participation but at the highest level in the organization.

**Constricted dynamics**   The Insight, 'A Fairly Routine Decision at Automotive Components' (chapter 3) is an example of a constricted decision. Once parameters had been set at the board level in the company the decision was delegated to a lower level to be implemented when the market conditions were right. Here the coalition was crisply managed by setting tight constraints on the performance of the decision.

From these examples a number of key aspects of the appropriate mode for management of the coalition during organizational decision making can be suggested.

**Performance norms**   As any decision issue arises a key question concerns the constraints set for decision makers by externally-imposed performance norms. Norms may include financial targets, other performance targets (such as market share), time constraints and deadlines, expectations of being invited into the coalition on the part of certain interests, the planning horizon, or other factors which are seen in some way to set constraints upon the decision processes and outcomes.

**Who should be there?** The organizational design problem is to provide the necessary expertise to cope with uncertainty and to provide the necessary involvement to get commitment, particularly at the implementation stage, while trying to reduce the managerial effort and keep within time constraints.

When complexity and politicality are high this inevitably seems to require an initially wide coalition as experts and interested parties move in and out of the decision. Who the participants are will depend upon the particular rules governing specialization and the allocation of tasks. The coalition may change its composition as the decision proceeds.

**Pacing** Time constraints and deadlines in particular suggest the pace at which the decision should proceed. However, this can often be a considerable bone of contention since participants may have a different idea of what the pace should be. In the case of sporadic processes it is a matter of building support and confidence around a solution. Implementation may involve incrementally testing partial solutions through, say, test marketing, experimentation, prototype building, and the like. Fluid processes have a much sharper sense of time often imposed by deadlines or the need to respond quickly to market conditions. Constricted processes are relatively undefined as regards pacing; the essence is for the timing to be delegated to a lower level.

**Integration** As has been emphasized, decisions occur within an organizational context and effort has to be expended to ensure both horizontal and vertical integration. Performance norms are the starting point for this but more precise parameters may also be laid down. For instance, the investment appraisal procedures in many organizations lay down certain steps to be taken in justifying an investment in terms of the rate of return, payback period, and the like (Butler *et al*. 1990). For horizontal integration there may be rules concerning the need to consult with different internal or external groups; a new product proposal may have to be routed around production, research and development, and purchasing, for instance.

**Achieving closure**    One problem in decision making is knowing when to bring the process to completion. As already pointed out in chapter 3 more work in defining, designing, and evaluating could always bring to light further nuances and solutions to a particular issue. However, from the viewpoint of the Principle of Requisite Decision-Making Capacity, to carry on indefinitely would lead to an error of decision overcapacity. The extra time and managerial effort involved would not bring sufficient improvement in the quality of the decision to make it worthwhile and may impose opportunity costs.

All decision makers need to consider how to achieve closure. This is particularly likely to be a problem in the case of sporadic processes. In the case of the Reorganization of Pathology Services (chapter 3), fortuitous events played an important part. Over a larger number of decisions this might be considered too chancy a procedure. Thompson (1967: 140) suggests that when there is a dispersed power base an inner circle needs to develop to conduct coalition business. This coalition may be elected or may emerge informally. Further, within this inner circle a single powerful person, who need not be the formal head of the organization but who shows especial competence in managing the inner circle, tends to emerge. It is this successive narrowing of the locus of complex and political decisions that can bring about eventual closure and is the implication of the apparent paradox found in the sporadic processes of high informal and dispersed involvement combined with high centralization. During the definition, design, and evaluation stages the decision creates a kind of vortex (Hickson *et al*. 1986) into which all relevant interests get sucked. After a certain point in the process, hierarchy takes over in order to bring the vortex under control.

## Power and ideology

One important aspect of successfully managing a disparate coalition concerns the ability to manipulate the local ideology in such a way as to produce a sufficient degree of cohesion necessary for an organization to demonstrate fitness for future action.

Pfeffer (1981: 303) has pointed to how power becomes stable when beliefs as to who has power are institutionalized and the power distribution remains virtually unquestioned. As Fox (1971: 124) argues, ideology is a resource in the struggle for power. Management seeks an ideology to justify its behaviour and this ideology, therefore, becomes an instrument of persuasion, a method of self-assurance, and a technique for seeking legitimacy.

As we have seen in our discussion of culture and ideology (chapter 8), ideology grows by accretion (Fox 1971: 128) by means of myths and martyrs which are used to strengthen socialization into an organization. This process is particularly noticeable in associations and voluntary organizations where ideology provides the social glue in place of economic motivation; to have a written history, as many voluntary organizations do, is a means of propagating its values to its members and to the outside world (Butler and Wilson 1990). This process can also be seen in business organizations where stories about the founding entrepreneur can hold great sway over present day decisions. Ideology is also deeply rooted in the affiliative web, whether originating from professional or craft affiliations, or class, gender, generational, or educational affiliations.

The skilful coalition manager is likely to be a person who can recognize the existing beliefs and values, understand the affiliative web (Simmel 1955), and manipulate this to produce gradually a satisficing degree of coherence over a wide range of decisions (Wilson 1982). Overtly strenuous efforts to propagate an ideology, however, may be counter productive (Fox 1971: 127) and delay the collective action that the coalition manager is trying to engender. Part of the understanding of the affiliative web must be an understanding of where in that web the ideology demands an inherent opposition to the plans of management. Such an opposition may be built into the socialization of many professionals, crafts, and trades unions, and needs to be recognized and worked around. For example, training in most professions emphasizes technical knowledge and the ideology of the right for the skilled professional to make independent judgements. This ideology often clashes with the managerial ideology that employs professionals; for example, in the British National Health Service, medical consultants sometimes find it difficult to accept that medical decisions have financial implications and hence find it difficult to accept the notion of budgetary constraint.

The more diverse the affiliative web the less likely is there to be a binary power distribution with the lines of two opposing sides drawn up. Diversity will demand the ability to manipulate symbols; in this way the coalition manager can move to a meta-level of concern taking participants' minds off their local differences and concentrating upon the organization's higher goals. This is where statements such as 'the customer comes first' or 'we must think of our clients' are useful. The customer-first ideology becomes symbolic of a higher-order goal upon which everyone can agree and the arguments have to centre upon how to achieve that goal. Hence, the dominant norm for a robust ideology must be the moral norm where a moral norm refers to the ability to generate agreement about ideas of the rightness of what an organization is trying to do.

## DESIGN IMPLICATIONS AND SUMMARY

An understanding of the processes of organizational power and of coalition management is critical if an organization is to achieve the requisite decision-making capacity and to demonstrate fitness for future action.

Five bases of interpersonal power have been suggested. Four of these bases – formal, reward, expert, and moral – are appropriate to conditions where instrumental, economic, referent, and moral ideologies are evident.

Power also derives from the strategic position of a manager and the sub-unit for which that manager has responsibility within the workflow of an organization. While some degree of centrality in the workflow of the organization is a necessary condition to exert power, the ability to cope with uncertainty – that is, with critical organizational problems – is a major power base. In this way managers that can show themselves as connected with developing the future fitness of the organization for action can gain power. Organizations, therefore, need to ensure that as contextual conditions change the decision rules permit such managers to have access to the decision-making coalition.

The problem of coalition management tends to be decision specific rather than organizational specific. Three dominant modes have been identified as providing the requisite decision-making capacity for differing circumstances. The sporadic is suitable for the most difficult conditions of high complexity and high politicality. Here, the coalition needs to be allowed to expand to include interested parties with power to affect implementation and to provide the necessary expertise. For this, fuzzy structures are needed. In order to avoid the most likely error of decision overcapacity with this mode, it is necessary to provide closure by moving the decision process into an inner circle which in itself needs a leader who will perform an important symbolic role in drawing together the various perspectives.

The simplest case of coalition management occurs with low complexity and politicality. Here, the coalition is deliberately constrained by means of crisp structures. The most likely error is that of decision undercapacity and it is necessary to provide the opportunity for these norms to be questioned from time to time.

# Chapter ten

# Learning and change

We have argued that structures need to reflect the degree of uncertainty facing an organization, high uncertainty calling for fuzzy structures, low uncertainty calling for crisp structures. Since the degrees of uncertainty experienced are likely to vary over time a critical concern is that of understanding how the process of change and adaptation takes place.

Uncertainty coping is at the centre of the problem of learning and change. We have already made a distinction between two types of learning cycle: inner and outer loop learning. Inner loop learning is comparable to Argyris's (1977) single loop learning and involves learning to be more efficient; over time this will result in a crisper structure as that learning is incorporated into decision rules.

Some types of change are more disruptive and deeper, involving significant changes in ideology via the outer loop or what Argyris (1977) and Argyris and Schon (1978) call double loop learning, and are more directly involved in the problem of achieving long-term survival. As already noted, a robust ideology copes with uncertainty by providing a shared body of ideas for making decisions but, whereas structures can be changed relatively easily, at the stroke of a pen so to speak, to change ideology requires changes in the beliefs and values of organizational participants – a much more difficult process. We have also argued that, although structure affects ideology in the sense that fuzzy structures are more able than crisp structures to develop a robust ideology, there is a time lag in this process. Hence, we can understand a common problem in organizations, namely, that the search for short-term efficiency can be detrimental to longer-term adaptation.

## INNER LOOP LEARNING

### Product innovation

The institutional model offers a general framework for considering the process of learning and change in organizations. When we look at inner loop learning in more detail we see that product and process innovation is one area where inner loop learning is important since organizations often routinely introduce new products in order to keep pace with changing customer expectations. Daft (1989) has proposed a horizontal linkage model to provide guidelines as to how an organization might be designed for effective management of product innovation.

According to this model successful product innovation involves the mounting of three steps:

1 Technical invention and prototype completion.
2 Commercialization and full-scale marketing.
3 Market success in terms of economic returns.

Generally, at each of these steps there is an attrition rate with ideas falling by the wayside; research in the pharmaceutical industry shows that only 12 per cent of projects started in the research and development department (R&D) actually achieve success at step 3 (Daft 1989: 279).

The horizontal linkage model proposes the development of strong horizontal linking mechanisms between research and development, production, and marketing functions. Research and development people will be linked to other professionals outside the organization (this is part of the boundary spanning function) and be concerned with developing their technical expertise, but it is also important that this is not done without reference to knowledge about the market – where marketing people have expertise – or about production, since products which are innovative and attractive to the market must also be capable of profitable manufacture in the required quantities.

However, concentration upon only horizontal linkages loses sight of the necessity for vertical linkages. It is here that strategic and financial parameters become vital. Bower (1971) describes the process whereby ideas for new products at the business unit level can be co-ordinated with overall corporate goals. Bower's prescription for the design of the resource allocation process sees an organization as consisting of essentially three levels: the corporate, the divisional, and the business levels. There are also certain processes connected to resource allocation giving us the two-dimensional diagram of Table 10.1. The primary function of the corporate level is to set aggregate financial targets and goals concerning the appropriate market/product mix (definition process) and to interpret these targets into meaningful structures; the divisional structure does this through a number of potentially competing divisions whose performances can be compared.

*Table 10.1* Vertical linkages: the resource allocation process

| Level | Phase | Process | | |
|---|---|---|---|---|
| | | *Definition* | *Impetus* | *Context* |
| Corp-orate | Corp-orate | Aggregate targets product/market mix | Yes or No | Design of corporate context |
| Divi-sion | Inte-gration | Financial aggregate ↑ ↓ Product Market | Company wants ↑ ↓ Business wants | Corporate needs ↑ ↓ Sub-unit needs |
| Busi-ness | Initia-tion | Product market | We've got a great idea | Product/market not served by structure |

Adapted from Bower, J.L. (1971) *Managing the Resource Allocation Process*, Homewood, Ill.: Richard D. Irwin.

The next part of the process occurs at the business level where detailed analysis of product/market opportunities takes place within the broad rules set by corporate level. The impetus for pursuing an idea comes from business units who approach corporate headquarters with investment proposals. The sequence is: 'I've got a great idea' from business unit to divisional management, to 'the business wants' from division to the corporate level, to a 'yes' or 'no' from corporate office back to division and business unit according to the defined context and the competing proposals submitted. The cycle will be completed by a feedback about the performance of the investment used to adjust future targets.

The divisional level fulfils an integrating role in this process. The divisional manager is responsible for passing on the corporate requirements in terms that have meaning to the individual businesses. Most likely there will be an investment review committee, or similar, to process individual investment applications.

Although the ideas are worked out primarily for a divisionalized corporation and fit the discussion of the divisional structure in chapter

7, the notion of the institutional function setting the broad rules for investment decisions would still apply to smaller organizations. The kinds of parameters set for investments might cover payback, market share, internal rate of return or other financial measurements (Butler *et al.* 1990).

There is a need for both horizontal and vertical linkages in product innovation, and for changing structures as products move through a life cycle from research, through prototype production, to full production; this need has led to the call for organizations to adopt an ambidextrous approach to innovation (Daft 1989: 275) by deliberately setting out to form fuzzy structures for the research and development stages but move to increasingly crisp structures as the product shifts to full-scale production. The problem lies in managing the coexistence of dissimilar structures each with their different ideology within a given organization. There are a number of proposed methods for this which can be broadly categorized under the headings of sequential and intensive approaches. It will be noted that these terms are closely related to the types of interdependence given by Thompson (1967) and outlined in chapter 5.

*Sequential structures* for innovation would have separate units or departments for research, development, prototype production, and full production; the product idea would move through the stages but the people stay in their units. As product 1 moves out of the research and development phase, research and development workers move to developing product 2, and so on. This is what happens in a functional organization and the general problems associated with this approach have been described in chapter 7. We would expect the structures of the various units in this chain to go from fuzzy for research to crisp for production. Horizontal integration in particular becomes difficult and various integrating devices might have to be used to overcome these problems (see chapter 7). People now lose ownership of their ideas and hence lose commitment to ensuring that the ideas are successfully put into full-scale production.

*Intensive structures* for managing product innovation create units of people and ideas which stay together over a substantial part of the life of a product from inception to full-scale production. Venture teams are an example of this approach whereby small self-contained business units are formed around a new idea and the team takes the idea through its stages. This now means that people have to change over time; in the early stages they will operate within a fuzzy structure but this will become crisper as the inner learning loop is cycled. The problem with this approach is that good research people do not necessarily make good production managers and they can have difficulty in making the needed change in ideology; this problem might be overcome by achieving a compromise structure whereby the venture team stops working on a project after a certain duration by which time, if successful, it is contracted out for full-scale production.

## Process innovation

Process innovation refers to changes in the core technology of the organization. We can point to two principal logics for process innovation:

1  As a result of product innovation whereby a new process is needed to make a new product; it should also be noted that the converse holds true, namely, that a new process can make available products not previously possible. An example of this is the development of injection moulding machines in the thermoplastics industry enabling the production of strong, highly accurate plastic items previously made in more expensive metal form (i.e., camera bodies) or not made at all (i.e., compact discs).
2  In the quest for greater efficiency for the making of existing products.

Both logics are outcomes of the strategic stance of the organization. As explained in chapter 6, a prospector strategy (Miles and Snow 1978) involves the constant developing of new products in order to gain strategic advantage in the market. Hence, we would see a positive relationship between a prospector strategy, product innovation, and hence to process innovation. This kind of process innovation will emphasize adaptability in the core technology since the primary organizational task is to adapt to change.

However, the prospector strategy does not emphasize efficiency; the defender strategy does this (Miles and Snow 1978). Process innovation derived via the efficiency route will be rather different to that derived via product innovation since the emphasis will be upon routinizing production as much as possible in order to achieve large production runs.

Product and process innovation are not limited to manufacturing organizations but also apply to service organizations. A new form of medical treatment can lead to new programmes of health care (products). The learning curve in previously rare operations such as heart transplants leads to process innovation due to pressures for technical efficacy and efficiency. Universities may introduce new courses (product innovation) as an outcome of a prospector strategy leading to process innovation such as the use of videos for teaching inter-personal skills; in this case the video is used as an interactive learning device. Conversely, the search for efficiency (a defender strategy) may lead to larger classes and the use of videos as a means of reaching larger student numbers, such as through distance learning techniques; in this case the video is used as a method of reproducing what has already been worked out.

## OUTER LOOP LEARNING

Outer loop learning involves a deep institutional change (Van de Ven 1986) to the organization, whereby not only do structures change but the ideology changes too. This is most likely to come about when there is a major shift in an organization's context and a major reorganization becomes necessary.

If we imagine an organization moving from a complex context of variability, interdependence, and heterogeneity to a simpler context, we can see that the form of the organization is going to have to change radically. According to the Principle of Requisite Decision-Making Capacity structures will become crisper as rules more closely govern actions, and ideology will also become more focused. The reverse can also happen. Context can become more variable, interdependent, and heterogeneous rather than less so. Structures will tend to make a shift towards fuzziness, and ideology towards robustness. Whichever direction the change, if the changes in context, structure, and ideology are significant we can speak of a major reorganization and organizational transformation.

Reorganization may involve a number of changes in key structural attributes such as reporting relationships, with some people increasing and others decreasing their status; number of participants, with some leaving (voluntarily or involuntarily) and others joining; departmentalization; skills; or working habits and practices. Not all the above factors necessarily change in any one reorganization but the overall feature of radical change is that a sufficient change occurs in the organizational variables to create a major shift in the rules of the game of which participants have to take note. We would expect that the more variables undergoing significant change, the greater the contentiousness surrounding a reorganization.

## Sporadic and fluid reorganizations

Daft (1989: 285) suggests that reorganizations (what he calls administrative changes) tend to be made more centrally than do technical changes, which involve participants in the technical core to a greater degree. Hickson *et al.* (1986) elaborate upon the manner in which reorganizations happen through their investigation of the processes of decision making. Out of their sample of 150 decisions, ranging across 10 topic categories, they note that reorganization decisions are the rarest with an average occurrence rate of 0.14 per year (or once every 7.14 years) whereas new technology decisions (or technical change decisions) were of intermediate rarity with an average occurrence rate of 0.53 per year (once every 1.88 years); Damanpour and Evan (1984) support this by noting that administrative reorganizations occur less frequently than technical changes. Reorganization decisions are concerned with changing the underlying decision rules of an organization and hence we could expect them to be amongst the rarest. Some organizations do reorganize frequently, however, which can be an indication of uncertainty concerning the correctness of its strategy or that it is facing a severe crisis.

Reorganization decisions are also seen as highly consequential to the organization and tend to be made in either a sporadic manner, suggesting that a great deal of effort goes into managing the coalition although in the end the decision to reorganize is made at the highest level in the organization, or they are made in a fluid manner, also indicating authorization at the highest level but that rather less effort goes into coalition management because these decisions are still complex but relatively non-political (Hickson *et al.* 1986). What does not generally happen is for reorganization decisions to be made in the constricted mode where decisions are authorized at lower levels (see chapter 9 for more details about the meaning of these decision types). What all reorganization decisions do have in common is the involvement of the highest levels of management. This is not surprising since they involve setting the basic rules of the organization.

### A sporadic reorganization

An example of a reorganization decision made sporadically involved a change in the committee structure of a large British university. This reorganization was complex in the sense that the specific triggering issue involved the procedures for evaluating faculty promotions but that this problem also raised wider issues about the decision-making apparatus of the university. Technically it is difficult to work out the ideal structure for such a system but the issue was also political in the sense that it cut across the interests of every department in the university and also involved the union, the Association of University Teachers (AUT). In issues of this nature it is impossible to disentangle the complexity and politicality dimensions since one feeds off the other. It was undoubtedly a reorganization where, if it had gone ahead, the essential rules of the game across a whole range of decision topics would be changed, especially as regards the all-important issue of promotions. The way in which the decision to reorganize was reached exemplifies the sporadic process of recycling, discontinuities, dispersed involvement, informal and formal interaction, but eventual authorization at the highest level (Wilson *et al.* 1986).

## *A fluid reorganization*

An example of a reorganization decided in the fluid mode involved a shift from a functional to a divisional structure in a subsidiary chemical company. As the company had come about through a forced merger between a number of previously separate businesses which had never truly melded, it was an issue where the owning group headquarters of the chemical company pressed for resolution and where the effective power lay outside the organization. Although the issue had its internal dissenters these were easily overruled, in one case through the firing of the manager of a once previously independent business. The fluid mode of the decision making is illustrated by the way in which the decision was made: in that there was not much recycling of the issue, since it was clear what headquarters wanted; there was fairly widespread involvement, but in the sense of informing people what needed to happen; and the decision proceeded rapidly to a conclusion through the highest level of authorization in this case, at the headquarters.

## Reorganization as an instrument of control

The above cases raise a vital aspect of reorganizations, namely that they are essentially about who governs (Dahl 1961). By setting the rules of the game they attempt to set the premises for a whole range of future decisions. It is, therefore, an instrument that may be used by top management or by outside owning groups to attempt to gain control over an organization which is seemingly out of control.

Daft (1989: 304) notes that reorganizations tend to happen more successfully in terms of rapidity and completeness of implementation in organizations with mechanistic structures, which are centralized and have a high proportion of administrative staff. This observation fits with the preceding discussion in that the externally imposed reorganizations involve an overwhelming power to impose the new structures. However, we would need to re-emphasize that reorganizations can occur through the sporadic mode of decision making indicating that they can be introduced without the overwhelming power of a higher authority but that this involves a considerable amount of coalition management.

The evolution of organizational structures is often portrayed as a fixed sequence of stages. This theory has been applied, particularly, to the development of the multidivisional business which, it has been suggested, will start out as a simple single product organization, move to a functional structure as greater specialization develops during which time the number of product lines will increase, and then shift to a divisional structure with a range of semi-autonomous businesses through organic growth or acquisition (Chandler 1962, Child 1977). For some organizations the development of autonomous divisions can come about by amalgamation with already existing organizations. Here the process of change tends to follow the path of increasingly trying to integrate the disparate parts into the overall mission of an organization. We need not assume that all organizations need develop in fixed sequences: there is organizational choice; the main thrust of the argument presented in this book is that structure flows from the organizational ideology and context.

## RESISTANCE TO CHANGE

Although the contextual conditions of an organization may shift there is nothing automatic in the process of change; organizations can muster up high degrees of resistance to change even though conditions as perceived by outside observers obviously demand change.

### Escalation of commitment to a previously chosen course of action

One aspect of resistance to change involves the degree of commitment to a previously chosen course of action even though negative information about that course is being accumulated. It is not a problem of misperception or bounded rationality; it is that we are faced with the possibility that a previous decision was wrong. What do we do?

We meet this situation when:

— we have bought a second-hand car which turns out to be a lemon; do we pour money into having it repaired or cut our losses and sell, admitting a mistake was made (Schelling 1978)?
— management has committed itself to an investment programme but technical problems are escalating costs; does management put more money in or cut its losses and admit a mistake has been made?
— government has committed itself to a war which it is losing; are more lives and money thrown in to justify the initial decision?

This is the problem of what Staw (1976) calls Knee-Deep in the Big Muddy. It might also be called the point of no-return. In general, it is the whole problem of understanding the conditions under which people and organizations develop a resistance to change and instead prefer to bolster previous mistakes.

Although Staw's original idea and research was fired by what he saw as the problem of the United States government pouring more and more resources into an unpopular and ineffective war in Vietnam, Staw and Ross (1978) later investigated this question by means of an experiment in which participants were asked to make decisions concerning a further investment in a failing business project. They also introduced another factor into the equation: whether individuals were personally held responsible for the outcomes of the decision to go ahead with the project in the first place.

The results showed that decision makers tended to invest more heavily after negative consequences of an initial investment decision became apparent, and especially when they were personally responsible for this initial decision. If the decision makers considering the follow up investment had not been responsible for the failing initial decision it was easier for them to follow a rational course and withdraw before getting further into the muddy. Staw explains this finding in terms of the self-justification, or cognitive dissonance, hypothesis (Festinger 1957), meaning that decision makers will justify a previous course of action by continuing the same course of action because it gives rise to psychological consonance. Failures tend to lead to a strengthening commitment to that previous course of action. In organizations, managers' promotion, salary, or career prospects may be dependent upon showing the correctness of their previous decisions. Not to continue the same course of action is to admit failure of earlier decisions which can also lead to loss of face and prestige.

Some practical implications can be drawn from this observation. Managers can develop self-awareness of such a tendency to avoid getting 'knee-deep in the big muddy' and if possible make incremental decisions to reduce the extent of the initial commitment if there is uncertainty. Each of these decisions needs to be considered as an independent event, that is, investment 2 should be treated as a separate issue from investment 1, and so on; developing critical awareness allowing managers to back down without loss of face would also help. More generally, by accepting that when there is uncertainty mistakes will happen, organizations can develop structures appropriate to learning.

A key structural dimension is the supportive–punitive dimension. One reason why people resist admitting previous mistakes and withdrawing can be because of the fear of punishment, perhaps loss of earnings, job, or promotion prospects. When rewards are directly linked to performance (see chapter 8) this is more likely than when collective rewards are involved.

## Bolstering by groupthink

A complementary approach to the question of bolstering is taken by Janis (1972) and Janis and Mann (1977) by putting more emphasis upon the social and organizational processes of bolstering, particularly through the notion of 'groupthink' whereby group norms and beliefs operate to filter out unacceptable or unpleasant information and to smother dissent.

Bolstering in this framework can take two slightly different forms: defensive avoidance and unconflicted adherence. Defensive avoidance occurs when decision makers are defensive about their actions and filter out information which does not conform to what they want to happen; under this condition there is perhaps an awareness that the wrong decision has been made. With unconflicted adherence there is not even this awareness of things not being right. The present course of action continues until disaster strikes.

A number of factors can lead to groupthink, according to Janis. There can be an illusion of invulnerability on the part of the group; strong group norms can make it difficult for dissent to emerge; top management of an organization can share a common sense of its own mission and rightness so that information which does not fit the existing policy is filtered out and existing policies are rationalized; there can be stereotypes of 'outgroups' adding to the sense of invulnerability because the outgroup is assumed not to be a major threat; there can be pressures put on dissenters to conform; there can be an illusion of unanimity; and self-appointed mind guards can enforce the group norms.

It is not suggested that all these factors are simultaneously at work in a group; indeed, as we have stressed, groups and organizations need to have common norms to survive. The problem arises when these are so strong that the possibility of admitting mistakes is denied. What we are seeing here is the negative side of a focused ideology. When uncertainty is high an ability to experiment is called for; but mistakes will happen and the problem is to develop structures whereby these do not become disasters through techniques such as loose coupling (Weick 1976), incrementalism (Lindblom 1959), or alternative maintenance. An ideology must also be developed to permit learning from mistakes; this is likely to require norms about openness to new information, even if it does not fit with existing norms.

## Robust versus focused ideology

It is at this point that we must re-emphasize the distinction between a focused ideology – what Brunsson (1985) calls a strong ideology – and a robust ideology. The focused ideology is heavily dependent upon one norm and is consistently held across participants. The robust ideology has a plurality and tolerance of norms but overarching these is a dominant morality. Within this pluralism must be ideas about competition and efficiency, instrumentalities, referents, and morality.

Business organizations are not usually associated with morality in the popular imagination so we need to translate the idea of robustness more specifically into an organizational context. A robust ideology would be present in a firm if decision makers have general understandings concerning the rightness of the products they are making and the markets they are serving and we often see these kinds of ideas expressed in mission statements and the like; the important feature, however, is the extent to which there is general agreement about these fundamental beliefs. Morality in this sense, however, is not enough. We would also expect to see decision makers with an awareness and ideas about the possible competition. They would also have to display ideas about appropriate other organizations and actors against which they compare themselves and are compared by others, that is, referent norms; in this way the firm can guard against obsolescence in new expertise. And they would also have technical ideas about how to achieve their goals, that is, instrumental norms; in this way what might remain as grand sentiments at the moral level are translated into specific actions in the technical core of the organization.

In addition to this plurality of norms there would be a tolerance and openness to new ideas and a conscious searching for them. This tolerance must extend across the existing notions about competition and efficiency, instrumentalities, referents, and morality.

## Robust ideology and complexity of context

Another significant aspect of robust ideology concerns its relationship to organizational context. As a robust ideology is based upon a richness and variety in the cognitive and social structures of decision makers such decision makers are also likely to select complex contexts. This can be illustrated by the difference between the defender and prospector strategies outlined in chapter 6.

Defenders take a focused view of the world. They will keep to a known technology/market combination and put their efforts into improving efficiency by cycling around the inner learning loop. Uncertainties are coped with by means of incremental computational-oriented decisions. Changes in technology or products will build upon what is already known. In this way the simple context, crisp structure, and focused ideology are in a mutually reinforcing cycle.

Conversely, prospectors take a robust view of the world. Their robust ideology helps them interpret the context as complex. They will explore unknown technologies and products and put their efforts into reaching out to do new things. Inspirational decision making becomes a way of life and their main management task is to maintain this mutually reinforcing cycle of complex context, fuzzy structure, and robust ideology.

Overall, we can see that decision makers have to interpret (Johnson 1987) their contexts, that is, the combination of the institutional environment, task environment, and technology. Ideology provides the underlying beliefs and values for this interpretation.

## CHANGING THE IDEOLOGY

Organizations can face crises which put their survival at stake; decision makers become aware of the need to change both structures and ideology. Changing ideology in particular can be the most difficult aspect to achieve but is an essential part of organizational transformations.

Wickens (1987) discusses the kinds of changes in social attitudes and relationships that were needed when Nissan set up a manufacturing plant in the North East of England. This was an area of high unemployment and poor industrial relations with traditional 'them and us' views on the part of both workers and management. The fundamental change was to move from the old working habits of rigid demarcations and status differences towards a system of single status working with an emphasis upon the team and flexible working practices. The old practices within industry reflect wider social attitudes and class distinctions within Britain. The shift to single status working required fundamental changes in the beliefs and values of the workers and the use of symbols and practices now well associated with Japanese management. Examples include the wearing of a uniform as a symbol of equality, a single cafeteria replacing the traditional management and workers' cafeteria, and the use of team working for production. The question is how to bring about these changes in ideology.

## Leadership

The role of leadership in organizations has, over the decades, received a great deal of attention and is generally considered to be of importance to the process of change. Much of the research has sought appropriate leadership styles (Likert 1961), particularly in terms of the value of participative versus directive leadership in raising group productivity or some other dichotomy based upon individual characteristics (Bass 1985). Greater attention is now being given to the importance of the interaction between the leaders and contexts in connection with leaders' ability to induce change into an organization (Pettigrew 1987).

Leaders cannot be divorced from followers; without followers there could be no leader and from this assumption Burns (1978) identifies two types of leadership. First, the transactional type, where leadership is an essentially homeostatic function whereby there is an exchange between leader and follower; in return for the follower's compliance the leader undertakes to provide certain benefits, rather in line with the notion of the reward/contribution balance outlined in chapter 8. In this way leaders can only effect a fairly limited change within the limits of the institutionalized rules. The metamorphosis of an organization requires the second type: transformational leadership. Here we see leadership in a more active role, looking for potential changes in motives of followers and appealing to higher-order values.

Pettigrew (1985), in his analysis of the transformation of the British chemical company Imperial Chemical Industries (ICI) from the 'slumbering giant' to the 'awakening giant', gives us more detail as to how the transformational leadership process works. The essential problem in ICI was that the company had for long rested upon its position as Britain's leading industrial company, with most of its production and employment being located within the United Kingdom and with relatively safe assured markets throughout the old British Empire. The post Second World War era saw a decline in this invincibility as safe markets disappeared and radical transformations became necessary, not just in terms of strategy, but also in terms of ideology.

Pettigrew shows how the radical changes were connected with changes in leadership. In the early 1960s Sir Paul Chambers and then in the early 1980s Sir John Harvey-Jones came in as chairmen to coincide with periods of great change. The main problem the leaders had to face was that of changing the beliefs, values, and culture of the organization. The actual strategy was worked out in a muddling-through way; major strategic decisions tended to follow a sporadic pattern (Hickson *et al.* 1986) but this took place alongside efforts to change the ideology through management development programmes, changes in administrative mechanisms, and generally challenging existing ways of doing things (Pettigrew 1987: 667).

The specific skills and techniques to bring about this change were based upon an underlying opportunistic surveillance rather than problematic decision making (Thompson 1967: 151) requiring an understanding of both the technical and the political dimensions of the organization, of how things have come to be as they are and of the history of the organization, and also a willingness to challenge that history by not allowing it to become a reason for inaction. Patience, perseverance, waiting for (or encouraging) potential opponents to retire, moving into political vacuums, knowing when to wait for opportunities in areas where the opposition is overwhelming, introducing sympathizers, and using succession opportunities to introduce new agendas (Pettigrew 1987: 667) are all part of a repertoire of needed skills. Such managers will not shirk from using naked power, either. These are all the skills observed in the processes of sporadic decision making (Hickson *et al.* 1986); central to these processes are their discontinuities and the need for coalition building.

## Some aspects of transformational leadership

Bass (1985) studied the possible dimensions of leadership to test whether a distinction can be found in practice between the transactional and transformational leadership types as suggested by Burns (1978). He collected questionnaire data from managers and supervisors in the military, public service, and industry. The study found support for the two-factor theory of leadership although it was also found that both the transactional and transformational leadership types could be further sub-divided into sub-factors: transactional leadership was found to consist of two sub-factors, contingent rewards and management by exception, while transformational leadership consists of three sub-factors, charisma, individualized attention, and intellectual stimulation. The salient features of each factor can be summarized as follows:


1 Transactional leadership
*Contingent rewards*
   Leader:
   Gives rewards related to effort and support given by subordinate
   Satisfies subordinate's needs in exchange for support
*Management by exception*
As long as things are going well people are left to get on with job

2 Transformational leadership
 *Charisma*
   Leader:
   Exudes enthusiasm
   Provides a model
   Encourages expression of ideas and opinions
   Excites with vision of what may be accomplished if we pull together
   Encourages understanding of other points of view
*Individualized attention*
   Leader:
   Gives personal attention to neglected people
   Finds out what can be done to help
   Expresses appreciation
 *Intellectual stimulation*
   Leader enables thinking in new ways about old problems

Burns' study is especially interesting in the sense that it is possible
to identify some of the specific actions that need to be taken by
managers pursuing one or the other type of leadership. What is
significant about the findings is that the transformational leadership
shows up as intensely active, exuding enthusiasm, and at the same
time giving personal attention to people and providing intellectual
stimulation. It identifies a management style that is very demanding
in terms of time and energy.

## The discontinuities of organizational transformation

Great changes in the major western industrial economies in the 1980s
have created much research activity into the process of organizational
change (Grinyer and Spender 1979; Peters and Waterman 1982;
Pettigrew 1985; Lawrence and Dyer 1983; Child and Smith 1987;
Whipp and Clark 1986) and into how organizations can cope with
the process of revival. All these studies emphasize the sheer hard
work and sometimes painful processes involved in such
transformations.

Child and Smith (1987) describe the changes that occurred in
Cadbury Ltd, a division of Cadbury–Schweppes, as it struggled to
develop a new ideology. They also emphasize the need to understand
the historical development of the organization in order to understand
how the change processes occurred. Child and Smith emphasize the
notion of a sector, or industry, as part of the analysis to understand
the origin of the particular beliefs and values that have accrued over
time and how these may help or hinder the change process. Two
aspects of the history of Cadbury are seen as important. First, is the
better-known notion of 'Cadburyism', the 'particular ideology
concerning welfarism' (Child and Smith 1987: 574) that Cadbury
shared with other Quaker manufacturers. This resulted in a number
of specific organizational arrangements designed to induce a strong
moral ideology, such as the use of an internal market for labour with
a commitment to long-term employment, the building of the Bournville
village in the period between the World Wars, the early development
of holiday and pension schemes, and health and safety provisions.
All these measures are a strong example of the Human Relations
(Burrell and Morgan 1979) movement and bear some comparison
to the producer co-operative, without the ownership and managerial
implications. The Cadbury family remained very much in control.

The other, and less well-known aspect of Cadburyism, lies in the linking of human relations measures to the drive for business efficiency – a kind of enlightened paternal capitalism. By 1913 Cadbury was at the forefront of the introduction of Taylorism and Fordism with the use of piecework payment, industrial engineering, and the hiring of American efficiency experts. The company continued this policy of mechanization, paid for out of retained income, to keep up with ideas of efficient production, but changes were generally absorbed through institutionalized change since the ideology had already been laid down and reinforced over years of successful operation.

The mid-1970s saw a dramatic downturn in the market position of the company due, in part, to American food and confectionery entrants into the UK. This change had already been foreshadowed in 1969 through the merger with Schweppes and the subsequent shedding of 5,000 jobs, marking an enforced break with previous practice of the internal market whereby jobs were found internally for workers displaced from one area of activity. The 'dynamic tension' (Child and Smith 1987) between the successful ideology of the past and the need for adaptability was already beginning to show. The company embarked upon a programme of rationalization, essentially pursuing an efficiency strategy (chapter 6) and then shifted in the early 1980s towards innovation through a massive investment programme. The departure from the old Cadbury ideology had by now become manifest: 1977 saw the first-ever company-wide strike which lasted over a month, and four-shift working, end of job demarcation, job flexibility, subcontracting, and significant job losses all became a fact of life.

### The process of transformation

The above two cases allow us to begin to draw some general conclusions as to the kinds of steps, activities, and skills associated with successful transformation.

**Triggers** The realization of a major problem builds up over time and involves a nexus of negative information from a variety of sources telling management that old recipes are no longer working. Typically, the first step in trying to resolve the problem will be to try and make the old structures work better, demonstrating the principle of bolstering discussed above. It is when these attempts can be demonstrated to have failed that real change can start.

**Long time**   As decision rules are built up over a long time and become institutionalized so too must we expect that transformations take time. What is a long time will have to be measured relative to the age of the organization and the cycles of working practices in the industry. When the change process is sponsored by a powerful top management, or especially from a powerful outside group, the change process will happen much faster and with less discontinuity; organizational change can happen by means of fluid decision processes as mentioned above.

**Change advocates**   We see organizational participants pressuring for change. These advocates are often quite low in the hierarchy, younger than the average management age, more highly qualified, have some experience outside the organization or from other distant parts of the same company if it is a large organization, as happened in the case of Cadbury (Child and Smith 1987: 583). Change advocates must not be marginalized, they need to have the ear of, without being part of, senior management. In this way they help avoid the problem of unconflicted adherence to an existing policy (Janis and Mann 1977). This would be an illustration of the tolerance dimension of ideology.

**Failures *en route***   As historical reinterpretations of the Japanese attack of Pearl Harbor indicate (Janis and Mann 1977) there is one particularly harsh way in which top management can force change lower down in an organization: let catastrophic failure occur as a demonstration of the problem in order to get the organization's attention upon overcoming a common problem. Two important conditions must obtain for this to work: the system must not be destroyed and top management's complicity must be hidden. Less dramatically, change advocates can also be helped by *en route* failures as events unfold. Hence management's failure in Cadbury to gain corporate backing for the four-shift working plan, enabled change advocates to point to the need to change the entrenched in Cadbury's paternalistic ideology and for flexible working to be eventually accepted.

**Use of power**   Research into the political processes of change (Pettigrew 1973, Wilson 1982) shows that people who get their way against opposition in an organization have superior political awareness and skills. Some aspects have been suggested previously in this chapter in the discussion of the ICI case (Pettigrew 1985), and the processes of sporadic reorganizations (Hickson *et al.* 1986) bring this out.

**Change agents** It may be worthwhile to describe a role for change agents who must, clearly, also advocate change but do something additional. In particular, they would seem to be high status people, maybe chief executives or chairmen (such as Harvey-Jones in the case of ICI) who are deliberately brought in for the purpose of achieving change, or they can be outside consultants.

**Articulation** Part of the role of advocates and agents of change is to articulate a vision in clear terms that can be understood (Peters and Waterman 1982). This articulation needs to be easily interpreted into measurable targets. Thus a strategy as was used in Cadbury of new investment and associated changes in working practices and redundancies can be interpreted into 'headcounts' of needed reductions (Child and Smith 1987: 587).

**Leadership** Transformational, rather than transactional, leadership will be evidenced.

**Rewards evidenced** Although a hard future is promised, it must be shown to be in support of a worthy cause and must, eventually, materialize into rewards for individuals. Transformational strategies in organizations are usually needed for survival and improvement in business performance. For workers who have been asked to change institutionalized behaviour the exhortations at some stage need to turn into improved pay and conditions and other tangible rewards; it must not always be a case of jam tomorrow. Hence, Child and Smith report that at Cadbury wage rates and pensions started to increase, and hours worked to decrease, while the transformation was in progress.

**Consolidation** Transformation is, at some stage, going to have to result in a new ideology and structure, and a period of consolidation follows the transformation. This requires setting up a new structure and a new set of norms, beliefs, and values. In the cases of ICI and Cadbury this required new ideas about each organization's mission, working practices, and organizational structures.

## Organizational design tracks

Some general ideas about the process of successful organizational transformations have been proposed; these have yet to be tested comparatively across a number of organizations and change events.

Nevertheless, we can see that the route to deep change is not easy for an organization but the above aspects of successful change appear to summarize a great deal of what has been written on the subject. Not all organizational changes need follow the same pattern, however, as Greenwood and Hinings (1988) have pointed out through their notion of organizational design tracks. They argue that, in instituting change, organizations develop archetypes both of where they are in the present and of where they wish to go in the future. An archetype is similar to a profile as discussed in chapter 7; it comprises a set of beliefs, or interpretive schemes, outlining ideas about organizational form, domain, and performance norms (Greenwood and Hinings 1988: 299). An archetype, therefore, presents consistent patterns of context, structure, and ideology. An organization embarking upon change, we may say, will have a present archetype (let us call this archetype A) representing the pre-change beliefs and values, but will develop archetype B during the course of change and this will then represent the new set of beliefs and values.

A coherent archetype is one in which structure and ideology continuously reinforce one another; here we should compare Greenwood and Hinings' ideas to the notion of outer loop learning already described. The conditions towards which an organization would try to move is that of archetypal coherence. However, the process of change involves the questioning of an archetype and this can produce a condition of schizoid incoherence when archetype A is under challenge and thoughts are turning to possible new archetypes. Greenwood and Hinings see an embryonic archetype B as emerging. This situation bears comparison with the description of change at Cadbury previously noted in this chapter where archetype A may be seen as the initial paternalistic form of organization providing a coherent picture of structure and ideology. The schizoid incoherence came about as a result of changes in context, and embryonic structures started to emerge taking the company towards a more aggressive consumer strategy more congruent with the demands of the market and changing technology. Archetype B, therefore, represents this consumer-orientated organization.

The process of change, as we have seen, is not painless and neither does the change always work or flow in the same way but can take, Greenwood and Hinings suggest, different paths or tracks as follows:

— Track A. Inertia. The organization stays with archetype A. No change occurs.

— Track B. Aborted excursions. The organization attempts to change, tastes the possible future, but aborts.
— Track C1. Linear transformation. The organization goes from archetype A, through the schizoid phase to embryonic archetype B and establishes itself finally in archetype B. This may be seen as the relatively smooth type of organizational change as represented in the fluid decision-making type of reorganizations.
— Track C2. Oscillating transformation. The organization finds it difficult to make up its mind, tries the new future, scurries back to the old but tries again and eventually finds a stable archetype B, maybe after a number of oscillations. Some of this aspect is evidenced in the Cadbury case.
— Track C3. Delayed transformation. Delays can happen in reorganizations as shown in the sporadic type of decision (Hickson *et al*. 1986); the reorganization of hospital pathology is an example of this (see chapter 3).
— Track D. Unresolved excursions. An organization may enter the schizoid phase, experiment with an embryonic B archetype, but not succeed in moving to a stable form.

By focusing upon change tracks, Greenwood and Hinings (1988) have opened up the possibility of introducing a comparative element in the understanding of organizational change which has been lacking due to the dominance of the literature on change by single case study descriptions. Some insights have been presented above as to how the context may affect the design track. Fluid changes come out of issues that are complex (due to rarity in particular) but non-contentious; this kind of change is likely to occur where participants are in agreement over what is needed and where power is fairly concentrated. On the other hand, sporadic changes come out of issues which are both complex and political in that there are many interests with conflicting beliefs and values.

## CHARISMA AND ITS ROUTINIZATION

Mintzberg (1990) points to the importance of leadership for inducing organizational change and argues for a high degree of centralized power for successful change. But we need to go further than this and say something about the characteristics such a leader would need to display, how these leadership characteristics may come about, and how they might change over time.

Organizational theory is rooted in Weber's theory of rational–legal authority and bureaucracy to the neglect of his theory of charisma and what he called the charismatic community. Rational–legal authority and charismatic authority provide two polar types of authority which relate well to our polar types of computational and inspirational decision making respectively.

In its ideal type Weber (1968: 241) applied the term charisma to certain extraordinary almost supernatural individual powers exhibited with a strong passion by an individual leader. This individual would be regarded by his/her followers to have some special insight in the making of decisions not available to them. Whereas under the rational–legal authority the motivation of those subject to the authority is to follow the rules, in the case of charismatic authority the followers focus their attention upon the characteristics of the person acting as leader.

Weber's presentation of charisma may sound a bit extreme for the modern business organization yet we can often learn a lot by looking at the extreme (or ideal) case and then make adjustments for the various mixtures and compromises that have to be made in practice. Weber makes a number of points of relevance to understanding how charisma may arise, be sustained, but eventually decline in modern organizations.

Charisma can be seen to be essentially unstable, coming to the fore at the entrepreneurial stage of organizational development, becoming routinized into rational–legal authority as crisper bureaucratic structures evolve, and then possibly coming to the fore again if that organization meets a crisis. Charisma rests upon the desires its subjects feel to follow the wishes of the leader (Weber 1968: 242). This condition is most likely to come about under conditions of extreme crisis or change (Eisenstadt 1968). Followers will look to the leader for salvation and hence the charismatic leader is likely to be someone who can provide evidence of success from other situations and who can persuade the followers that further success will be forthcoming.

Charisma is therefore fed by success and if evidence of success evades the leader for long and if the leadership fails the followers it is likely that the charismatic authority will fade. We can now see why the ability to demonstrate success *en route* during change in an organization acts as a kind of regenerator of charisma.

According to Weber a group subject to charismatic authority is a charismatic community. This community forms a band of disciples;

there is no hierarchy, no career, no promotion. The leader simply intervenes in individual cases to make decisions in an inspirational way.

Charisma is foreign to economic and efficiency considerations. Hence in business organizations charisma needs to be kept on a tight reign. Too much reliance upon charisma, and the economic survival of the firm may be threatened. More appropriate for the fuzzy organization is the notion that charisma can change from one person to another with different decisions. Charisma can provide a vital driving force to decision making as viewed through the eyes of the garbage can model. Participants are entering and leaving the can, carrying their solutions; the impetus for participants, problems, and solutions to come together to make a choice could be the use of charisma. But different decisions would bring different individuals to the fore as leaders. Thompson and Tuden (1956) pointed to the apparent paradox that when ends/means relationships are unclear and there are uncertainties over the ends to be reached, inspirational decision making seemed to be the only way in which decision makers can get action. Charisma would offer a resolution to this problem but there is no reason why the charisma need continuously reside in the same person.

## Succession

In purposive organization, where a degree of rationality must pervade its activities, it is unlikely that an organization can remain in a perpetual state of charisma with one leader coming to dominate affairs. The image that the fuzzy organization gives would be one in which charisma is at work but the actual leader changes according to circumstances and issues.

There is no well-defined theory of how leaders get selected by organizations. As indicated, leadership succession can coincide with a crisis (Mintzberg 1990) and the organization selects a new leader in accordance with a view of how that crisis might be resolved and the kinds of qualities a leader would need. The process of selection can often be highly political as Hickson et al. (1986) show; Alwyn, in their case of Toxichem, came to power as chief executive only after a prolonged tussle with his opponent. The question over which this contest was fought concerned the issue of electricity generation from spare steam which was produced as a by-product of chemical production – hardly an issue of great strategic importance to a chemical manufacturer in itself. Nevertheless, it became a strategic issue in so far as it became a testing ground for the political skills of the two main contenders. In the end Alwyn's superior political skills seemed to be highly valued by the organization and he became chief executive.

Top management succession can often involve the bringing in of an outsider. Gouldner's (1965) study of the gypsum mine shows how a new outside leader can be brought in as a means of an owning group or headquarters trying to exert more control over an operation that is considered to have become slack or 'gone native', that is, become dominated by the local community ideology.

## DESIGN IMPLICATIONS AND SUMMARY

Learning is vital to ensuring an organization's fitness for future action. Inner loop learning involves successive cycles of uncertainty coping enabled by a fuzzy structure which will, however, become crisper as learning proceeds and more defined decision rules are developed. The dilemma is that inner loop learning also develops a more focused ideology which makes the organization less adaptable in the long term.

Outer loop learning is longer term and directed towards developing a robust ideology which is also a means of coping with uncertainty. The significant aspect of the robust ideology is that it permits longer-term adaptability through continuing selection of a more complex context.

Product and process innovation tend to involve inner loop learning. Reorganizations involving a major transformation of the organization tend to involve outer loop learning, and the key problem here is to unfreeze an old ideology and create a new ideology appropriate to a changed context.

Mistakes are an inherent aspect of an organization operating under conditions of uncertainty. Bolstering of a previously chosen course of action for which evidence of failure is accruing is a common phenomenon and is accentuated by groupthink. This problem may be alleviated by fostering a robust ideology.

It has been suggested that the process of successful organizational transformation involves a number of attributes, specifically: a long time horizon, change advocates and agents, ability to deal with *en route* failures, use of power, articulation, leadership, evidence of rewards, and consolidation.

In terms of the variables of the institutional model of organization we have posited relationships between the variables as shown in Figure 10.1.

*Figure 10.1* The contingent institutional model of organization: salient variable relationships discussed in this chapter

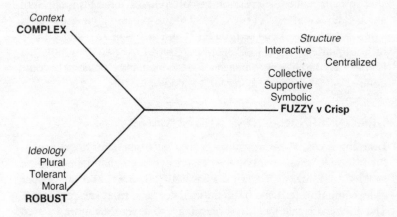

We have emphasized the processes that are needed for successful organizational transformations and the structures that are likely to achieve that transformation. The trigger for transformation, according to the model, comes from a change in context making existing structures inappropriate. Generally an organization needs to change both its structure and ideology.

The kinds of structure likely to permit this kind of change are those which are fuzzy to the extent of being interactive, collective, and supportive. However, we have also suggested that centralization is needed. This leaves an organization with the problem of managing a tension between the need for interaction and centralization. Particularly important in this process will be the use of symbolic leadership.

# Chapter eleven

# Conclusion

After an impetus given to the issue of organizational design in the mid-1960s and early 1970s by a number of publications (e.g., Haberstroh 1965, Rubenstein and Haberstroh 1966, Clark 1972, Galbraith 1973) the interest in this field failed to be maintained in the organizational literature. Nystrom and Starbuck's (1981) *Handbook of Organizational Design* revived some interest in the topic and was followed by Daft's (1986, 1989) integrative work.

I have premised this book upon the notion that organizational design is an important subject of study but that any effective design must rest upon a coherent theory of organization. Throughout I have stressed the need for a model of organizational design capable of integrating the many strands of organizational theory developed over the years and one that is transferable in time and in space. The institutional model of organization has been suggested as the means of achieving these aims and the body of the discussion has centred upon developing the variables of this model and their interrelationships.

In part, I see the problem of organizational design to be concerned with finding structures suitable for the context within which an organization lives. This much has been well established in the organizational theory literature. Not so well established in organizational theory is the importance of ideology and its relationship to structure and context; we have had to accept that our understanding of these relationships is not yet well developed.

At the organizational level the overall framework for the institutional model is taken to comprise the variable categories of context, structure, and ideology, the constituent variables interacting in a triangular relationship. Part of the task has been to develop an understanding of the processes connecting these categories.

At the centre of the institutional model is a theory of decision making providing our understanding of organizational processes. Decision making is, so to speak, the driving force – the dynamic of the model. Hence the institutional model operates at two levels with the decision level fitting within the wider organizational level. At the decision level participants make decisions but within constraints and opportunities provided by an organization's context, structure, and ideology. However, in the process of making decisions over many topics the outcomes from decision making come to alter the organizational level variables.

Also established has been one further overall requirement of a theory of organizational design. In the language of economics and operational research organizational design implies a normative theory, an objective function to be optimized. This proves to be most difficult to conceptualize since organizations can be seen to have many outputs. Organizational theory has attempted to overcome this problem by means of the notion of effectiveness, taking care to distinguish this concept from that of efficiency.

Organizational effectiveness is concerned with an organization achieving a dynamic equilibrium within its environment, the primary requirement being to gain support in this environment; to do this an organization needs a requisite decision-making capacity to enable sufficiently responsive actions to be taken in accordance to the changing patterns of support, while at the same time achieving sufficient operating efficiency to ensure that it performs satisfactorily relative to its rivals. This requirement has been encapsulated by the Principle of Requisite Decision-Making Capacity. The overall problem for an organization is to maintain sufficient fuzziness of structure for responsiveness while maintaining sufficient crispness of structure for efficiency.

## CONTEXT: COMPLEXITY VERSUS SIMPLICITY

The institutional model starts from a view of an organization acting within a task environment from which it obtains support in exchange for certain performances. Also in the task environment are rivals who compete for the same pool of support. This makes up the resource component of an organization's context. There is also a technical aspect to the context. An organization has to carry out an internal transformation function converting inputs into outputs for exchange in the environment.

Overarching the task environment is the institutional environment providing a normative aspect to actions within the task environment. In particular, there are norms of performance defining constraints and opportunities for the actors in the task environment. Norms provide benchmarks against which an organization's performance is assessed and also define the entry and exit of actors from the task environment.

## The variables of context

In general, complex contexts produce more uncertainty than do simple contexts. Complexity is an outcome of a number of variables that have been discussed with these variables defining context in the following ways.

**Ambiguous versus clear**    Ambiguity of purpose makes assessment of decisions more difficult. In the technical core ambiguity leads to unanalysability of task.

**Unique versus comparable**    An organization that defines itself as unique in its task environment will lack other organizations against which to evaluate itself. Within the technical core uniqueness also makes the evaluation of units difficult.

**Variable versus stable**    An organization that frequently changes its products, or for which the norms or technology are changing, will create uncertainty of decision making.

**Heterogeneous versus homogeneous**    A wide range of types of elements in the task environment is more likely to give rise to unexpected problems and hence increase uncertainty. Conversely, homogeneity reduces the range of problems to cope with. Heterogeneity in the technical core leads to a greater variety of technologies and problems arising.

**Interdependent versus autonomous**    When external elements or internal units are interrelated in the sense that actions in one part of the environment or organization have a wide impact upon other parts, uncertainty is increased. When elements and units are relatively autonomous the uncertainty becomes less. A similar situation exists if there is interdependence in the technical core.

## STRUCTURE: FUZZINESS VERSUS CRISPNESS

The key organizational design problem is to devise structures that set rules for coping with uncertainties. What is needed are rules that permit the requisite decision-making capacity. The theme running throughout this book is the contrast between the fuzzy and crisp structures and the way in which each of these structures provide the requisite decision-making capacity to cope with differing levels of uncertainty – the fuzzy for high uncertainty, the crisp for low.

The fuzzy–crisp terminology has been introduced from the mathematical theory of fuzzy sets (Zadeh *et al*. 1975, Lerner and Wanat 1983, Karwowski and Mital 1986). For what reason do I propose new terms when we already have terms such as the machine bureaucracy, mechanistic, rigid, or hierarchical organizations to cover the crisp end of the spectrum, and we have terms such as organic, flexible, garbage can, or anarchic organizations to cover the fuzzy end of the spectrum? The terms fuzzy and crisp have been introduced partly in hope; we can continue, and undoubtedly many will, to use the established terms in their own way. By locating the terminology in a mathematical theory the hope is that developments in that theory may, in time, be transferred to organizational theory. Regardless of whether this happens or not the words 'crisp' and 'fuzzy' have a useful onomatopoeic value-free ring to them. From time to time there has been a tendency to consider that organic organizations are to be preferred to mechanistic, rigid, or bureaucratic ones, the very words – especially in times of ecological concerns – suggesting the preferred structure. To assume this, however, is to miss the thrust of the argument; fuzziness is not to be preferred to crispness at all times; fuzziness and crispness each have their place according to context – fuzziness for coping with conditions of high uncertainty, crispness when the context is well defined and problems can be categorized by inelastic rules (Lerner and Wanat 1983).

The language of fuzzy set theory is particularly appropriate to considering organizational structures. Organizations categorize decision issues (Lerner and Wanat 1983). To decide whether to invest in a new machine to make widgets is to involve a number of categorizations, such as who gets involved in the decision (categories of experts), what procedures to use for making assessments about outcomes of the investment (categories of standard procedures), or at what level in the hierarchy will the decision be authorized (categories of centralization). Other categories could be thought of; the important factor is not so much what the categories are as the degree to which they are precisely defined. Crisp structures define these categories very closely so there is no doubt as to where a decision belongs, whereas fuzzy structures provide imprecise definitions. Fuzziness provides elastic constraints (Zadeh *et al.* 1975: 1) as to the values that may be assigned to a variable. In organizational terms this means that in treating decision issues as fuzzy we are not precisely sure who should participate, what the desired outcomes are, or how to evaluate the decision.

From the organizational perspective the purpose of designing the fuzzy structure is to provide the ill-defined constraints and degrees of freedom as to issues that are considered, who participates, and the procedures to be followed; that is, a high decision-making capacity not permitted in a crisp structure. High decision-making capacity does not mean that all and sundry are participating all the time. It means an awareness that whatever rules exist in the organization should not be treated as tablets of stone, that the rules are indeed elastic.

## The variables of structure

We have defined structure as the enduring decision rules of an organization and a number of variable dimensions have been defined.

**Implicit versus formal** Organizations set standard operating procedures, often formalized in manuals or computer programs, for making decisions. The issue for the fuzzy organization is not so much the quantity of these rules but the flexibility with which rules get interpreted as decisions arise. In the crisp organization, rules will be applied inelastically; the fuzzy organization will rely upon implicit understandings in its interpretation of rules with justifications for decisions often being completed after a decision has been made.

**Expert versus local** The fuzzy organization will use much expertise to cope with uncertainties. Experts will tend to be cosmopolitan (Gouldner 1957) in that they will have been, more often than not, professionally trained outside the organization; the primacy here is to keep in touch with scientific and technical developments at large. The origin of knowledge and training for the crisp organization will tend to be acquired locally through in-house training and local experience. This dimension does not suggest that local knowledge is less skilful or to be less preferred than cosmopolitan knowledge but rather describes the source of that knowledge.

**Differentiated versus demarcated**   The fuzzy organization may be differentiated and full of experts but they operate in a generalized way. Watertight demarcations between experts are not allowed to develop and if someone thinks they have a solution, even if not formally categorized as the expert on the subject, those views are noted. The crisp organization will expect people to keep within their job descriptions.

**Interactive versus parametric**   Fuzzy organization relationships require high interaction and mutual adjustment between participants horizontally and vertically; there is little respect for formal position within this organization. The crisp organization will govern inter-dependencies by means of rules defining, let us say, that action B follows action A; that P gets involved not Q; or that target X not target Y must be achieved. The fuzzy organization will, on the other hand, say that action B might follow action A, but then so might action C; that P, Q, R, etc. could get involved; that target X is this today but could be something different tomorrow. What the fuzzy organization is doing tomorrow will be a result of today's interactions.

**Active versus analytic**   The fuzzy organization will emphasize inspirational action-packed decision making rather than the extensive search and analysis associated with computational decision making. Fuzziness does not mean no attention to computation; rather that computations are used as guidelines and to provide information, often after the decision has been made.

**Decentralized versus centralized**   Fuzzy organizations are decentralized, but again it is not so much the degree of centralization that is important as the notion that decisions can be authorized by those to whom they are most relevant. The crisp organization will insist on going through channels to get decisions authorized.

**Collective versus individualistic**   Rewards in the fuzzy organization are determined and distributed collectively, perhaps on the basis of teams. In the crisp organization rewards will be more on an individual incentive basis.

**Supportive versus punitive**   Under uncertainty errors occur; the mode of treating errors is critical to the successful operation of the fuzzy organization. The fuzzy organization accepts the inevitability of errors and provides appropriate learning opportunities for participants. The crisp organization will set up reward systems to punish under-performance; output related pay is an example of this.

**Symbolic versus literal**   Fuzzy structures will tend to develop symbolic means of communicating the values of the organization whereas crisp structures will rely upon facts, hard data, and a legalistic interpretation of the rules.

### Inner loop learning: from inspirational to computational decision making

The fuzzy organization provides high decision-making capacity and inspirational decision making, not for its own sake but to permit the organization to cope with the problems of uncertainty and to achieve efficiency. Over many decision cycles we could expect learning to occur and for uncertainty to be attenuated via the negative feedback loop as shown in Figure 11.1; decision making would gradually shift towards the computational. We call this the inner learning loop which is comparable with Argyris's (1977) single loop learning. It means that the organization will step by step crispify its structure in order to match the decision-making capacity to the uncertainty. It is essentially learning to do the task better and more efficiently. It is what Thompson (1967) means by technical rationality which has the associated logic of increasing routinization of activities.

## IDEOLOGY: ROBUSTNESS VERSUS FOCUSED

Ideology has been defined as the body of ideas shared amongst an organization's participants. It is important to distinguish this notion of a body of ideas from the notion of ideology as associated with an ideologue – a person who pursues an idea to the exclusion of all else. Ideology comprises the underlying beliefs and values held by decision makers; it forms a kind of organizational cognitive structure or mental map for problem solving.

A robust ideology is contrasted to a focused ideology. By robustness is meant the ability of the body of ideas to be applicable to many different decisions, a kind of ideology for all seasons. By focus is meant the ability of the body of ideas to concentrate upon the conditions holding in a particular decision.

The following variables of ideology have been identified:

**Plural versus singular**    An ideology is robust when it contains a broad range of norms and singular when one norm dominates.

**Tolerant versus particular**    Robustness will be tolerant of new and unusual ideas whereas the focused ideology will want to concentrate upon the particular.

**Moral versus efficiency**    Although the robust ideology will consist of a broad range of norms the moral norm will predominate in order to give a strong sense of the rightness of what the organization as a whole is doing. The focused ideology will emphasize the instrumentality of what the participants are doing.

### Outer loop learning: striving for adaptability

The robust ideology is organizationally very demanding and the obvious question is what kind of structures are needed to foster such a body of ideas within an organization? I have posited a positive link from fuzziness to ideology (see Figure 11.1), pointing to the notion that the kinds of decision rules contained within such a structure would encourage robustness. This is an area where we need to know more as regards organizational theory but some indications have been given in chapter 10 and elsewhere as to the nature of the process. For example, the transformational leadership referred to by Pettigrew (1985) emphasizes symbolic actions; Brunsson (1989) has pointed to the need for the leadership to keep a distance from the instrumental actions in the organization in such cases. Clark (1972: 43–4) has argued for an 'alternatives and differences approach' to organizational design thereby recognizing that design changes will only be effected when the values and beliefs of an organization's participants are in line with the proposed structural changes. The actual process of changing an organization must, therefore, primarily rest upon encouraging decision makers to think through for themselves the form of the appropriate structures.

Although we have to accept that the present state of our knowledge concerning the nature of the link between fuzzy structures and robust ideologies is sparse we can see the possibility of another learning loop – what I call the outer learning loop – whereby a robust ideology is fostered by a fuzzy structure which in turn reinforces a complex context. The outer learning loop is comparable to Thompson's (1967) organizational rationality, Argyris's (1977) double loop learning, or Lawrence and Dyer's (1983) process of readaptation.

As we can see from Figure 11.1 there is a tension between inner and outer loop learning. Cycling via the inner loop reduces fuzziness; the organization is on a cycle of learning which is efficiency driven and will lead to increasing crispness and contextual simplicity. However, the reduction in fuzziness will have the longer-term effect of reducing robustness.

This phenomenon appears in organizations when short-term expediency leads organizations to tighten up structures, with apparent immediate return achieved through greater efficiency, centralization, and the like, but leads the organization into a vicious cycle of decline as the ability to adapt to future exigencies decreases.

*Figure 11.1* The contingent institutional model of organization

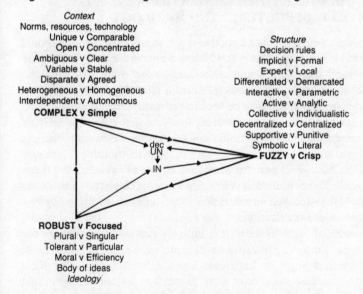

*Context*
Norms, resources, technology
Unique v Comparable
Open v Concentrated
Ambiguous v Clear
Variable v Stable
Disparate v Agreed
Heterogeneous v Homogeneous
Interdependent v Autonomous
**COMPLEX v Simple**

*Structure*
Decision rules
Implicit v Formal
Expert v Local
Differentiated v Demarcated
Interactive v Parametric
Active v Analytic
Collective v Individualistic
Decentralized v Centralized
Supportive v Punitive
Symbolic v Literal
**FUZZY v Crisp**

dec
UN
IN

**ROBUST v Focused**
Plural v Singular
Tolerant v Particular
Moral v Efficiency
Body of ideas
*Ideology*

*Notes*: UN = uncertain; IN = inspiration; dec = decision.

## Robustness and complexity

Another factor in the dynamics of the model concerns the connection robustness and complexity. I argue that decision makers under robustness are more likely to negotiate a complex context for themselves; it takes robustness to create complexity.

The connection between robustness and complexity can be illustrated by the discussion of the negotiated environment (Pfeffer and Salancik 1978) where we noted that organizations are not just passive recipients of an environment. An organization can negotiate improved terms for itself assuming it has the power to do this. If we look at this from the perspective of organizational decision makers we can see that for this to happen and to result in increased complexity, a robust body of ideas would be required. Decision makers would have to interpret the environment as negotiable. Similarly concerning technology: decision makers would have to be capable of understanding the opportunities presented by technical developments if they are to move into new technical areas which would then increase complexity.

## THE TRIANGLE OF ORGANIZATIONAL DESIGN: CONTEXT, STRUCTURE, AND IDEOLOGY

Ultimately any model is a hypothesis and this is how this one should be treated. It is a hypothesis in which some areas are more thoroughly discovered than others and other areas need more development. Context, structure, and ideology form a triangle of interaction. In general, organizations may be seen to maintain themselves as simple, crisp, and focused, or as complex, fuzzy, and robust. The triangle of interactions tends to be mutually reinforcing. However, there is nothing automatic in the maintenance of these relationships. Strategic choice (Child 1972) and organizational choice (Trist *et al*. 1963) can intervene. Either approach is a viable strategy: as already stated, the simple–crisp–focused organization is not inferior to the complex–fuzzy–robust organization.

As with all organizations it is unlikely that we will ever see the pure type. Fuzzy organizations will contain areas of crispness, crisp organizations areas of fuzziness; some rules for the hierarchical ordering of these areas have been suggested. It does not mean that the fuzzy organization can have no concern for efficiency, nor does it mean that the crisp organization can have no concern for the moral component. Ultimately we are considering the relative weights of concern for the contrasting variables presented in the model.

# IMPLICATIONS FOR METHODOLOGY

As mentioned, some areas of the model are lacking development and it is appropriate to conclude with a note concerning methodology. As a theoretical model describes a way of knowing about the phenomenon at issue the methods by which we claim to know something need to be considered.

My approach has been to deduce a model based upon some fairly basic notions of how an organization works internally and how it relates to its environment. I have called this the institutional model of organization because the institutional environment is the starting point for considering the rules of the game under which an organization operates.

In developing the model and assessing its validity I have drawn upon the basic tenets of decision-making theory and the general contingency theory framework that underlies much of organizational theory. The approach to theory building has been to reflect the particular against the general, the ideographic against the nomothetic (Mohr 1982). The case study gives us access to the ideographic and provides insights and a richness concerning process; it is especially useful in stimulating thought. But as the aim has also been to produce a transferability of theory, curiosity makes us ask whether these insights hold elsewhere, either at a different time or a different place; that is, we wish to gain access to the nomothetic understanding. This leads to the need for concepts that can be expressed in variable form to allow comparisons to be made; for instance we need to be able to judge whether organization X is more or less fuzzy than organization Y, and so on.

Contrasting the ideographic to the nomothetic method in this way inevitably leads to the comparison of qualitative to quantitative research. Case studies rely upon an intensive inquiry into happenings in one particular situation. However, because there are an infinite number of questions that a researcher can ask in any one situation, a theoretical framework is needed to help define the limits to the kinds of information that is sought. The advantage the researcher has in this instance is that the theory and data can interact as the research proceeds. This is why this kind of qualitative research is useful for raising issues and exploring questions.

Comparative studies have to work more closely to a predefined framework: for comparisons to work the same questions have to be answered across all the units being studied in a standardized way and on scales which permit the allocation of values to the units of analysis. This methodology inevitably leads to the use of quantitative analysis. Although there is considerable scope for interaction between theory and data during analysis there is obviously less scope for such interaction within the boundaries of a particular study than there is in the case method, although a study might suggest changes to be made in the model to be examined in future studies. Hence, the nomothetic method can lead to a programmatic approach to theory building (Donaldson 1985) whereby knowledge is built up incrementally. The advantage of this kind of quantitative research is that it widens our horizons in terms of the applicability, or otherwise, of case study observations to other situations.

In the social sciences, arguments often arise as to the superiority of qualitative research relative to quantitative research (Pettigrew 1979, Donaldson 1985). I suggest that both methods are needed since each provides its own strengths and weaknesses; case studies need to complement comparative studies, and vice versa. The outstanding area for further research suggested by this book is the area of organizational ideology; case studies of this concept are needed and should be conducted within individual organizations and comparatively across organizations and nations. Comparative research, inevitably involving the use of quantitative methods, will also be needed to enable wider generalization. It would indeed be a pity if the ideologues of social science became barriers to the understanding of organizational ideology by setting up artificial conflicts between different research methods.

This book has, I hope, shown that the study of organizations and of their design is an exciting topic of investigation and one of great importance to societies in general. It is not suggested that the ideas contained within the institutional model are a final solution to what organizations are and how they work. Underlying the model is the belief that greater attempts at integrating previously disparate threads of thought need to be made and a model of this nature, at the least, provides a framework for such integration.

# References

Abell, P. (1975) 'Organizations as bargaining and influence systems: measuring intra-organizational power and influence', in P. Abell (ed.) *Organizations as Bargaining and Influence Systems*, ch. 1, London: Heinemann.

Abell, P. (1988) *Small-scale Industrial Producer Cooperatives in Developing Countries*, Oxford: Oxford University Press.

Adams, S. (1965) 'Inequity in social exchange', in L. Berkowitz (ed.) *Advances in Experimental Social Psychology*, New York: Academic Press.

Allison, G.T. (1971) *The Essence of Decision: Explaining the Cuban Missile Crisis*, Boston: Little, Brown & Co.

Argyris, C. (1977) 'Organizational learning and management information systems,' *Accounting, Organizations and Society* 2 (2): 113–29.

Argyris, C. and Schon, D.A. (1978) *Organizational Learning: a Theory of Action Perspective*, Reading, Mass.: Addison-Wesley.

Arrow, K.J. (1974) *The Limits of Organization*, New York: W.W. Norton & Co.

Asch, S.E. (1956) 'Studies of independence and conformity: I. A minority of one against a unanimous majority', *Psychological Monographs* 70: 1–70.

Ashby, W.R. (1956) 'Self-regulation and requisite variety', in F.E. Emery (ed.) *Systems Thinking*, ch. 6, 1969, Harmondsworth, England: Penguin. Originally in W.R. Ashby, *Introduction to Cybernetics*, ch. 11, 1956, New York: Wiley.

Barnard, C.I. (1938) *The Functions of the Executive*, Cambridge, Mass.: Harvard University Press.

Bass, B.M. (1985) *Leadership and Performance Beyond Expectations*, New York: Free Press.

BBC (1980) 'Horizon programme on the Mondragon Co-operative'. Television programme broadcast by the British Broadcasting Corporation, London, November 17.

Beattie, J. (1964) *Other Cultures: Aims, Methods and Achievements in Social Anthropology*, London: Cohen & West.

Beer, S. (1972) *Brain of the Firm*, London: Penguin.

Bendix, R. (1956) *Work and Authority in Industry*, New York: Wiley.

Berger, P.L. and Luckmann, T. (1966) *The Social Construction of Reality: A Treatise in the Sociology of Knowledge*, New York: Doubleday.

Blau, P.M. (1955) *The Dynamics of Bureaucracy*, Chicago: University of Chicago Press.

Blau, P.M. and Scott, W.R. (1963) *Formal Organizations: A Comparative Approach*, London: Routledge & Kegan Paul.

Blauner, R. (1964) *Alienation and Freedom*, Chicago: University of Chicago Press.

Bower, J.L. (1971) *Managing the Resource Allocation Process*, Homewood, Ill.: Richard D. Irwin.

Bradley, K. and Gelb, A. (1982) 'The replication and sustainability of the Mondragon experiment', *British Journal of Industrial Relations*, 10 (1): 20–3.

Bradley, K. and Gelb, A. (1983) *Worker Capitalism: The New Industrial Relations*, London: Heinemann Educational Books.

Brunsson, N. (1985) *The Irrational Organization: Irrationality as a Basis for Organizational Action and Change*, Chichester: Wiley.

Brunsson, N. (1989) *The Organization of Hypocrisy: Talk, Decisions and Actions in Organizations*, Chichester: Wiley.

Buckley, W. (1967) *Sociology and Modern Systems Theory*, Englewood Cliffs, N.J.: Prentice-Hall.

Burns, J.M. (1978) *Leadership*, New York: Harper & Row.

Burns, T. and Stalker, G.M. (1961) *The Management of Innovation*, London: Tavistock.

Burrell, G. and Morgan, G. (1979) *Sociological Paradigms and Organisational Analysis: Elements of the Sociology of Corporate Life*, London: Heinemann Educational Books.

Butler, R.J. (1980a) 'User satisfaction with a service: power, task and the personal touch', *Journal of Management Studies* 17, 1 (Feb): 1–18.

Butler, R.J. (1980b) 'Control through markets, hierarchies and collectives', paper presented to European Group for Organization Studies Conference on Markets and Hierarchies, Imperial College, London, December. Also reprinted in Rose A., Turk, J., and Wilman, P. *Power, Efficiency and Institutions: A Critical Appraisal of the Markets and Hierarchies Paradigm*, ch. 7, 1983, London: Heinemann.

Butler, R.J. (1983) 'A transactional approach to organizing efficiency: perspectives from markets, hierarchies and collectives', *Administration and Society* 15 (3): 323–62.

Butler, R.J. and Carney, M.G. (1983) 'Managing markets: implications for the make or buy decision', *Journal of Management Studies* 20 (2): 213–31.

Butler, R.J. and Carney, M.G. (1985) 'Strategy and strategic choice: the case of telecommunications', *Strategic Management Journal* 7: 161–77.

Butler, R.J. and Carney, M.G. (1987) 'Public choice, ambiguity and regulation', *Scandinavian Journal of Management Studies* 3: 3–4.

Butler, R.J., Davies, L., Pike, R., and Sharp, J. (1990) 'Strategic investment decision making: complexities, politics and processes', *Journal of Management Studies*, 27, Sept.

Butler, R.J., Hickson, D.J., and McCullough, A. (1974) 'Power in the organizational coalition', paper presented at the Conference of International Sociological Association, Toronto, August.

Butler, R.J., Hickson, D.J., Wilson D.C., and Axelsson, R. (1977/8) 'Organizational power, politicking and paralysis', *Organization and Administrative Sciences* 8, 4 (winter): 54–9.

Butler, R.J. and Wilson, D.C. (1990) *Managing Voluntary and Non-Profit Organizations*, London: Routledge.

Cameron, K.S. and Quinn, R.E. (1983) 'Organizational life cycles and shifting criteria of effectiveness: some preliminary evidence', *Management Science* 29: 23–61.

Carney, M.J. (1984) 'Organizational strategy and industry regulation: responses to deregulation in the United Kingdom telecommunications and bus transport industries', unpublished Ph.D. thesis, University of Bradford Management Centre.

Carrell, M.R. and Dittrich, J.E. (1978) 'Equity theory: the recent literature, methodological considerations and new directions', *Academy of Management Review*, April: 202–10.

Carzo, R. (Jnr.) and Yanouzas, J.N. (1969) 'Effects of flat and tall organizational structures', *Administrative Science Quarterly* 14, 2 (June): 178–91.

Champion, D.J. (1967) 'Some impacts of office automation upon status, role change and depersonalization', *Sociological Quarterly* 8 (winter): 71–84.

Chandler, A.D. (1962) *Strategy and Structure: Chapters in the History of the Industrial Enterprise*, Cambridge, Mass.: MIT Press.

Chandler, A.D. (1977) *The Visible Hand*, Cambridge, Mass.: Harvard University Press.

Child, J. (1972) 'Organization structure, environment and performance: the role of strategic choice', *Sociology* 6: 1–22.

Child, J. (1977) *Organizations: A Guide to Problems and Practice*, London: Harper & Row.

Child, J. (1984) *Organizations: A Guide to Problems and Practice*, 2nd edn, London: Harper & Row.

Child, J. (1987) 'Organizational design for advanced manufacturing technology', in T.D. Wall, C.W. Clegg, and N.J. Kemp (eds) *The Human Side of Advanced Manufacturing Technology*, ch. 6, Chichester: Wiley.

Child, J. and Smith, C. (1987) 'The context and process of organizational transformation – Cadbury Limited in its sector', *Journal of Management Studies* 24, 6 (Nov.): 565–93.

Clark, P. (1972) *Organizational Design: Theory and Practice*, London: Tavistock.

Clark, R. (1979) *The Japanese Company*, London: Yale University Press.

Clegg, S. (1979) *The Theory of Power and Organization*, London: Routledge & Kegan Paul.

Coase, R.H. (1937) 'The nature of the firm', *Economica N.S.* 4: 386–405.

Cohen, M.D. (1989) 'Organizational learning of routines: a model of the garbage can type', paper presented at the conference on the Logic of Organizational Disorder, Venice, Italy: April.

Cohen, M.D., March, J.G., and Olsen, P.J. (1972) 'A garbage can model of organizational choice', *Administrative Science Quarterly* 17: 1–25.

Commons, J.R. (1979) *The Economics of Collective Action*, Madison: University of Wisconsin Press.

Crozier, M. (1964) *The Bureaucratic Phenomenon*, London: Tavistock.

Crozier, M. and Friedberg, E. (1980) *Actors and Systems*, Chicago: University of Chicago Press. Published in French by Editions du Seuil 1977.

Cyert, R. and March J.G. (1963) *The Behavioral Theory of the Firm*, Englewood Cliffs, N.J.: Prentice-Hall.

Daft, R.L. (1986) *Organization Theory and Design*, 2nd edn, St. Paul, Minn.: West Publishing Co.

Daft, R.L. (1989) *Organization Theory and Design*, 3rd edn, St. Paul, Minn.: West Publishing Co.

Dahl, R.A. (1957) 'The concept of power', *Behavioral Science* 2: 201–18.

Dahl, R.A. (1961) *Who Governs? Democracy and Power in an American City*, New Haven: Yale University Press.

Dalton, M. (1959) *Men Who Manage*, New York: John Wiley & Sons.

Damanpour, F. and Evan, W.M. (1984) 'Organizational innovation and performance: the problem of organizational lag', *Administrative Science Quarterly* 29: 392–409.

Davis, S.M. and Lawrence, P.R. (1977) *Matrix*, Reading, Mass.: Addison-Wesley.

Didrickson, J. (1989) 'A framework for performance management in a local authority social services department', unpublished MBA dissertation, University of Bradford Management Centre.

DiMaggio, P.J. and Powell, W.W. (1983) 'The cage revisited: institutional isomorphism and collective rationality in organizational fields', *American Sociological Review* 48: 147–60.

Donaldson, L. (1985) *In Defence of Organization Theory: A Reply to the Critics*, Cambridge: Cambridge University Press.

Dore, R. (1973) *British Factory–Japanese Factory: The Origins of National Diversity in Industrial Relations*, London: George Allen & Unwin.

Duncan, R.G. (1972) 'Characteristics of organizational environments and perceived environmental uncertainty', *Administrative Science Quarterly* 17 (2): 313–27.

Duncan, R.G. (1979) 'What is the right organization structure? Decision tree analysis provides the answer', *Organizational Dynamics*, winter 1979: 59–80.

Dunkerley, D., Spyby, T., and Thrasher, M. (1981) 'Interorganization networks: a case study of industrial location', *Organization Studies* 2 (3): 229–48.

Eisenberg, D.J. (1984) 'How senior managers think', *Harvard Business Review* 62 (Nov.–Dec.): 80–90.

Eisenstadt, S.N. (1968) 'Charisma and institution building: Max Weber and modern sociology', in S.N. Eisenstadt (ed.) *Max Weber on Charisma and Institution Building*, introduction, Chicago: University of Chicago Press.

Emerson, R.M. (1962) 'Power-dependence relations', *American Sociological Review* 27 (Feb.): 31–40.

Emery, F.E. and Trist, E.L. (1965) 'The causal texture of organizational environments', *Human Relations* 18: 21–32.

Emery, F.E. (ed.) (1967) *Systems Thinking*, Harmondsworth: Penguin.

Etzioni, A. (1964) *Modern Organizations*, Englewood Cliffs, N.J.: Prentice-Hall.

Evans, G.W. and Karwowski, W. (1986) 'A perspective on mathematical modelling in human factors', in W. Karwowski and A. Mital (eds), *Application of Fuzzy Set Theory in Human Factors*, pp. 3–27, Amsterdam: Elsevier.

Fayol, H. (1930) *Industrial and General Administration*, London, Pitmans.

Festinger, L. (1957) *A Theory of Cognitive Dissonance*, Evanston, Ill.: Row, Peterson.

Fiedler, F.E. (1967) *A Theory of Leadership Effectiveness*, New York: McGraw-Hill.

Filby, I. and Wilmott, H. (1988) 'Ideologies and contradictions in a public relations department: the seduction and impotence of living with myth', *Organization Studies* 9 (3): 335–49.

Form, W.H. (1972) 'Technology and social behaviour of workers in four countries: a sociotechnical perspective', *American Sociological Review* 37 (Dec.): 727–38.

Fox, A. (1971) *A Sociology of Work in Industry*, London: Collier Macmillan.

Francis, A. (1983) 'Markets or hierarchies: efficiency or domination?', in A. Francis, J. Turk, and P. Willman (eds) *Power, Efficiency and Institutions: A Critical Appraisal of the 'Markets and Hierarchies' Paradigm*, London: Heinemann Educational Books.

French, J.R.P. (Jnr.) and Raven, B.H. (1959) 'The bases of social power', in D. Cartwright (ed.) *Studies in Social Power*, Ann Arbor, Mich.: Institute for Social Research.

Galbraith, J.R. (1973) *Designing Complex Organizations*, Reading, Mass.: Addison-Wesley.

Galbraith, J.R. (1977) *Organization Design*, Reading, Mass.: Addison-Wesley.

Galbraith, J.R. and Nathanson, D.A. (1978) *Strategy Implementation: The Role of Structure and Process*, St. Paul, Minn.: West Publishing Co.

Gilbreth, F.B. and Gilbreth, L.M. (1917) *Applied Motion Study*, New York: Sturgis & Walton Co.

Glaser, B.G. and Strauss A.L. (1967) *The Discovery of Grounded Theory: Strategies for Qualitative Research*, Chicago: Aldine.

Glueck, W.F. (1980) *Business Policy and Strategic Management*, 3rd edn, Tokyo: McGraw-Hill Kogakuska Ltd.

Goldthorpe, J.H. (1968) *The Affluent Worker: Industrial Attitudes and Behaviour*, London: Cambridge University Press.

Goodman, P.S. and Friedman, A. (1971) 'An examination of Adam's theory of inequity', *Administrative Science Quarterly* 16: 271–88.

Gouldner, A.W. (1954) *Patterns of Industrial Democracy*, New York: Collier Macmillan.

Gouldner, A.W. (1957) 'Cosmopolitans and locals', *Administrative Science Quarterly* 2, 3 (Dec.): 282–92.

Gouldner, A.W. (1965) 'The problem of succession and bureaucracy', in

A.W. Gouldner *Studies in Leadership: Leadership and Democratic Action*, pp. 644–64, New York: Harper & Row.

Greenwood, R. and Hinings, C.R. (1988) 'Organizational design types, tracks and the dynamics of strategic change', *Organization Studies* 9 (3): 293–316.

Grinyer, P.A. and Spender, J.C. (1979) *Turnaround: The Fall and Rise of the Newton Chamber Group*, London: Associated Business Press.

Haberstroh, C.J. (1965) 'Organization design and systems analysis', in J.G. March *Handbook of Organizations*, Chicago: Rand McNally.

Hall, R.H. (1987) *Organizations: Structures, Processes and Outcomes*, 4th edn, London: Prentice-Hall International.

Halsey, R.W. (1980) 'A case study of a large site organization and its implications for management', unpublished Ph.D. thesis, Department of Management Studies, Teeside Polytechnic.

Hannan, M.T. and Freeman, J. (1977) 'The population ecology of organizations', *American Journal of Sociology* 82: 929–64.

Herzberg, F. (1966) *Work and the Nature of Man*, World Publishing Company.

Hickson, D.J., Butler, R.J., Cray, D., Mallory, G.R., and Wilson, D.C. (1986) *Top Decisions: Strategic Decision-Making in Organizations*, Oxford: Basil Blackwell; San Francisco: Jossey-Bass.

Hickson, D.J., Hinings, C.R., Lee, C.A., Schneck, R.E., and Pennings, J.M. (1971) 'A strategic contingencies theory of intraorganizational power', *Administrative Science Quarterly* 16 (2): 216–29.

Hickson, D.J., Pugh, D.S., and Pheysey, D.C. (1969) 'Operational technology and organizational structure: an empirical reappraisal', *Administrative Science Quarterly* 14, 3 (Sept.): 378–97.

Hickson, D.J. and Thomas, M.W. (1969) 'Professionalization in Britain: a preliminary measurement', *Sociology* 3, 1 (Jan.): 37–54.

Hinings, C.R., Hickson, D.J., Pennings, J.M., and Schneck, R.E. (1974) 'Structural conditions of intraorganizational power', *Administrative Science Quarterly* 19 (1): 22–43.

Hirschman, A.O. (1970) *Exit, Voice and Loyalty: Responses to Decline in Firms, Organizations and States*, Cambridge, Mass.: Harvard University Press.

Hofstede, G. (1980) *Culture's Consequences: International Differences in Work Related Values*, London: Sage.

Hofstede, G. (1981) 'Management control of public and not-for-profit activities', *Accounting, Organizations and Society* 6 (3): 193–211.

Huber, G.P. and McDaniel, R.R. (1986) 'The decision making paradigm of organizational design', *Management Science* 32 (5): 572–89.

Issack, T.F. (1978) 'Intuition: an ignored dimension in management', *Academy of Management Review* 3: 917–22.

Janis, I.L. (1972) *Victims of Groupthink*, Boston: Houghton Mifflin.

Janis, I.L. and Mann, L. (1977) *Decision Making: A Psychological Analysis of Conflict, Choice and Commitment*, New York: Free Press.

Johnson, G. (1987) *Strategic Change and Management Process*, Oxford: Basil Blackwell.

Jurgens, U. (1989) 'The transfer of Japanese management concepts in the international automobile industry', in S. Wood (ed.) *The Transformation of Work?*, London: Unwin Hyman.

Kanter, R.M. (1984) *The Change Masters: Corporate Entrepreneurs at Work*, London: George Allen & Unwin.

Karpik, L. (1972) 'Les politiques et les logiques d'action de la grande enterprise industrielle', *Sociologie du Travail* 1: 82–105.

Karwowski, W. and Mital, A. (1986) *Application of Fuzzy Set Theory in Human Factors*, Amsterdam: Elsevier.

Katz, D. and Kahn, R.L. (1966) *The Social Psychology of Organizations*, New York: John Wiley.

Knight, K. (1976) 'Matrix organization: a review', *Journal of Management Studies* 13 (May): 111–30.

Koontz, H. and O'Donnell, C. (1959) *Principles of Management*, New York: Knopf.

Lawrence, P.R. and Dyer, D. (1983) *Renewing American Industry*, New York: Free Press.

Lawrence, P.R. and Lorsch, J.W. (1967) *Organization and Environment: Managing Differentiation and Integration*, Homewood, Ill.: Richard D. Irwin.

Lerner, A.W. and Wanat, J. (1983) 'Fuzziness and bureaucracy', *Public Administration Review* (Nov.–Dec.): 500–9.

Likert, R. (1961) *New Patterns of Management*, New York: McGraw-Hill.

Lindblom, C. (1959) 'The science of muddling through', *Public Administration Review* 19: 79–88.

Littler, C.R. (1982) *The Development of the Labour Process in Capitalist Societies: A Comparative Study of the Transformation of Work Organization in Britain, Japan and the USA*, London: Heinemann.

Lockett, M. (1980) 'Workers' co-operatives as an alternative organizational form: incorporation or transformation', in D. Dunkerley and G. Salaman (eds), ch. 10, *The International Yearbook of Organization Studies 1980*, London: Routledge & Kegan Paul.

Lukes, S. (1974) *Power: A Radical View*, London: Macmillan.

Lupton, T. and Bowey, A. (1976) *Wages and Salaries*, Harmondsworth: Penguin.

Lupton, T. and Gowler, D. (1969) *Selecting a Wage Payment System*, London: Kogan Page.

Luthans, F. (1981) *Organizational Behavior*, 3rd edn, New York: McGraw-Hill.

McGregor, D. (1960) *The Human Side of Enterprise*, New York: McGraw-Hill.

Mangham, I.L. (1987) *Organization Analysis and Development: A Social Construction of Organizational Behaviour*, Chichester: Wiley.

Mann, F.C. and Hoffman, L.R. (1960) *Automation and the Worker: A Study of Social Change in Power Plants*, New York: Holt, Rinehart & Winston.

Mannheim, K. (1936) *Ideology and Utopia: An Introduction to the Sociology of Knowledge*, New York: Harcourt Brace and World Inc.

March, J.G. and Olsen, J.P. (1976) *Ambiguity and Choice in Organizations*, Bergen: Universitetsforlaget.

March, J.G. and Simon, H.A. (1958) *Organizations*, New York: Wiley.

Maslow, A.H. (1943) 'A theory of human motivation', *Psychological*

*Review*, 50: 370–96.

Maslow, A.H. (1965) *Eupsychian Management*, Homewood, Ill.: Dorsey-Irwin.

Mechanic, D. (1962) 'Sources of power of lower participants in complex organizations', *Administrative Science Quarterly* 7. 349–64.

Merton, R.K. (1968) *Social Theory and Social Structure*, New York: Free Press.

Meyer, J.W. and Rowan, B. (1977) 'Institutionalized organizations: formal structure as myth and ceremony', *American Journal of Sociology* 83 (2): 340–63.

Meyer, J.W. and Scott, W.R. (1983) *Organizational Environments: Ritual and Rationality*, Beverly Hills, Calif.: Sage.

Michels, R. (1949) *Political Parties*, New York: Free Press.

Miles, R.E. and Snow, C.C. (1978) *Organizational Strategy, Structure and Process*, New York: McGraw-Hill, international edition.

Miles. R.H. (1980) *Macro Organizational Behavior*, Santa Monica, Calif.: Goodyear Publishing Co.

Miles, R.H. and Cameron, K.S. (1982) *Coffin Nails and Corporate Strategies*, Englewood Cliffs, N.J.: Prentice-Hall.

Milgram, S. (1975) *Obedience to Authority*, New York: Harper & Row.

Miller, D. and Mintzberg, H. (1983) 'The case for configuration', in G. Morgan (ed.) *Beyond Method*, pp. 57–63, Beverly Hills, Calif.: Sage.

Mills, C.W. (1956) *The Power Elite*, New York: Oxford University Press.

Mintzberg, H. (1973) *The Nature of Managerial Work*, New York: Harper & Row.

Mintzberg, H. (1983a) *Power In and Around Organizations*, Englewood Cliffs, N.J.: Prentice-Hall.

Mintzberg, H. (1983b) *Structure in Fives: Designing Effective Organizations*, Englewood Cliffs, N.J.: Prentice-Hall.

Mintzberg, H. (1990) 'The design school: reconsidering the basic premises of strategic management', *Strategic Management Journal* 11 (3): 171–96.

Mintzberg, H., Raisinghani, D., and Therot, A. (1976) 'The structure of "unstructured" decision processes', *Administrative Science Quarterly* 21, 2 (June): 246–75.

Mohr, Lawrence B. (1982) *Explaining Organizational Behavior*, San Francisco: Jossey-Bass.

Morischima, Michio (1982) *Why has Japan 'Succeeded': Western Technology and the Japanese Ethos*, Cambridge: Cambridge University Press.

Nystrom, P.C. and Starbuck W.H. (1981) *Handbook of Organizational Design*, vols 1 & 2, London: Oxford University Press.

Ouchi, W.G. (1980) 'Markets, bureaucracies and clans', *Administrative Science Quarterly* 25 (March): 129–41.

Ouchi, W.G. (1984) *The M-Form Society: How American Teamwork can Recapture the Competitive Edge*, Reading, Mass.: Addison-Wesley.

Palm, G. (1977) *The Flight from Work*, Cambridge: Cambridge University Press.

Perrow, C. (1970) *Organizational Analysis: A Sociological View*, London: Tavistock.

Peters, T.J. and Austin, N. (1985) *A Passion for Excellence: The Leadership of Difference*, New York: Random House.

Peters, T.J. and Waterman, R.H. (1982) *In Search of Excellence*, New York: Harper & Row.

Pettigrew, A. (1973) *The Politics of Organizational Decision Making*, London: Tavistock.

Pettigrew, A. (1979) 'On studying organizational cultures', *Administrative Science Quarterly*, 24 (4): 570–81.

Pettigrew, A. (1985) *The Awakening Giant: Continuity and Change in Imperial Chemical Industries*, Oxford: Basil Blackwell.

Pettigrew, A. (1987) 'Context and action in the transformation of the firm', *Journal of Management Studies* 24, 6 (Nov.): 649–70.

Pettigrew, A. (1990) 'Studying deciding: an exchange of views between Mintzberg and Waters, Pettigrew and Butler', *Organization Studies* 11 (1): 1–16.

Pfeffer, J. (1978) 'The micropolitics of organizations', in J.W. Meyer and W.R. Scott, *Organizational Environments: Ritual and Rationality*, Beverly Hills, Calif.: Sage, pp. 29–50.

Pfeffer, J. (1981) *Power in Organizations*, Marshfield, Mass.: Pitman Co.

Pfeffer, J. and Salancik, G.R. (1974) 'Organizational decision making as a political process: the case of a university budget', *Administrative Science Quarterly* 19 (2): 135–51.

Pfeffer, J. and Salancik, G.R. (1978) *The External Control of Organizations: A Resource Dependence Perspective*, New York: Harper & Row.

Porter, M.E. (1985) *Competitive Advantage*, New York: Free Press.

Pugh, D.S. (1966) 'Modern organization theory: a psychological and sociological study', *Psychological Bulletin* 66 (4): 235–51.

Pugh, D.S. (1976) 'The Aston approach to the study of organizations', in G. Hofstede and M.S. Kassen (eds) *European Contributions to Organization Theory*, ch. 3, Van Gorvan, Netherlands.

Pugh, D.S. and Hickson, D.J. (1989) *Writers on Organizations*, 4th edn, Newbury Park, Calif.: Sage; London: Penguin.

Pugh, D.S., Hickson, D.J., Hinings, C.R., and Turner, C. (1968) 'Dimensions of organization structure', *Administrative Science Quarterly* 13 (1): 65–104.

Pugh, D.S. and Hickson, D.J. (eds) (1976a) *Organizational Structure in its Context: The Aston Programme I*, Farnborough, Hants: Saxon House.

Pugh, D.S. and Hinings, C.R. (eds) (1976b) *Organizational Structure: Extensions and Replications: The Aston Programme II*, Farnborough, Hants: Saxon House.

Roethlisberger, F.J. and Dickson, W.J. (1939) *Management and the Worker*, Cambridge, Mass.: Harvard University Press.

Rowe, C. (1989) 'Analyzing management decision making: further thoughts after the Bradford Studies', *Journal of Management Studies*, 26, 1 (Jan.): 29–46.

Roy, D. (1952) 'Quota restriction and goldbricking in a machine shop', *American Journal of Sociology* 57, 5 (March): 430–7.

Roy, D. (1954) 'Efficiency and "the fix": informal intergroup relations in a piecework machine shop', *American Journal of Sociology* 60 (3): 255–66.

Rubenstein, A.H. and Haberstroh, C.J. (eds) (1966) *Some Theories of Organization*, revised edn, Homewood, Ill.: Irwin & Dorsey.

Sako, Mari (1988) 'Japanese company-subcontractors relationships', lecture given at University of Bradford Management Centre, 23 May.

Sathe, V. (1983) 'Implications of corporate culture: a manager's guide to action', *Organizational Dynamics*, autumn: 5–23.

Schein, E. (1984) 'Coming to a new awareness of organizational culture', *Sloan Management Review*, winter: 3–15.

Schelling, T.C. (1978) *Micromotives and Macrobehavior*, London: W.W. Norton & Co.

Sharp, J.A. (1989) 'Capital investment: an optimal control perspective', working paper, University of Bradford Management Centre.

Silverman, D. (1970) *The Theory of Organisations: A Sociological Framework*, London: Heinemann.

Simmel, G. (1955) *The Web of Group Affiliations*, trans. by R. Bendix, New York: Glencoe Press.

Simon, H.A. (1947) *Administrative Behavior: A Study of Decision Making Process in Administrative Organizations*, New York: Free Press (2nd edn 1957).

Simon, H.A. (1957) *Models of Man*, New York: Wiley.

Simon, H.A. (1960) *The New Science of Management Decision*, New York: Harper & Row.

Simon, H.A. (1964) 'On the concept of organizational goal', *Administrative Science Quarterly* 9, 1 (June): 1–22.

Simon, H.A. (1987) 'Making management decisions: the role of intuition and emotion', Academy of Management Executive 1 (Feb.): 57–64.

Smircich, L. (1983) 'Concepts of culture and organizational analysis', *Administrative Science Quarterly* 28: 339–58.

Smith, A. (1937) *Wealth of Nations*, New York: Modern Library Edn.

Staw, B.M. (1976) 'Knee-deep in the big muddy: a study of escalating commitment to a chosen course of action', *Organizational Behavior and Human Performance* 16 (1): 27–44.

Staw, B.M. and Ross, J. (1978) 'Commitment to a policy decision: a multitheoretical perspective', *Administrative Science Quarterly* 23 (1): 40–64.

Taylor, F.W. (1911) *Principles of Scientific Management*, New York: Harper & Row.

Thomas, H. and Logan, C. (1982) *Mondragon: An Economic Analysis*, London: George Allen & Unwin.

Thompson, J.D. (1967) *Organizations in Action*, New York: McGraw-Hill.

Thompson, J.D. and Tuden, A. (1956) 'Strategies, structures and processes of organizational decision', in J.D. Thompson, *Comparative Studies in Administration*, pp. 195–216, University of Pittsburgh Press. Also in W.A. Rushing and M.N. Zald (eds) (1976) *Organizations and Beyond: Selected Essays of James D. Thompson*, ch. 5, Boston, Mass.: Lexington Books, D.C. Heath & Co.

*Times, The* (1988), 25 June.

Titmuss, R.M. (1970) *The Gift Relationship: From Human Blood to Social Policy*, Harmondsworth: Penguin.

Trist, E.L. and Bamforth, K.W. (1951) 'Some social and psychological consequences of the longwall method of coal-getting', *Human Relations* 4: 3–38.

Trist, E.L., Higgin, G.W., Murray, H., and Pollock, A.B. (1963) *Organizational Choice*, London: Tavistock

Twaalhoven, F. and Hattori, T. (1982) *The Supporting Role of Japanese Enterprises*, Schiphol: Indivers Research.

Van de Ven, A.H. (1986) 'Central problems in the management of innovation', *Management Science*, 590–607.

Van de Ven, A.H., Delbecq, A.L., and Koenig, R. (1976) 'Determinants of coordination modes within organizations', *American Sociological Review* 41: 322–38.

Walker, C.R. and Guest, R.H. (1952) 'The man on the assembly line', *Harvard Business Review* 38 (3): 71–83.

Weber, M. (1968) *Economy and Society: An Outline of Interpretive Sociology*, G. Roth and G. Wittick (eds). Berkeley, Los Angeles, and London: University of California Press.

Weick, K.E. (1969) *The Social Psychology of Organizing*, Reading, Mass.: Addison-Wesley.

Weick, K.E. (1976) 'Educational organizations as loosely coupled systems', *Administrative Science Quarterly* 21 (1): 1–19.

Weick, K.E. (1979) *The Social Psychology of Organizing*, 2nd edn, Reading, Mass.: Addison-Wesley.

Whipp, R. and Clark, P. (1986) *Innovation and the Auto Industry*, London: Francis Pinter.

Whittington, R. (1989) *Corporate Strategies in Recession and Recovery: Social Structure and Strategic Choice*, London: Unwin Hyman.

Wickens, P. (1987) *The Road to Nissan: Flexibility, Quality, Teamwork*, Basingstoke: Macmillan.

Williamson, O.E. (1975) *Markets and Hierarchies: Analysis and Anti-Trust Implication*, New York: The Free Press.

Williamson, O.E. (1985) *The Economic Institutions of Capitalism*, New York: The Free Press.

Wilson, D.C. (1982) 'Electricity and resistance: a case study of innovation and politics', *Organization Studies* 2: 119–40.

Wilson, D.C., Butler, R.J., Cray, D., Hickson, D.J., and Mallory, G.R. (1986) 'Breaking the bounds of organization in strategic decision making', *Human Relations* 39 (4): 309–32.

Withey, M., Daft, L., and Cooper, W.C. (1983) 'Measures of Perrow's work unit technology: an empirical assessment and a new scale', *Academy of Management Journal* 25: 45–63.

Wood, S. (1989) 'The transformation of work?' in S. Wood (ed.) *The Transformation of Work*, ch. 1, London: Unwin Hyman.

Woodward, J. (1965) *Industrial Organization: Theory and Practice*, Oxford: Oxford University Press.

Woodward, J. (1980) *Industrial Organization: Theory and Practice*, 2nd edn, introduction by S. Dawson and D. Wedderburn, Oxford: Oxford University Press.

Worthy, J.C. (1950) 'Organization structure and employee morale', *American Sociological Review* 15 (April): 169–79.

Wrong, D.H. (1968) 'Some problems of defining social power', *American Journal of Sociology* 73.

Zadeh, L.A., Fu, K.S., Tanaka, K., and Shimura, M. (1975) *Fuzzy Sets and Their Applications to Cognitive and Decision Processes*, New York: Academic Press.

# Author index

# Subject index